The David & Charles Book of
HISTORIC ENGLISH INNS

Ted Bruning
& Keith Paulin

DAVID AND CHARLES
Newton Abbot London North Pomfret (Vt)

To Our Mums and Dads, and to Robert Swainson,
who knows a good pint when he's had a few

British Library Cataloguing in Publication Data
Bruning, Ted
  The David and Charles book of historic inns.
  1. Hotels, taverns, etc.—England—History
  I. Title   II. Paulin, Keith
  647'.942   TX910.G/
  ISBN 0-7153-8178-4

Filmset in Monophoto Plantin
by Latimer Trend & Company Ltd, Plymouth
and printed in Great Britain by
Butler & Tanner Limited, Frome and London
for David & Charles (Publishers) Limited
Brunel House   Newton Abbot   Devon

Published in the United States of America
by David & Charles Inc
North Pomfret   Vermont 05053   USA

CONTENTS

FOREWORD

by Terry Jones

People are never asking me why I think pubs and beer are so relevant to the way we live. I wish they would. I'd tell them that pubs and beer form a microcosm of our society—which is just the sort of thing to put anyone off asking me that sort of thing again. Nobody likes to hear about anything being a microcosm of anything else, in my experience. Still, it's a pity really, because I do think it's a valid point, and one which could interest someone, somewhere.

Take yourself, for example. You've just picked up this book to read about good old English pubs, and jolly interesting you'll find it too; it's packed with fascinating details: did you know, for example, that pubs are disappearing at a rate of 1,000 a year? Or that the replacement of pewter tankards with glasses actually changed the sort of beer that was brewed because people . . . well, perhaps you'd better turn to page 79 at once and find out, because I'd better get back to what I was talking about.

What *was* I talking about? Oh! I know—I was talking about you. It's not often that a foreword-writer can talk about his readers because in the general nature of things he doesn't know anything about them. But in this case, I know you must be at least slightly interested in pubs and beer, otherwise you wouldn't have picked up this book in the first place (assuming the author isn't your brother, which must be pretty unlikely). So it's quite possible that you actually *are* interested in why I think pubs and beer form a microcosm of our society . . . oh blow it! You've just put the book down again! I knew I shouldn't have mentioned the microcosm bit, but somehow it just slipped out . . . Oh well, I suppose I'll just have to write the rest of this foreword for myself.

As far as I can see, few things demonstrate the lunacy of the profit motive as clearly as running pubs and brewing beer. What I mean is this; if a brewer wants to make ever greater profits, he needs to brew ever more beer. So, like any modern businessman, he applies the philosopher's stone of Expansion to his business and hey-presto! profits rise as if by magic. But here's the rub: beer is a living thing and like all living things it needs love. The brewer whose first love is profit, however, finds that he has so many outlets and has to send the beer over such long distances that it no longer makes economic sense to go to all the trouble of keeping the beer alive and well until the moment of consumption. So he kills the beer off in the brewery by sterilization and filtration and ships out the carcass to his customers, with carbon dioxide pumped in to give it a ghastly semblance of life. And thus he turns the pub into a funeral parlour, tarting it up maybe so that his less-discerning customers don't notice. In this way brewers all over the world have demoted themselves to producers of alcoholic pop, and have killed the very thing they set out to create.

And the same thing goes for running a pub. If you run pubs *purely* for profit and for no other reason, they cease to be pubs, because a lot of what makes a pub a pub is nothing that shows up on an accountant's books. Oh sure, accountants can measure the cash spent on putting in mock-Tudor plastic beams or hiring topless go-go dancers for Friday lunchtimes, but look through all the account-books in the world and you won't find recorded anywhere that the landlord of the Lamb & Flag is a jolly soul, whom everyone likes to have a drink with, or that the public bar of the Bell is just a good place to sit, and you'll always find old Fred waiting for you with a cure for hangovers even if you haven't got one. What makes a good pub is indefinable in terms of modern business. It isn't something you can buy or put a price on . . . it's spirit . . . it's human . . . it's beyond the mean computation of profit and loss and the accountant's deadening hand, and as such it provides a touchstone for how we might organise ourselves in the future. Pubs and beer form a microcosm of our . . . oh damn it!

I've got all this way without mentioning microcosm again and then all of a sudden out it comes . . . Oh well, lucky you're not reading this.

Ted Bruning and Keith Paulin's book provides a fascinating history of the pub in general, and of many of Britain's oldest and most interesting pubs in particular. It celebrates the fact that a pub is not just somewhere where you pay to drink, nor something that can be simulated by the calculating entrepreneur merely in the pursuit of profit. A pub is a manifestation of humanity and of individuality. It is history. It is a precious thing that we should strive to keep.

INTRODUCTION

The England our ancestors knew is vanishing fast. Affluence and modernity are catching up with us, and while they offer the advantages of better health and greater comfort, they do seem to spell the death of much that has always been considered uniquely English. For while the industrial society does have a culture of its own, it is an international one that crosses borders and even oceans. It has no national identity.

It is true that foreigners flock to England by the million, and spend thousands of millions of pounds every year, to see our cathedrals, castles, great monuments and stately homes. But these, the grander parts of our national heritage, are museums which can be maintained by government subsidy. It is the peasant culture, the way of life of the everyday people of the past, which is in danger of vanishing. And perhaps that is not all bad. The squalid slums of the city and the often savagely dictatorial squirearchy of the countryside deserve to be obliterated. Enthusiasts struggle to keep some areas of peasant culture alive, such as folk music and morris dancing; but they are no more than quaint curios, irrelevant to modern life.

There is, however, one ancient institution which is very much alive; and that is the English pub. There are some 60,000 of them in the United Kingdom, and, although in concept they go back to Roman times and beyond, they still provide the most important milieux of social life today. This book has been written in an attempt to examine their development, and to place it against the background of the broader canvas of English history. In the first part we trace the outline of the story of the pub, while in the Gazetteer we try to fill in the detail by taking an individual look at a hundred or so of the best-known and most historical old inns, taverns, and ale-houses.

We make no apology for leaving London out of Part Two altogether; for the ground there has already been covered quite thoroughly enough. To those regional partisans who believe we have paid unfair attention to the South East at the expense of their native districts, our answer is that until the rise of the great cities of the North and Midlands in the last century, the South East was the most heavily populated part of the country, and therefore has a higher concentration of old buildings and pubs. Others may think we have ignored pubs which they know to be ancient and worthy of inspection. But of the 60,000 pubs available, something like a quarter or even a half must have fascinating stories to tell; we could not visit them all.

Finally, this is a book about pubs, not about beer. In the last ten or so years, a great deal has been written and spoken about beer, and the quality of our national drink has improved noticeably. We salute the Campaign for Real Ale (CAMRA) and its work; and to that organisation and its sympathisers we leave the task of writing about a subject they know better than anyone else.

This book would never have been written without the help, both moral and practical, of a great many people; we would like to thank them now. They are John Kay, John Norton, Katherine Moss, Geoff and Margaret Hine, Rose and Richard Meade, Pete and Lou Bruning, Clem Bruning, Mr and Mrs G. J. Bealey, Jon Marsh, Robert and Pat Swainson and the monks of Downside Abbey in Somerset.

1
ORIGINS 1066-1534

The pub is English.

This may come as a surprise to countless Scottish, Welsh and Irish publicans and their customers; nevertheless, the pub is a peculiarly English institution which has spread to the rest of the British Isles along with the English tongue.

Underlying this are the different social and economic structures of the Anglo-Saxons, who took possession of the English lowlands, and the Celts, who were left with the barer highlands of Scotland and Wales. The Sassenachs were not merely plunderers: they came as colonists and quickly settled down to become villagers, in time each village developing its own manor, church, forge, mill, common and alehouse. But for the dispossessed Celts, poorer land meant leaner livings and thus a more scattered population. Well into the eighteenth and even nineteenth centuries, Celtic shepherds and their flocks were semi-nomadic, fattening up on the high pastures in summer and sheltering in the valleys in winter. (In Wales you can still see, in many places, the shells of long-abandoned 'hafods', or summer cots, gathering moss high above the tree-line.) So the popular conception of the village and all that goes with it, including the village pub, is English rather than British.

The word 'inn' is now regarded as rather 'twee': few people would seriously suggest spending the evening down at the 'inn'. A similar fate has befallen the word 'tavern'. There may be a tavern in the town, but only in ballads of the most direly sentimental kind. But at one time these words had quite separate meanings. The inn was the hotel of its day, where a traveller could eat, drink and find shelter for himself and stabling for his horse. If we speak of the village inn today, we almost always mean the village alehouse; for the alehouse was the tap where the locals resorted, and where the occasional traveller paused to wet his throat and spread a little gossip, while the tavern was its urban cousin where wine was the principal drink. You could not spend the night at a tavern or alehouse, except in an emergency, and you cannot today at their modern equivalents.

For while the inn existed for the 'receipt, relief, and lodging of wayfarers', the alehouse had but one *raison d'etre*: ale. This, too, was an English rather than a British feature: weak ale was known to the Britons of Tacitus's day, but for serious drinking they resorted to mead or, much later, to whisky. Ale was the drink of the Anglo-Saxons. The Norman and Angevin aristocracies preferred wine: taverns served it, grapes were grown in southern England throughout the Middle Ages and Bordeaux was a vital part of the Angevin empire. But ale was the drink of the rural peasantry, who then made up the bulk of the population. Every village had its ale-wife, whose husband toiled in the fields along with the other men, and whose kitchen was the village pub. At the smithy, too, a traveller would normally be offered a wooden piggin of ale while the smith shod his horse; an account of the goings-on in the outside world was generally considered part of the price. (In some cases, when the smithy itself closed down, the refreshment side of the business was carried on—hence the great number of Smith's Arms and Horseshoes about the country.)

Like inn and tavern, the word 'ale' has acquired a sentimental quaintness, and the man who calls for a pint of it is normally the same pompous character who calls the landlord 'mine host' and bespeaks a repast rather than orders a meal. But it, too, once had a technical meaning. Originally it was brewed without hops, which were introduced by the Flemish settlers in the reigns of Edward III (1327–77) and Richard II (1377–99). Ale was a very different drink from the beer we know today. Without hops it would have been very much sweeter, and it was usually flavoured with anything from sage to honey. The advantages of hopped ale (or beer) were

14

eventually becoming an inn. Many royal manors held no tenants, but were run entirely by stewards who regarded the tips left by travellers as justifiable perks. Not that prices were very high: the bill for a day's travel for a party of three in 1331 came to 2/3d, which was fairly lavish in those days; but of that only 1½d went on beds and ¾d on candles.

The early Norman economy was a pastoral one in which the lords lived on and by their estates, with towns playing no important part. The slow rise of the towns and the bourgeoisie which inhabited them plays a vital part in English history, and is, of course, accompanied by the development of town pubs. Burgesses were first admitted to Parliament by de Montfort in 1264, and the towns became the homes of the great fairs which played an important role in trade. But the towns did not reach their full potential until the fourteenth century when Edward III, whose wife Philippa was Flemish, decided it would be more profitable to export finished cloth rather than raw wool. To do this he had to create a weaving industry, which entailed importing a great number of Flemish weavers (the same migrants who introduced the hop). By Richard II's time, the towns in which they settled had begun to encroach on the economic predominance of the land-owning classes, and there was much aristocratic opposition to their development. But it was the Crown which granted charters, and the Crown wanted the fledgling weaving industry to succeed, so it is not surprising that the town taverns often took their names from the arms of their patron, the King. Thus the principal hotel in many towns— Lincoln, Lewes, Retford and others—is called the White Hart, this being the personal emblem of Richard II. After Richard's murder in 1399, civil unrest and war troubled the country until the reign of Edward IV (1461–83) brought peace and a new period of urban expansion—and a flock of town taverns called either the White Lion or the Sun after his insigne. After his death, the Wars of the Roses enjoyed a brief resurgence, and with the coming of the Tudors we find a large number of Rose & Crowns named in honour of Henry VII and Henry VIII.

Before turning from town taverns to the great monastic, pilgrims' inns, it is worth dealing with the irksome, contentious and really quite irrelevant question of the country's oldest pub; but it is a delicate subject, particularly with landlords who believe their patently sixteenth- or seventeenth-century establishments to be pretty hoary. Earnest assurances that there are pubs three hundred and more years older tend to induce frostiness and hostility in the bluffest of licensees. Nevertheless, the authors' candidate for the dubious honour is the Ostrich at Colnbrook, practically on the main runway of Heathrow Airport. This was built in 1106 by one Milo Crispin as a guest-house for Abingdon Abbey. Shortly afterwards, it became a secular inn under a Saxon named Aegelward, but it achieved real notoriety some years later when the then landlord, John Jarman, and his wife were convicted of the murder of Thomas Cole, a Reading clothier. The murder weapon in this case was a bed built on a trapdoor above the kitchen; at the touch of a lever, the trap fell, the bed tilted and the sleeping victim was shot down into a vat of boiling water. His possessions were then stolen, and it was given out that the victim had decamped without paying his bill. When the law caught up with the Jarmans, they confessed to sixty such murders, and a working model of their 'death-bed' is proudly displayed in the bar. The seventeenth-century chronicler, Thomas Deloney, who wrote up the murders, puts them in the reign of Henry I (1100–35); but he mentions Thomas Becket as a friend of Cole's, so he may mean Henry II (1154–89). That still makes the Ostrich older than Nottingham's Trip to Jerusalem, whose claim of 1189 as a date of origin is unsubstantiated. The *Guinness Book of Records* mentions many older pubs, some claiming to date back to the tenth century, and in the next chapter we shall see some monastic pubs which claim even earlier dates. We discount them all, either because they have been rebuilt so often and so extensively that nothing of the original survives, or because, like the Fighting Cocks at St Albans, they are genuinely ancient buildings which have only been licensed for a mere 300 or 400 years. So our vote goes to the Ostrich.

The Ostrich, Colnbrook, Buckinghamshire. Built in 1106 as a monastic guest-house, the Ostrich probably became an inn during the reign of Henry II (1154–89) and is the oldest in England

Whether it is the oldest or not, the survival of the Ostrich for 870 or so years proves that the medieval monks built their inns, like their cathedrals, to last. For if the alehouses and taverns that served the ordinary folk have not survived the centuries, the pilgrims' inns certainly have, in some glory and in surprising profusion.

2

PILGRIMS' INNS

Throughout the Middle Ages, the cultural and political influence of the Church was as important as that of the Crown or the nobility. The leading prelates played a central role in government, and since a fifth or more of the country's cultivated land was held by abbeys or bishoprics, they had a major effect on the economy too. Universities flourished under Church patronage, hospitals were invariably religious foundations, and in the Templars, the Hospitallers and other lesser orders, the Church even had its own fighting arm. Further down the social scale, country parsons enjoyed as much influence over the peasants as did the lords of the manor. Parish priests were entitled to a tenth of all the manor produced and held glebe lands which their parishioners were obliged to work. Many barons were the vassals not of a secular liege, but of a diocese or an abbey.

The Church had been accustomed to wielding temporal power since it was first recognised by the Emperor Constantine, but its real constituency was spiritual. To peasants and gentry alike, there was more to the world than met the eye: Heaven and Hell, white magic and witchcraft, and the unending battle between the Archangel Michael and the fallen angels of Satan were as real to them, and as relevant to daily life, as the trees and the fields. The only guiding light through this frightening otherworld was the Church; for all its abuses and shortcomings, it alone could promise eternal salvation, and therein resided its power.

A people so deeply in the grip of religion made religious practice a central plank of their daily lives. Church-going, prayer, and observance of the liturgical calendar were one aspect of this, but an equally important part was pilgrimage. Prayers at the shrine of a martyr or the scene of a miracle not only conferred grace on the unworthy, they also brought healing to the sick. Pilgrimage offered not only a spiritual and physical salve in an age that was disease-ridden, poverty-stricken, oppressive and often violent: for many, it was the only chance of a break from the harsh routine of subsistence farming; for one group, the palmers, it was a way of life; while for a serf tied to the land, it even offered a chance of freedom since the lord could not prevent his serfs going on pilgrimage, and if they managed to stay away from the manor undetected for a year and a day, they were free.

The Church, too, did well out of pilgrimage. On an unofficial and purely personal basis, there had always been pilgrimage, but it was not until the Second Council of Nicaea decreed in 787 that all churches should possess sacred relics in some form that it became a major institution. The great numbers who left their homes to visit some far-off shrine had to put up somewhere; there were too many of them to put up at manor-houses, where, bearing in mind the anarchic nature of pilgrimage, they would not have been welcome anyway. While the Church was obliged to extend its charity to the poor and infirm, there was a healthy business potential in catering to the healthy and wealthy. At times, the unacceptable face of capitalism was very much in evidence, as when a nasty squabble blew up as to which abbey really possessed the bones of the English protomartyr, St Alban, whose reputation for healing was a big draw for pilgrims. The abbot of St Albans swore that the bones had never left his church, while at Ely they were protesting furiously that the bones had been committed to them for safekeeping. Eventually, in 1155, the Pope himself intervened, appointing a committee of three bishops who settled the dispute in favour of St Albans.

The best-known shrines in England, and the only ones capable of attracting foreigners in large numbers, were the tomb of St Thomas Becket at Canterbury and the scene of Richelda de Faverche's vision of Our Lady at Walsingham. But there were, if

24

not hundreds, certainly dozens of other places of pilgrimage across the country: Westminster boasted the tomb of St Edward the Confessor; Glastonbury had the thorn tree of Joseph of Arimathaea; Gloucester had the tomb of Edward II; Norwich, York, Lincoln, Hereford, Oxford and many lesser places also had sacred relics with the power to attract pilgrims by the hundred.

But Canterbury was the greatest of them all, England's Compostella or Tours, and the Pilgrims' Way, connecting the eastern city with the interior of the country and the south coast ports, was certainly the most important route of pilgrimage. It started properly at Winchester, where groups of pilgrims from the West Country, the Midlands and Wales, along with foreigners who disembarked at Southampton, joined up for a journey of over a hundred miles via Farnham, Guildford, West Malling, Aylesford, Maidstone and Charing.

Along this route were many places set aside by monks to receive footsore pilgrims. In Winchester itself they could shelter at the hospitals of St Cross and St John or at the Hundred Men's Hall. At Farnham there was Waverley Abbey, and at Guildford the Black Friars' hospice. Then there was St Mary's Abbey at West Malling; the White Friars' Pilgrims' Hall at Aylesford; Bishop Boniface's Hospital at Maidstone; Boxley Abbey; Hollingbourne Priory; the Archbishop's Palace at Charing; and in Canterbury itself two abbeys, two friaries and two hospitals.

All of these were free, decent and clean. But why sleep on bare stone in a cheerless dormitory with a stomachful of simple, unexciting food when for 4d a night (quite an inflated price) you could enjoy a warmer fire, livelier company and something a deal more satisfying in the line of food and drink at such inns as the Godbegot at Winchester, the Bush at Farnham, the Angel (then the Salutation) at Guildford, the White Hart at Bletchingly, the Crown or the Old Bell at Oxted, and the Chequers, the White Hart (now the Falstaff) and the Sun in Canterbury itself? In their day they were extremely popular, and they are still flourishing; six of the nine were founded not by businessmen but by monks.

Similarly, setting out from London, one would find charity at St Mary Overy's, now Southwark Cathedral, at Bermondsey Abbey and its daughter foundation St Thomas's Hospital, at the Templars' hospice at Strood and at St Bartholomew's Hospital, Chatham. On the other hand, one could stay at the Tabard in Southwark (immortalised by Chaucer but shamelessly pulled down in the 1860s), the Crown, the Bull or the King's Head at Rochester, the Red Lion at Sittingbourne, or the Maison Dieu at Ospringe (of which little survives but a few courses of stone in the wall of the Crown).

The monks' charity and the facilities of their inns were not only at the disposal of pilgrims. Bad roads were a condition of life in the Middle Ages and for a long time afterwards, and the country was only said to be at peace when a fair maid with a bag of gold in her bosom could travel without fear of rape or robbery—and that was not often. Many of the monastic inns which have come down to us, such as the Talbot at Towcester and the King's Head at Aylesbury, stand on no obvious pilgrim's routes, but they were prosperous enough to survive the Reformation as going concerns. In the major ports, as well, there were *maisons dieux*, hostels for those entering or leaving the country.

At this point, the question of England's oldest inn once more raises its ugly head, and it is true that many inns can claim a longer history than the Ostrich at Colnbrook. The Godbegot at Winchester was the guest-house of St Swithun's Abbey in 1002, while the Bingley Arms at Bardsey near Leeds was a 'priests' inn' in 953. The Grosvenor at Shaftesbury was another Saxon monastic guest-house. But the Godbegot has been through several major rebuildings; the Bingley Arms was pulled down and replaced in 1738; and the Grosvenor, although it survived the Reformation and was known as the Red Lion in the seventeenth century, was demolished and rebuilt in 1836. So although all these inns are older, in a sense, than the Ostrich, what you actually see is comparatively recent.

The Ostrich, however, is only one of a clutch of twelfth- and early thirteenth-century inns that survive. The Oxenham Arms in South Zeal, Devon, was a small religious foundation in 1150 or thereabouts; the Crewe Arms at Blanchland was part of a Premonstratensian Friary founded in 1163; the Old Bell at Hurley in Berkshire was also monastic and of a similar date; and the Trip to Jerusalem has already been mentioned. The earliest part of the complex of buildings making up Oxford's Golden Cross was founded in the reign of Richard I (1189–99) by the Augustinian Canons of Osney; and there are traces of early thirteenth-century work in the George at Stamford, founded by the Hospitallers, and in the Angel & Royal at Grantham, founded by the Templars and visited by King John in 1213.

The thirteenth and fourteenth centuries have been dubbed by historians the Age of Faith, so it is not surprising that they have

The Lord Crewe Arms, Blanchland, Northumberland. The Lord Crewe stands on the site of a monastic guest-house of the twelfth century. Although the present building is some four hundred years younger, it closely follows the ground plan of the friary

left us a good crop of monastic inns. There is the George & Dragon at Codicote in Hertfordshire, founded by St Alban's Abbey in 1297, and the Green Dragon at Lincoln was the hospice of St Catherine's Priory only a little later. The Crown at Chiddingfold in Surrey, widely held to be one of the country's finest half-timbered inns and praised by Pevsner for its king-post roof, was first let as an inn in 1383; before then it had been a rest-home for monks shattered by the peace and quiet of the contemplative life. Another fine king-post, octagonal and sitting on a moulded base, is to be found at the Pilgrims' Rest at Battle in Sussex, built in the fourteenth century as a new hospice for the abbey founded by William I to celebrate the victory at Hastings.

But the golden age of the monastic hospices came in the fifteenth century, when many of the country's finest inns were first built. Typical of this golden age was the George at Norton St Philip in Somerset, founded in 1397 by the monks of Hinton Charterhouse. The Carthusians, along with the Cistercians, played perhaps a greater part than any other order in the development of the wool trade on which England's medieval prosperity was based. In building the George, they killed two birds with one stone, for they provided themselves with not only a splendid guest-house for the accommodation of travellers, but also a warehouse and exchange for their principal product. The stone stair running up to the slightly elevated door furnished a loading bay for waggons, while a great hall on the first floor served as the wool exchange. Doubtless the hospice sheltered not only pilgrims making their way to Glastonbury, but also the sleek and prosperous wool merchants who built so many fine houses and endowed so many splendid churches in the county. Originally the George was all of stone, but

---

The George, Norton St Philip, Somerset. The rear of the building survived the fire of about 1500 and shows more clearly than the front the ecclesiastic formality of the inn's architecture. The short gallery on the left dates to about 1300 and is probably the earliest example of its type; the stone stair turret can also be seen

the half-timbered upper floors date from the aftermath of a fire in about 1500. This gives the front of the inn an informal and friendly air which contrasts strongly with the rear, where the stone stair-turret and mullioned windows are evidence of the more disciplined ecclesiastic architecture of the original.

The rear of the George also possesses a gallery, perhaps the earliest example of a style which became more and more popular over the next two centuries. The courtyard and gallery plan became the model not only for many coaching inns, but also for the Elizabethan theatre. It is argued that the Crusaders—surely the most determined of all medieval pilgrims—brought the style back with them from the Middle East, where they had been impressed by the arcaded pleasure gardens of their enemies. If this is so, then the Saracens may have copied it from the Byzantines, who in turn inherited it from Rome—which makes pilgrims' inns such as the New Inn at Gloucester and the George at Huntingdon the distant cousins of villas such as Fishbourne in Sussex, whose remains are still to be seen grouped round a peristyle, or courtyard-garden.

The New Inn is certainly one of the best surviving examples of the galleried inn. It was built in 1455 by John Twyning, Abbot of Gloucester, to accommodate the floods of pilgrims who came to visit the tomb of Edward II in the abbey church. Edward was murdered at nearby Berkeley Castle in circumstances of particular brutality on the orders of his queen, Isabella, and her lover, Roger Mortimer, in 1327. His body was buried in state in Gloucester Cathedral, and it was not long before the tomb became a martyr's shrine and miracles were being attributed to the hapless Plantagenet. Over the next hundred years, the number of pilgrims rose so sharply that the New Inn had to be built, and among its regulars were troupes of actors who performed in the yard while the multitude watched from the galleries. These strolling players were the fathers of Tudor drama. Shakespeare himself performed in many an inn yard, including that of the George at Southwark, and theatres such as the Globe bore an obvious resemblance to the galleried inn.

The new design also heralded another innovation. About this time private rooms became more commonplace. Had you arrived at the Crown at Chiddingfold, or the Ostrich, or a host of others, you would have eaten with the rest of the guests round trestle tables in the great hall. The hall would also be your bedchamber, for at night, when the trestles had been stacked away, you would have curled up to sleep in your cloak, perhaps on a straw mattress, but quite likely on the rushes strewn on the floor, and as near to the fire as possible. Sleeping in travel-stained clothes on rushes that probably contained fleas, lice, scraps of food, spilt ale and possibly dog-droppings was hardly the most hygienic of activities; one inn at least, the George at Winchcombe, had in the yard a big trough in which pilgrims were encouraged to enjoy a well-deserved bath. But during the Middle Ages, tastes naturally changed: whereas at first only the great had demanded private chambers—and even they would have slept with a bodyguard or two—the gradual introduction of such creature comforts as glazing and proper chimneys raised common people's expectations until they demanded, and were given, a greater degree of sophistication and privacy.

The George at Dorchester in Oxfordshire, the Star at Alfriston in Sussex, the Angel & Royal at Grantham, the George & Pilgrims at Glastonbury, the King's Head at Aylesbury—all these great fifteenth-century monastic inns seem to attest that the Church was alive and flourishing—indeed, was at its peak. Many other national treasures come down to us from the same period: St George's Chapel at Windsor, Magdalen College Tower, Oxford, King's College Chapel, Cambridge, and Henry VII's chapel at Westminster, by the Florentine Torrigiano; they seem to say that all was well, that the country and its institutions, Church and Crown, were peaceful, wealthy and secure. But for most of the century, the truth was somewhat different. The Hundred Years' War had ended in defeat. The French empire gained by Edward III and Henry V on the fields of Poitiers and Agincourt had dwindled until only Calais was left. The Wars of the Roses, which lasted from the first Battle of St Albans in 1455 to the Battle of Stoke in 1487, with the accompanying brigandage and disorder, rate as one of the bloodiest and most protracted dynastic struggles in our history. The Crown had been badly shaken. Four out of eight kings between 1399 and 1485—Richard II, Henry VI, Edward V and Richard III —had been supplanted and killed by ambitious nobles. The Church, too, was in decline: the only orders which did not lose members were the more ascetic ones—the Carthusians, the Franciscans, the Brigittines—for, in an age of increasing literacy, when the alternative careers of commerce and the law were becoming more attractive and accessible, men no longer took vows for mere advancement.

That so many fine buildings—the inns not least among them— were erected and survive, bears witness to the continuing prosperity of the wool trade, and to the rise of the bourgeois and merchant classes, whose stabilising influence was enough to counterbalance the turbulence of the age. Stability and peace was what commerce needed, and the towns supported strong monarchs such as Edward IV who were able to provide it. The new Tudors were aware of it, too, and set about gaining the solid support of the towns for their still insecure and challenged regime.

The result was the end of feudalism. Henry VII was perhaps the first man since Edward the Confessor who could truly call himself King of the English people rather than hereditary leader of the barons, and he and his son used this new political situation to tackle and break the power of the independent aristocracy. Once the last Plantagenet heir had been beheaded and the last proud baron become a courtier, it was inevitable that the other medieval centre of power, the Church, should be confronted. Church and Crown had been through periods of rivalry since the assassination of Becket and before. When Henry VIII joined battle, he was not short of allies.

32

3

REFORMATION
TO REVOLUTION 1534-1688

In 1534 Henry VIII declared himself head of the Church in England. More, Fisher and one or two others who refused to swear an oath of loyalty were beheaded, but the greater part of the population, including the merchant classes, backed their King. Even in the Church itself, there were few serious dissidents.

The beginning of the Dissolution two years later seemed hardly any more revolutionary. The first Act of Suppression was aimed only at the smaller and poorer religious houses, and was presented as a measure of reform so moderate that many of the communities that fell within its scope, including all seventeen houses of the order of St Gilbert of Sempringham, were spared.

But Henry badly needed the assets and revenues commanded by the greater monasteries and convents. After the Act had closed down 243 out of some 800 religious communities, the royal coffers were hardly any fuller, and there seemed no excuse to begin the real work until the Pilgrimage of Grace provided one.

This rebellion, which began in October 1536, was an ill-timed and poorly organised demonstration by the deeply conservative northerners of their support for traditional ways. Suppression was high on their list of grievances, and they naturally expected the sympathy of monks and abbots. Henry bided his time, and before long the rebellion collapsed. During the mopping up, five abbots, including the Abbot of Jervaulx, were executed for complicity, and their abbeys and estates were forfeited to the Crown. It was the way in which a sixth, the Abbot of Furness, saved his neck that in-

terested the King. Rather than face the block, the abbot 'surrendered' his house and all its property to the Crown.

This was an invaluable precedent for Henry. Surrenders could
be negotiated by private deed, so Parliament's support for the King
never had to be put to the test, and the Church itself had no chance
to present a united opposition. The King felt so secure that the
pretence of sensible reform was dropped altogether—the deeds
concluding each surrender clearly stated that the monastic way of
life was superstitious and unchristian. Those who showed signs of
resistance, such as the Abbot of Glastonbury, went to the block,
and in March 1540 the last abbey in England, Waltham in Essex,
founded by Harold Godwinsson five centuries before, closed its
doors.

The Dissolution was a financial flop. Thanks to the French war,
the King could not afford to hold on to the great estates and enjoy
their income, and by his death in 1547 two-thirds of the appro-
priated land had been sold. Furthermore, the Government was
obliged to meet the pensions promised to some 10,000 displaced
monks, nuns, friars, and canons. Before long, all that the Treasury
was left with were the guns cast from church bells, the bullets made
from roofing lead and the church plate reduced to bullion.

Many of the guest-houses which for centuries had been the
traveller's principal resort were now closed. Charles Brandon,
Duke of Suffolk, for instance, purchased the estates of St Catherine's Priory, Lincoln; perhaps he had only done so out of an
obligation to the King and now needed to recoup as much of his
outlay as possible, for he quickly sold the abbot's guest-house to a
merchant as a private residence, which it remained for 150 years
before reopening as the Green Dragon. Others, however, survived
the upheaval as secular inns. Elizabeth I donated the former guest-
house of Bruern Abbey in Gloucestershire to the village of Shipton-
under-Wychwood on the understanding that £20 a year of its
profits should go to the poor. Richard Bewforest, a cousin of the
last abbot of Dorchester-on-Thames, bought up the abbey's
estate for £150, donated the valueless abbey church itself back to

the parish, and settled down to enjoy the profits of his latest commercial acquisition, the George Inn.

It was businessmen like Bewforest who first realised the potential of owning a well-founded inn, and so the old guest-houses and hospices prospered. One factor behind this was the growing popularity—indeed, necessity—of travel. The roads were still bad: the Great North Road was impassable for much of the year in Elizabeth's reign, and the Dissolution and the new Enclosure Acts had filled them with vagrants in unprecedented numbers. But the decay of feudalism had softened the strictures on population movement, and the growth of commerce had increased the number of merchants on the road. It was a period of growing affluence and sophistication, and the inn trade did well. Old houses continued to be turned into inns, as had the manor-houses of an earlier period: the Bull at Long Melford, Suffolk, was a wealthy wool merchant's home until 1570; the Lion at Shrewsbury was a dwelling until 1618; the Feathers at Ludlow, built as a residence in 1603, was made an inn about 1619. One building that became an inn had not even been a house before: the Fighting Cocks at St Albans was an eleventh-century dovecote which opened its doors to travellers in 1599. New inns were built, too: the George at Andover in 1546, the George at Odiham, Hampshire, in 1547, and yet another George, at Keswick, during Elizabeth's reign.

But this new generation of travellers was not prepared to put up with the rough-and-ready halls their fathers had known. The great men and women of the land were moving out of their draughty castles and building themselves palatial mansions such as Haddon, Hardwick, Burghley and Longleat, and humbler folk expected at least some of that grace and elegance to rub off on them. The galleried inns mark a move away from the old hall-house type; now travellers could have private rooms facing onto the bustle of the inn yard, and the eating and drinking accommodation was also split up into a maze-like complex of tiny parlours bearing names like the Peacock, the Flower-de-Luce, the Pomegranate, or the Dolphin. In their 'chamber-lies' or bedrooms, the travellers could

The George, Odiham, Hampshire. Despite its later façade, the George is a Tudor inn, one of those which owed its building and prosperity to the 'boom' which followed the Dissolution. The George has been licensed since 1547, and recently discovered wall-paintings date to about 1550

expect to find curtained four-posters, draught-proof and private enough for most activities, a truckle-bed on wheels for a servant or two, a chest for baggage, and perhaps another innovation: decorative wall-paintings.

Such paintings, in vogue for a while before panelling became popular, echoed the tapestries which were hung up in castle halls to keep out the draught and hide the cold, grey stone behind a splash of colour. They were not long in fashion, and not too many examples have survived. One of the best known is at the White Swan, Stratford-on-Avon, which illustrates the story of Tobias and the Angel from the Apocrypha. Others are in the Bell at

Thetford and the Black Horse at York, while in the George at Odiham cartoons of birds, including an owl that says 'tewet tohw' and a rook or crow cawing 'knave, knave', have recently been uncovered in an upstairs room and dated to about 1550.

One diarist, William Harrison, writing in 1583, was mighty pleased with the inns he called at:

> Every man may use his inn as his own house. Our inns are also very well furnished . . . with bedding and tapestry. Each comer is sure to lie in clean sheets, wherein no man has been lodged since they came from the laundress. If he lose aught while he abides at the inn, the host is bound by a general custom to restore the damage, so there is no greater security anywhere for travellers than in the greatest inns of England.

The testimony of two foreigners, a Dutchman and a Scot, is more flattering for being disinterested. The Dutchman, Levinus Lemnius, a doctor who visited England during the reign of Elizabeth, was almost embarrassingly effusive:

> The neat cleanliness, the exquisite fineness, the pleasant and delightful furniture in every point of the household wonderfully rejoiced me; their nosegays, finely intermingled with sundry sorts of fragrant flowers in their bedchambers and privy rooms, with wonderful smell cheered me up and entirely delighted all my senses.

The Scot, Fynes Moryson, writing in about 1620, described how on arriving at the inn, his travel-stained boots were whisked away to be cleaned while a fire was prepared in his bedroom. For 6d or less he could eat the 'ordinary'—a set meal round a communal table with the other guests, the landlord carving at its head—or for a few pence extra he could have his victuals sent up to his chamber. Even musicians were employed to send the guests away in good humour in the morning, and he concluded that, 'the world affords not such inns as England hath'.

In the past the monarchs themselves, on progress through their realms or on campaign, had been known to sojourn at an inn when no better accommodation was available, and in the sixteenth and seventeenth centuries this custom was still maintained. Elizabeth stayed at the George at Cranbrook in Kent, the Bear at Devizes and the King's Head at Chigwell in Essex. Charles I when on campaign clearly preferred an inn to a tent: he was such a frequent visitor at the King's Arms at Southwell (as indeed his father had been) that when he was executed, the management felt it necessary to change its name to the Saracen, the name it bears today. He also passed what must have been a rather dismal night in 1646 at the Red Lion in Hillingdon, Middlesex, on his way to surrender to the Scots at Newark. At the same time, many local Justices of the Peace found that the building best-appointed for their needs was the local hostelry: the George at Odiham, the George at Cranbrook, the White Bull at Ribchester in Lancashire, the New Inn at Pembridge in Herefordshire and the Speech House in the Forest of Dean all served as court-houses, as did many others, in some cases well into the nineteenth century. Many inns were so profitable that in the 1650s, when coinage was scarce, they minted their own in the form of trade tokens which were good in the immediate neighbourhood and were backed by the personal wealth of the innkeeper. The landlords of the Ostrich at Colnbrook, the Red Lion at Colchester and the Swan at Lavenham were among the many rich enough to stimulate local trade in this way.

But there was a reverse side. Harrison discovered that there was often an ulterior motive behind the solicitude of the innkeeper and his servants:

> For when he cometh into the inne and alighteth from his horse [wrote the diarist] the hostler is very busie to take his budget or capcase in the yard from his saddle-bow, which he passeth slilie in his hand to feel the weight thereof.

Having been given a preliminary once-over by the ostler, the traveller's baggage received a more thorough casing later on from the chambermaid and he is watched hawkishly as he eats and drinks to determine just how much cash he has about him. Should he leave his valuables with the landlord for safe-keeping, he will not be robbed—at least, not until he has left the inn and is a safe distance away. In 1654 a Mr Kidderminster of Cambridge vanished with a bag containing £600. Over the next few years he was reported in Cork, Amsterdam, even Barbados; in fact he had been murdered and robbed, but his killers were not even suspected until his body was accidentally uncovered in the back yard of the White Horse at Chelmsford. Attention naturally focussed on the man who had been landlord at the time, one Sewell—who was promptly poisoned by his wife in order to keep his mouth shut. But the evidence of a maid, Mary Kendall, and of neighbours who remembered hearing poor Mr Kidderminster's dying screams, was enough to send Mrs Sewell and her accomplice, Moses Drayne, the ostler, to the gallows.

Other innkeepers also suffered at the rope's end for such conduct. Jonathan Bradford of Oxford was found standing over the body of a guest, Mr Hayes, with a lantern in one hand and a bloody knife in the other, and swung for it, although Hayes's servant subsequently confessed. James Batson, a highwayman turned innkeeper, along with his ostler, robbed a sleeping guest and slit his throat; the ostler turned King's evidence. The Van Berghens, Dutch immigrants who ran the Black Bull in Aldgate, London, along with the ostler Dromelius, were seen dropping the battered body of a Mr Norris into the Thames. (The ostler, you will observe, was the butler of his day—he always did it.)

Such melodramas were, however, exceptional, since landlords were generally too exposed to suspicion to make successful villains. Far more usual was the kind of complaint that John Taylor, the Water Poet, had to make after a tour of the West Country in 1649. The inn at Nether Stowey in Somerset he found to be so filthy, so cobwebbed, and so filled with stinging smoke that he sat outside while the landlord, who was staggering drunk, prepared him some beef. Three hours elapsed, and the landlord came out saying there was no beef after all, and would Mr Taylor make do with eggs? The poet assented, and the man stumbled off to fetch them. But after a while he was back, explaining that there were no eggs, either, so poor Taylor, who had been travelling all day, had to go to bed on nothing but bread and butter. No sooner had he turned in than he was assaulted by an 'Ethiopian army of fleas', which he managed to beat off after killing, in his own estimation, some 500 of them. At that point the landlord's baby started crying, and all the local dogs joined in, so the luckless poet, having neither eaten nor slept, got up in the middle of the night and quit the place.

He had no better luck at Mevagissey in Cornwall where the inns failed to fulfil their function; there he asked for a bed at seven inns without success. At the eighth he tried to insist, and found himself in a fight with the landlady's son; luckily he was rescued by a passing gent who turned out to be a local Justice and who insisted on putting the poet up at his own home for the weekend free of charge.

The Government was not totally insensible to the defects and abuses prevalent in inns and alehouses. In the reign of Edward VI, wine shops in London had been limited to forty, while other boroughs were allowed only two (except Shrewsbury which, for some reason, was allowed three). However, this measure had been aimed at curbing French wine imports rather than regulating the quality of taverns. The Justices already had the power to close the worst offenders, although in Mevagissey, at least, this power seems not to have been exercised, and the next step was to give them the power to prevent anyone they considered unreliable from setting up as an innkeeper.

This Licensing Act of 1552, for all its drawbacks, was a momentous piece of legislation. In forbidding the sale of alcohol from any premises without the consent of two Justices, it laid the foundations of the system we drink under today. The idea was not entirely new: there had been licences before, but these were private agreements between a land-owner and a tenant who wanted to brew and sell ale. The new legislation was not an unqualified success: for a start, the Justices could not always know the character of an applicant, and even if they knew it to be bad, they could be bribed, or they could choose to turn a blind eye anyway. The Justices of Mevagissey had obviously been less than assiduous, as were the Justices of

Colchester and Ripon. In Colchester, in 1598, the Puritan Town Assembly complained so bitterly about the villainous nature of local taverns and alehouses that the complacency of the Justices was shattered: they had to close down half the town's drinking-dens on the spot. The same happened in Ripon in 1623. The Act was equally seriously discredited in the reign of James I when the licensing of wine shops was made the subject of a monopoly. The first to hold it was Sir Walter Raleigh, and nobody knows what abuses he might have committed. The antics of his successor, Sir Giles Mompesson, however, were less discreet and were very much resented. For four years he systematically took bribes from the worst licensees and blackmailed the blameless; eventually he was tried at the Bar of the House of Commons, stripped of his Parliamentary seat and his knighthood, fined £10,000 and banished.

Repeated attempts were made to back up the 1552 Act. In the 1590s, a curfew was imposed of nine o'clock in summer and eight in winter, although with only the parish constable, himself an honorary and part-time official, to enforce them, these closing times cannot have been over-successful. Parliament went even further in 1604 with an Act that pompously asserted:

> The ancient, true and proper use of inns, alehouses and victualling houses was for the receipt, relief and lodging of wayfarers . . . and not for the entertainment and harbouring of lewd and idle people.

This Act prevented taverns and alehouses (or beerhouses, as we should by now be calling them) from offering accommodation, which was a good thing in that it prevented drunks from sleeping off their excesses in situ, to commence anew as soon as they revived. But it also prevented decent inns from allowing any but travellers to drink on the premises except for an hour at noon, which was a bad thing for the inns and for their local regulars. The problem of enforcement which dogged the government at the time, however, would have rendered this Act as ineffective as the curfew. A more significant move came not from Parliament but from the King himself: an Order in Council of 1618 decreed that licences should be renewed annually, and this was supported in 1627 when the punishment for running an inn, tavern or beerhouse without a licence was set at a guinea fine or a whipping.

Oliver Cromwell, whose grimly Puritanical image is perhaps exaggerated, knew and appreciated the worth of a well-kept inn. On campaign he put up at an inn whenever he could—the King's Head at Aylesbury and the Fighting Cocks at St Albans both enjoyed the patronage of Parliament's general—and, as a country squire and JP himself, he perhaps understood the problems in licensing and enforcement better than the high-born. In 1656 he commanded his fellow JPs to be more active in using their powers of suppression against the unruly and lax (although he probably did not get the Water Poet's approbation for this, since Taylor was an ardent and much-persecuted Royalist). At the same time Cromwell put an end to one abuse in which the Church itself was involved—the dispensing of church ales.

This practice began long before the Reformation, when parishioners were lured to church on Sundays with the promise of a drink after Mass to make their journeys worthwhile. At the same time, local benefactors were bequeathing money to see that ale was brewed for the poor, and before long church houses were springing up. These functioned rather like the church halls of today, and were equipped with dining-halls, kitchens, and brew-houses to enable all the parishioners to celebrate such feasts as Easter and Whitsun communally. They also brewed 'bid' or 'gift' ales to raise money for the tower restoration appeal, or whatever, an idea that many a hard-pressed modern Vicar might find worth reviving. For many years this friendly and most Christian institution continued quite happily; but the abuses which inevitably crept in horrified high Churchmen and Puritans alike. In one church the whole south aisle was so packed with barrels as to be unusable; while in at least one other, divine service was seen as no reason for breaking off the convivialities, so that the poor priest could scarcely make himself heard above the cheery chat of his quaffing flock. The problem of enforcement seems to have been as insurmountable to the Church authorities as it was for the Government; at any rate, pastoral letters and episcopal injunctions made not the slightest difference. The Protector, however, was used to being obeyed, and had troops as well as Puritan divines to see that his commands were enforced. Church ales were brewed no more, but many of the church houses survived as beerhouses: the fifteenth-century Golden Cross in Shrewsbury was known originally as the Sextry, since it had been both sacristy and tap-room for St Chad's Church; while the Church House Inn in Harberton, Devon, built possibly in the thirteenth century to house masons working on churches in the area, served for a while as a chantry and then became a beer-house.

Part of the reason for so much Government interest in what we may now call the licensed trade must have been the bawdy and indisciplined custom attracted by many urban taverns and beer-houses. In many cases this custom was drawn from the theatre, of which many sober and God-fearing Puritans thoroughly dis-approved. Actors and playwrights (there were no actresses at this time) worked hard and played hard. They drank and they brawled —indeed Marlow died in a tavern-brawl, although it has been whispered ever since that his murder was carefully planned, since he was thought to have been involved in espionage. The villainies of Falstaff and his cronies in *Henry IV Part I* are set in the Boar's Head, Eastcheap (which, it should be noted, was a proper wine-serving tavern—Mistress Quickly's husband in the *dramatis personae* was a 'vintner', and Falstaff's tipple was sack, not ale). Shakespeare himself was often to be found in the Mermaid, Bread Street, or the Bush, Aldersgate; Ben Jonson, who died an alcoholic in the reign of Charles I, used the Devil in Fleet Street; and the actors Burbage and Tarleton frequented the Bull in the City. (Tarleton turned tavern-keeper after quitting the stage, and is credited with the invention of the 'ordinary' in the 1560s.)

The introduction of a wonderful new beverage from the mys-terious East, coffee, in 1612, gave a powerful boost to this nascent café society, which soon began to take on a more political complexion. The first coffee-house was set up by a Turk called Pasha who had come to England as a servant of Daniel Edwards, a Smyrna merchant. Later known as the Jamaica, it was situated near St Michael's, Cornhill, and although it did a roaring business it was for a long time a novelty. The coffee bug did not in fact catch on until 1657, when James Farr, a former barber, opened the second coffee-house, the Rainbow in Fleet Street. It was soon followed by Peele's, Anderton's, Nando's, Groom's, Dick's and a galaxy of others. Lawyers, writers, brokers, shippers and others of every degree and interest could soon be 'heard of' at this or that coffee-house, where clients could see them and mail could reach them. At the Crown in Wells (Somerset), which joined the vogue as soon as possible, the local doctor, Claver Morris, even held his surgeries. But the coffee-houses were principally the stamping-ground of politicians. Buckingham and Shaftesbury set up their Green Ribbon Club in opposition to Charles II and his Chancellor, Lord Danby, at the King's Head tavern and coffee-house in Fleet Street in 1676; in the 1680s and '90s Dryden and the Tories haunted Will's in Covent Garden, while across the road at Button's, or at the Grecian Coffee House near the Temple, Steele, Addison and the Whigs (as the Green Ribbon Club had by now become) were to be found. This was despite an attempt as early as 1675 to prevent the spread of coffee-drinking: an Order in Council made in December that year had sought to stop any further coffee-houses opening, partly because they provided centres for political opposition, partly because the Government was alarmed at the rapid growth in coffee imports. This alarm was well-founded: by 1699 a hundred tons of coffee was being imported annually, at £14 a ton.

It is to the coffee-houses that such gentlemen's clubs as White's and the Athenaeum owe their birth. With Dr Johnson, Boswell, Goldsmith, Reynolds and Hogarth frequenting taverns and chop-houses such as the Mitre, Ely Place, and the Cheshire Cheese in Wine Office Court off Fleet Street, the brilliance of this café or tavern society continued well into the eighteenth century.

But in 1688 a new drink was introduced, one that was destined to wipe the glitter away for good, and transform the image of the town beerhouse from the civilised resort of great minds to the temple of wantonness and depravity. Perhaps the Whigs were to blame, but in ousting James II in favour of William of Orange, they could hardly foresee that one of the side-effects of their Glorious Revolution would be the introduction of a Dutch drink that was to become the curse of the working classes in the eighteenth century— mother's ruin, the blue devil—gin.

4

DEAD DRUNK
FOR TWOPENCE 1688-1830

Gin, to be fair to William and his Dutch entourage, was not wholly unknown in England before the Glorious Revolution. Distilling had been carried on since the early Middle Ages, and a monopoly on the production of spirits had long been enjoyed by the Distillers' Company. But William inherited from the Stuarts a shaky economy and a poor balance of trade, and when war with France loomed, it became imperative that French brandy imports should be curbed. Gin, a clear spirit flavoured with coriander and juniper, was encouraged as a substitute: by the Acts of 1690 and 1703 the Distillers were relieved of their monopoly, and an absurdly low and easily evaded duty of twopence a gallon was fixed. The same Acts also raised the duty on beer.

The result was that over the next fifty years production of gin shot up from half-a-million gallons annually to twenty million. The advertising slogan 'drunk for a penny, dead drunk for twopence, clean straw for nothing' became the maxim by which the poor and underprivileged lived, flocking in droves to the sordid gin shops which sprouted in slums all over the country. Even the most sedate cathedral cities and market towns had their corners of filth, overcrowding, and decay.

Poverty already had much of the kingdom in its grasp. In 1688, the year of the Glorious Revolution, Gregory King estimated that over half of the country's population of $5\frac{1}{2}$ million would never be able to support themselves without poor relief, however hard they worked. They often faced winters of short commons, if not of actual starvation. Countrymen were deterred from supplementing their diet with poached game by armed gamekeepers, mantraps and spring-guns, and in the urban slums, conditions were worse. As well as hunger and overcrowding, they faced cholera, typhus, rickets and a host of other diseases, and the hangings, floggings, prison hulks and transportation of the 'Bloody Code' awaited them if they tried to alleviate their plight by theft.

It is hardly surprising that the poor turned to gin as a cheap and ever-available means of escape from their surroundings. In the worst slums, deaths outweighed births by two to one, but a constant influx of starving peasants from the country (most of the whores with whom Boswell disported in the 1760s came, or claimed to come, from rural districts) kept the population topped up, and erosion of slum areas by redevelopment ensured that the 'rookeries' were packed ever tighter. Writing in 1751 (by which time the gin epidemic was showing signs of abating), Henry Fielding believed that 100,000 Londoners lived more or less on gin alone, swilling pints of the poison—and poison it was, being adulterated with anything from turps to sulphuric acid—every day. When a drunk collapsed, he or she would be thrown into a bare room set aside for the purpose, to begin drinking again as soon as the last bout had been slept off. The gin shops of London, said Tobias Smollet, were 'the haunts of idleness, fraud, and rapine, and the seminaries of drunkenness, debauchery, extravagance, and every vice incident to human nature'. Hogarth's 'Gin Lane', in which squalor and death caused by drink seem a normal condition of life, can in the circumstances hardly be an exaggeration.

The disease-ridden, idle and gin-sodden mobs of eighteenth-century England regarded petty crime as a legitimate trade and the public punishments enshrined in the Bloody Code as an occupational hazard, or as a spectacle laid on especially for their amusement. The heroes of the day were master criminals like Blueskin and Jonathan Wild, and highwaymen like Jack Shepherd who, when hanged in 1724, aged 22, had broken out of Newgate itself no fewer than three times. The body of Dick Turpin, hanged at

York for horse-stealing in 1739, aged 34, was borne in triumph round the city on a door by an adoring mob which had succeeded in seizing it from the prison authorities. Until they were abolished in 1868, public hangings always provided a good revenue for those taverns lucky enough to overlook the gaol square and for gin-sellers in their mobile booths. Many of the latter toured the country, going from hanging to hanging and attending any other public event— race-meeting, horse-fair or prize-fight—where they could expect to make a fortnight's usual profit in an afternoon. Often there were riots in which property was damaged and lives lost—forty people were crushed to death in the disturbances which followed the execution of the murderers Holloway and Haggerty at Newgate in 1807. But the outgoings of the trade were not high, and the owner of a booth destroyed in such a riot could easily set himself up again.

The degeneracy which scars the eighteenth century was not confined to the mob. In time it spread upwards until the once-brilliant café society of the seventeenth-century coffee-house was itself polluted. In 1715 the playwright and Whig Sir Richard Steele, touring London after the death of Louis XIV, found (although his view tended to the satirical) that the political nature of coffee-house clientele was very much unchanged:

> I called in at Giles's, where I saw a board of French Gentlemen sitting upon the life and death of their Grand Monarque. . . . At Jenny Mann's I saw an alert young fellow who cocked his hat upon a friend of his and accosted him after the following manner: 'Well, Jack, the old prig is dead at last. Sharp's the word. Up to the walls of Paris directly!'

By the 1760s, taverns and chop-houses such as Rule's in Maiden Lane, Stone's in Panton Street, and the Poulter's Arms in Free-man's Court were still the haunts of such luminaries as Garrick, Sheridan, Boswell, Dr Johnson and many others, and as late as the 1790s Coleridge and Charles Lamb were to be found holding court at the Salutation & Cat, Smithfield. But by that time the rot had set in: in 1761 the Duke of Ancaster was one of many to be found betting 100 guineas a match at the cockpit in St James's Park, and very heavy gambling was to become a feature of high society around the turn of the century. The barrister Andrew Steinmetz found General Scott, Canning's father-in-law, winning £200,000 in a single sitting of whist at White's, while the fishmonger turned casino-operator, William Crockford, relieved two peers of £50,000 each in a game of hazard at his club. Gone was the age of earnest and animated political or artistic debate: the best people in the land now gathered in gambling hells such as Almack's, Graham's and the Cocoa-Tree, where they wagered small fortunes on which of two raindrops running down a window-pane would reach the bottom first. (One young blade wagered £1,500 that a man could live twelve hours under water. A volunteer desperate enough to try the experiment was found: the blade lost his money, the volunteer his life.) Steinmetz blamed for all this the great number of French immigrants fleeing the Revolution—the 'muddy flood . . . whose vices contaminated the very atmosphere', he called them. He was certainly right in identifying foreigners as the prime movers of great changes in social life, as shall be seen in Chapter 6, though his accusations of moral degeneracy were probably more attributable to his own chauvinism than any basis in fact.

No government of the time could be expected to legislate on the behaviour of the ruling classes; but there were attempts to tackle the gin epidemic. The Gin Act of 1736 sought to impose a £50 annual licence on gin shops and at the same time clamp down on the tobacconists, grocers, chandlers and other tradesmen who also sold gin, but the mob reacted with an outburst of violence so fierce that the attempt came to nothing. The gin-sellers carried on as ever, and only two of the licences are recorded as having been issued. The epidemic peaked in the 1740s, and began to die away in the following decade.

A number of factors underlie the decline in gin consumption. In 1751 the Government succeeded in raising the duty which, combined with a sharp rise in grain prices, had the effect of trebling the cost of gin. It was no longer ridiculously cheap, although it was still not ruinously expensive. Perhaps a better explanation is that a fundamental social change was taking place.

The first textile mill, a silk-mill, opened in Derby in 1724. Soon, mills were springing up wherever there was water-power, and they and the engineering industries which serviced them needed man-power. There was no shortage of labour to fill the demand: despite transportation of vast numbers to Australia and the Americas, the population nearly trebled in the eighteenth century. Conditions in the countryside, however, had not improved since King's investigation in 1688, and in the urban slums they had certainly worsened. The mill-owners and industrialists—Darby, Boulton, Paul, Wedgwood, Guest, Arkwright and Strutt—offered the chance of a better life. To attract new workers they constructed neat and even pleasant mill-towns such as Belper, Cromford and Hebden Bridge where there was at least some sanitation, where the houses were solid and weatherproof and where there was enough, if not too much, living space.

These places were far from workers' paradises. The work was hard, the hours were long, industrial diseases and accidents were commonplace and wages were not high. Striking or 'turning-out' was punishable not only by dismissal and eviction, but frequently also by imprisonment or transportation. But compared to, say, the hand-loom weavers, whose piece-work system almost guaranteed a life on the fringes of destitution, the mill-workers were well off. Family incomes varied from 15/- (75p) to £2 a week, which ensured a reasonable standard of living without leaving room for any luxuries, the housing was decent, and the bosses generally took a benevolent, if sanctimonious, interest in their workers' welfare. Whole families migrated from the slums and the inhospitable countryside to the new mill-towns, and it was in these sober and industrious places, where Methodism and other nonconformist sects first flourished, that gin truly met its nemesis.

Gin was not done for, of course; a pint of hot gin continued as a much-favoured tonic well into the nineteenth century, and there was enough of a revival of the gin epidemic after the Napoleonic

War for the distillers to begin building gin-palaces on a lavish scale, but from the middle of the eighteenth century onwards, beer began to reassert its old dominance in the market.

At the same time a revolution was going on in the countryside, too. The expanding population of the new towns meant a larger market for farm produce, and improved agricultural methods ensured that the demand could be filled. The exhausting burden of the rural poor was also being reduced, and this prosperity made itself felt in the licensed trade. Many a country pub dates from the eighteenth century, particularly in market towns, where beer-houses sprang up which would be empty six days a week and packed to the doors on market day. Along the drove-roads which led from Wales and Scotland to London, over a million beasts a year were herded, and although many of the hedge-alehouses which catered for the drovers failed after the advent of steam—for their inac-cessibility usually denied them the possibility of finding new patrons once the drovers had stopped passing—some survive today. The Feathers at Ledbury in Herefordshire was much used by drovers and, surprisingly in view of its modern opulence, so was the Lygon Arms at Broadway. The packhorse drivers, or jaggers, who carried much of the country's wool, lime and salt, also supported many inns and alehouses, as did the 'navigators' who built the canals and railways which superseded both drover and jagger. They were a troublesome brood, the 'navvies', much given to brawling and poaching and utterly contemptuous of the heavily outnumbered constables and gamekeepers who opposed them. But they were thirsty and well-paid, and much of their pay found its way into the pockets of the country beerhouse-keeper.

During this period the beerhouse licensing system took a number of steps closer to the present system. The 1552 Act had stipulated that a licence should be granted by two Justices, and the Order in Council of 1618 made annual renewal compulsory. These pro-cedures could be carried out in private, and there was much corrup-tion. An Act of 1729, by bringing all licensing before the open court, certainly made corruption more difficult, though not impossible. The Consolidation Act of 1828 removed the power of JPs to delicense except at 'Brewster Sessions', and made some other changes, but more important was the royal proclamation of 1787.

This proclamation was one of the two main factors behind the growth of the big breweries and the tied-house system which so worried later governments. The proclamation's introduction of closing times, Sunday closing and certain other restrictions on trade, hit the smaller brewers, particularly the home brewers who still occupied the largest part of the market, much harder than the big brewers who were on the rise. The big brewers, with higher profit margins and bigger capital reserves, were much better placed to weather any trading difficulties or artificially imposed restrictions; they were already turning out thousands of barrels a year at competitive prices, and by the end of the century they had made their stranglehold on the licensed trade still tighter.

The other factor behind the rise of the big brewers was the technical advance which made mass-production possible. Isinglass, a gel extract of the swim-bladders of fish, made its appearance as a fining agent early in the century, and before long hydrometers and thermometers were also in use. At the same time the work of pioneer chemists such as Lavoisier and Leeuwenhoek was contributing to the understanding of the mysterious process of fermentation, and the varying characters of the local water supplies were discounted as brewers learnt how to add or extract mineral salts according to their needs. These innovations meant that big breweries could now turn out a product of a consistent standard and enabled them to go on brewing throughout the year—previously they had had to shut down in the summer months. One of the first beers to be mass-produced was 'entire', later known as 'porter' because of its popularity with workers in London's markets. Originally known as 'three-threads', it started out as a mixture of different beers drawn by the landlord from three or more barrels to the customer's own taste. It was first brewed as entire in 1722, and survived as market leader until the use of glass drinking vessels became common in the middle nineteenth century and made brighter beers, particularly bitter, more popular.

Many of the big brewers who put up their signs in the eighteenth century are still in the market-place today. Benjamin Wilson of Burton was founded in 1708 (now part of Ind Coope), Whitbread was founded in 1742, followed by Worthington in 1744, Charrington in 1766, Bass in 1777 and Courage in 1789.

The licensing system, the beer and the brewers were all coming closer to their modern counterparts. But perhaps the most striking change of the eighteenth century was taking place actually inside the beerhouses and chop-houses of the towns and cities. In the sixteenth and seventeenth centuries, these interiors had resembled the kitchens and parlours of private homes, but an innovation adopted from France was to change all that. The *limonadière* of a Continental salon operated from within a booth situated in the corner of the room. It was her duty to dole out to the maids and waiters the liquor, the pipes and tobacco, to receive the money and to count out the change. Early in the eighteenth century, this booth with its functionary—generally the landlord's wife—made its appearance on this side of the Channel too. Enterprising landlords soon realised the value of having a strikingly pretty girl as *limonadière*, and by the middle of the century the booth, or bar, had become the focus of the room. The pot-boys and maids who plied between bar and table were phased out as customers began to go up themselves, and by the early nineteenth century, 'perpendicular drinking', to use a phrase coined by Gorham and Dunnett in *Inside The Pub*, had arrived.

In country beerhouses and market-town taverns, the bar-counter followed a similar evolutionary path, but much later. Indeed, at a time when the bar-counter was an accepted feature in the cities, Goldsmith was able to base *She Stoops To Conquer* on Marlow's failure to recognise that the squire's house is not, as he has been told, the Three Jolly Pigeons. The development of the bar-counter in the country beerhouse started with the enclosure of a space at the rear of the kitchen as the 'tap', where the day's supply of beer could be brought in from the brew-house. In the tap, the landlord or his wife would preside, and there the pot-boy would repair to refill his jug and get the customers' change. George Morland's *Alehouse Kitchen*, painted in 1788, shows the pot-boy entering the kitchen with a jug which, presumably, he has had to fill in the brew-house across the yard, but in Rowlandson's 1810 version there is a tap screened off at the rear. Eventually the tap became the focus of the room, around which the customers would gather, but this was a later development. Loudon's architectural *Cyclopaedia* of 1833 published a number of designs for country beerhouses, none of them showing a recognisable bar-counter.

But King Gin, as we have seen, was not dead yet. The resurgence in gin-drinking which occurred after the Napoleonic Wars was principally due, odd as it may sound, to the advances made in steam-power. The improved steam engines of Watt and Trevithick created the coal- and copper-mining boom of the 1760s and '70s, but more important, they enabled the manufacturing industries to move down from the inaccessible hillsides of water-powered days to cities such as Manchester, where communications were far easier. Watt and Matthew Boulton teamed up in 1769 to produce their improved steam engine, and in 1775 were granted a 25-year patent. If any single event could be said to mark the birth of the big northern industrial cities, it is this. That the developments which followed were good for business is shown by the tremendous rise in textile exports in the last two decades of the eighteenth century—from less than £½m a year to over £10m—but the cost in human suffering was incalculable.

The old-style mill-owners, for all their shortcomings, at least built their mansions amongst their workers' cottages and took a personal interest in their employees' welfare. Not so the new-style industrialists. They built palmy rural retreats, and let speculators provide homes for the workers. To add to the old-fashioned rookeries such as London's Holy Land, which stretched from Great Russell Street to Seven Dials, there were now abysmal shanties of jerry-built back-to-backs, put up as small, as cheap and as tightly packed as possible to save money. These were purpose-built slums, natural breeding grounds for rickets, typhoid, consumption and cholera. Small wonder that the dangerous classes, as the Victorians called the slum-dwellers, turned back to gin and rioting.

What made disturbances such as the Spa Fields Riots in London in 1817 and the prolonged Chartist troubles of the early nineteenth century seem more sinister to the authorities was the overt political expression which accompanied them. Republicanism, Socialism, Chartism, the combinations, Parliamentary radicalism and, most dreaded of all, Jacobinism—these seemed far more of a threat to the established order than had the merely boisterous effusions of the mobs of a century ago. In the misery that followed the end of the Napoleonic Wars, the Government struck back in the only way it knew: troops, transportation and gaol sentences.

It was not long before the recourse of sending in the dragoons was seen to be futile. The late 1820s saw the beginning of a pro-gramme of reform which was to extend to almost every area of public life: poor relief, Parliamentary enfranchisement, penal reform, policing, public health, factory conditions and child labour, cruel sports—all were examined and to varying degrees reformed. One of the measures contained in this package of reforms was the 1830 Beer Act.

The reasoning behind the Act was threefold. First, gin had made something of a comeback in the industrial slums. Second, tea and coffee imports were rising and threatened the balance of trade. Third, the commanding position established by the big brewers through the tied-house system had almost become a monopoly, with consequent effects on prices and quality. The Act aimed to knock all three on the head by the simple expedient of doing away with beer duty and Justices' licences, and introducing a two-guinea excise licence which would entitle anyone to sell beer. Thus, it was believed, anyone would be able to set up as a beerhouse keeper in-dependently of the big breweries, while demon gin and upstart tea and coffee would be replaced in public favour be traditional manly and virtuous beer. The result of this simple piece of legislation was, however, to be somewhat different from that anticipated.

5

THE COACHING ERA

As we drove into the great gateway of the inn, I saw on one side the
light of a rousing kitchen fire beaming through a window. I entered,
and admired for the hundredth time that picture of convenience,
neatness, and broad, honest enjoyment, the kitchen of an English
inn. . . . Hams, tongues, and flitches of bacon were suspended from
the ceiling; a smoke-jack made its ceaseless clanking beside the
fireplace, and a clock ticked in one corner. A well-scoured deal table
extended along one side of the kitchen, with a cold round of beef and
other hearty viands upon it, over which two foaming tankards of ale
seemed mounting guard. Travellers of inferior order were preparing
to attack this stout repast, while others sat smoking or gossiping over
their ale, on two high-backed oaken settles beside the fire. Trim
housemaids were hurrying backwards and forwards under the direc-
tion of a fresh, bustling landlady, but still seizing an occasional
moment to exchange a flippant word, and have a rallying laugh with
the group round the fire.

Washington Irving's eulogy, taken from *Travelling At Christmas*,
which he wrote at the height of the coaching era, evokes all the
nostalgic romance which still clings to coaching and its inns: the
rumble of the coach, the clatter of the horses' hooves and their
snorting breath and the belling of the post-horn answered by a
hunting horn across the misty meadows on a bracing November
morning. Usually such romantic notions of the past are misplaced,
but perhaps in this case they are not entirely unjustified.

The coaching era, which was at its peak roughly between the
1780s and the 1830s, marked a high point in the fortunes of the
inn unknown since the days of pilgrimage. New inns were opened
by the dozen, old ones refurbished by the hundred, and many of

the attributes of the modern hotel—notably the large dining-room and the ballroom—came into being. Not hundreds, but thousands of inns made their living wholly or in part out of coaching. At the height of the boom in 1825 (the year, ironically, in which the first steam-hauled passenger rail service opened), over two million people travelled by stage-coach, mail-coach, post-chaise, gig or flyer. Apart from the government's mail-coaches, the whole industry was owned, run and co-ordinated by the innkeepers themselves. In their heyday, the coaches had an almost complete monopoly on long-distance travel; even the rich, who had their own vehicles, or those like Cobbett who chose to go about on horseback, depended on the coaching inns for food and shelter.

Coaching was the solution to a problem which had become more and more acute throughout the sixteenth and seventeenth centuries—the abysmal state of transport. As the industrial and agricultural revolutions gathered force, there had to be a corresponding revolution in the transport industry or they would have ground to a halt. The jaggers or pack-horsemen who had hitherto been responsible for much of the carriage of goods and raw materials were eventually replaced by the canal system; but salesmen and businessmen had to move about as well, and even those who did not use commercial coach services were extremely glad of the improved roads and the convenient network of inns provided by the coaching industry.

The process of improving the miry and rutted roads of England had a tentative beginning in 1555, when an Act of Mary I obliged parishes to levy a rate, elect 'waywardens' and conscript local labour to work on the highways. The state of the roads depended therefore on the wealth and energy available in the parishes through which they passed, which often left plenty to be desired. Land-owners were unwilling to pay, men of any calibre were unwilling to serve as waywardens and agricultural workers tended to regard their six days' obligatory annual labour on the roads as a holiday. By the reign of James I, the state of the roads was so poor that weight restrictions, in the form of limiting four-wheeled waggons to only five horses, had to be enacted. As late as 1660 the antiquary Ralph Thoresby had difficulty tracing the line of the Great North Road between Tuxford and Barnby Moor in Nottinghamshire; beyond Doncaster it petered out completely, and he became utterly lost. This sorry state of affairs had been quickly apparent to the Civil War commanders who could only stand by and curse as their troops, guns and supply trains floundered deeper and deeper in the rutted quagmires that passed as roads. It was equally apparent, too, to the hauliers who often took a whole day to shift a load four or five miles.

The first Turnpike Trust was set up at Ware in Hertfordshire by an Act of Parliament of 1663, when a consortium of interested parties undertook to maintain a stretch of the Great North Road, raising funds from tolls levied on all users. The turnpike system was not an immediate success. Local opposition was fierce, and the second trust was not set up until the 1690s. For many years after it was not uncommon for turnpikes to be set upon and destroyed: the City of Hereford was shaken by riots when a Turnpike Act was passed for the area in 1732. Nevertheless, between 1751 and 1772 nearly 400 new trusts were set up, and by the early nineteenth century there were some 20,000 miles of turnpike roads.

The idea was not wholly new. Bridge-building had been funded by tolls since the Middle Ages: the Rose Revived at Newbridge in Oxfordshire is just one inn whose early prosperity depended on the tolls levied from the neighbouring bridge. Many of the new trusts, however, were run by businessmen whose first concern was not merely to profit from the tolls: they were far more anxious to secure an easy passage for their goods. They could be depended upon to discharge their work conscientiously which, out of pure self-interest, benefitted the whole community. But not all trusts were so well-managed, and it was easy to tell where a turnpike was operated by mere profiteers. John Scott, in his *Digests Of The General Highway And Turnpike Laws* of 1778, bitterly attacked the system by which laxer trustees 'farmed' or contracted out the upkeep of turnpikes to agents:

The Trustees, once a road is farmed, have nothing to do but meet once a year to eat venison, and pay the farmer his annuity: the farmer has nothing to do but work as little and pocket as much money as he possibly can; he has other fish to fry, other matters to mind, than road-mending. . . . At length, perhaps, the universal complaint of travellers, or menaces of indictment, rouse the Trustees for a moment: a meeting is called, the farmer sent for and reprimanded, and a few loads of gravel buried among the mud serve to keep the way barely passable.

Since the Middle Ages there had been box-like covered carts, but perhaps the true ancestor of the coach was the unsprung palanquin copied from France by the Earl of Arundel in the reign of Elizabeth I. At first, such vehicles were considered effete and sneered at, but they soon became fashionable after 1565, when the Queen herself was presented with one by a Dutchman. Although she appeared in martial splendour on horseback before her troops at Tilbury during the Armada crisis, it was this coach she used on her many and prodigious royal progresses about the country, and so the innovation caught on. Though these early carriages bounced, jarred and jostled, often stuck in the deep mud and just as often broke down, so did horses. At least a coach preserved the traveller from the worst excesses of the climate. By 1657 there was a regular public service running thrice weekly between London and Chester, taking four days at a charge of 35/6d (£1.77½). Soon there were services from the capital running to Preston, Lancaster and Kendal, and to Exeter and Plymouth, and a commentator in 1669 described them as possessing 'an admirable commodiousness'. But there were the inevitable grumblers too, one of them being the pamphleteer John Cresset, who wrote in 1672:

> What advantage is it to man's health to be called out of their beds into these coaches an hour before day in the morning, to be hurried in them from place to place till one hour, two, three, within night . . . in the summertime stifled with heat and choked with dust; in the wintertime starving and freezing with cold. . . . They are often brought into their inns by torchlight, when it is too late to sit up and get a supper; and the next morning they are forced into their coach so early that they can get no breakfast.

59

The grim picture that Cresset presented of the hazards of early coach travel is convincing enough: vehicles stuck in the mud and passengers forced to wade clear to wait for a team of horses to come up and haul out the coach, breakdowns, which meant another wait and often a hectic drive through the night to make up lost time, poor inns without suitable accommodation, cheating innkeepers and 'surly, dogged, cussing, illnatured coachmen' who refused to throw out their schedules by stopping either for calls of nature or even for genuine cases of illness. Nevertheless, Cresset rather spoiled his argument by inconsistency, adding that the convenience of travel afforded by coaches lured good women from their hearths to the vice-ridden cities, where exposure to fashionable clothes and plays bred in them 'such a habit of idleness and love of pleasure as to make them uneasy ever after'. But whether so inconvenient as to be a health hazard or so convenient as to be immoral, the new industry developed regardless.

True, the coaching trade made a hesitant start, as such new systems often do. Quite apart from the parlous state of the roads and the ubiquitous highwaymen who plagued them (the successors, incidentally, of Royalist officers who turned to robbery after the Civil War, which is why so many highwaymen were accorded spurious military ranks), the design of the coach itself had yet to be perfected. Arundel's was a clumsy, unsprung oaf of the road, and its immediate successors were little better. The coaches of which Cresset complained were not much more than covered waggons and they were superseded by vehicles resembling sedan chairs on wheels. A London service started by the landlord of the Pheasant in Shrewsbury in 1730 and dubbed the Gee-Ho was probably of this latter type, as was the coach shown in a Hogarth engraving of 1747. One particular feature of this picture is that although there are no seats and no guard-rail on the roof, there are a few passengers clinging on precariously and only saved from falling off by the vehicle's lack of speed. Life for the 'outsiders' was always tough, and the annals of coaching abound with gruesome tales of such unfortunates found frozen to death at the end of a long journey, or having their heads struck off by low bridges and archways.

By 1753 there was another oddity on the London to Shrewsbury road: the Long Coach, which was drawn by six horses and took four days to reach its destination. However, by this time a greater degree of sophistication was becoming available, and the Long Coach was soon withdrawn from service. In 1720 the average speed between London and York had been 5mph; by 1750 it was 7mph. Fowler's Stage to London, which started from the Raven in Shrewsbury in the same year as the Long Coach, took only three and a half days to cover the distance; in 1754 the Flying Coach took four days between London and Manchester; and in 1761 the Farewell reached the Green Dragon, Whitechapel, from Colchester's Red Lion in eight hours at a cost of 25/- (£1.25).

The greatest drawback in the early years was the lack of springing, which not only caused much discomfort to passengers but also enforced a severe limitation on speed, and without speed the trade's full potential could not be realised. One of the entrepreneurs who recognised this and tackled the problem in many ways was Robert Lawrence, who took over the Raven in Shrewsbury from his father in 1771 when he was only 22, and became one of the most important figures in coaching history. His attack on the speed limits of the time was threefold. First of all, punctuality which had always been a virtue prized by coach operators, for if two coaches which were supposed to arrive at an inn with an interval of half-an-hour or twenty minutes pulled in together, the resulting confusion could set both services back several precious minutes. Lawrence was as much a stickler for punctuality as any other conscientious coach operator, and his services were among those by which local people swore they could tell the time. Secondly, Lawrence played an important part in the development and improvements along Watling Street, and was doubtless instrumental in Thomas Telford's appointment as Shropshire's county surveyor in 1786. It was due in great part to him that Shrewsbury became a major coaching town on the Holyhead road when Holyhead was as important a port as Liverpool, and the landlords of the many other coaching inns which proliferated in the town must have, or at any rate should have, revered his memory. Finally, he started up one of the first services to use sprung vehicles, the Fly, which, in his first two years as landlord, ran regularly between Shrewsbury and Birmingham.

Although he died young, in 1806, Lawrence nonetheless accomplished much. He was constantly innovating and experimenting, and in all his ventures speed and reliability were the keys. In 1773, in partnership with a Stratford-upon-Avon innkeeper named Payton, he came up with the New Machine, which went to London, and in 1774 both the Fly and the New Machine were succeeded by the New Fly. The Diligence, which he started in 1776, made London inside a day, as compared with the four days taken by the Long Coach fifty years before, carrying three passengers who paid a guinea each. In 1779 he set up another fast service, a post-chaise running between London and Holyhead. When he moved from the Raven to the Lion in 1780, he took his business with him, and in 1784, when the Government replaced the old system of mounted post-boys with mail-coaches, Lawrence succeeded in winning the contract to service all mails passing through the town. Even after his death, the Lion maintained the unassailable position in the town's affairs which he had created for it: one of the most famous coaches of the whole era was the Wonder, which started up in 1822 and took just sixteen hours between London and the Lion. In 1825 the Lion boasted seven daily coaches on the London–Holyhead run, thirteen local services per day and regular mails to Chester, Welshpool, Newtown and Aberystwyth.

Lawrence was a combination of daring pioneer and hard-headed businessman, but although he deserved his great success he was a far from unique phenomenon. By 1775 he, and the many others like him, had evolved the classic coach design which was to remain almost unchanged for over sixty years, and were running some 400 main-road services with a fleet of nearly 17,000 vehicles. At the same time, road technology, in the hands of civil engineers such as Blind Jack Metcalfe, Telford and, a few years later, Macadam, meant shorter and more comfortable journeys. The Lion, though Shrewsbury's leading coaching inn, had plenty of rivals in the town, and there were many other coaching inns across the country just as well-known. One such was the Castle at Marlborough, originally built as a residence for Lord Seymour in the reign of Charles II. In 1740 it became the home of Lady Hertford (who astounded the locals by wandering the newly laid-out gardens in the guise of an Arcadian nymph), and in 1751 the property passed to the Duke of Northumberland who, having more of a head for commerce than for classical legend, promptly leased it out to a Mr Cottrell as an inn. It changed hands again in 1752, and under the proprietorship of Mr George Smith soon became perhaps the most prominent stop between London and fashionable Bath. In Smith's day the 106-mile journey took less than eight hours, so there cannot have been much time to dally at the Castle. But one client who did enjoy a prolonged stay was Pitt the Elder, in 1762, who had been taking the waters at Bath as a cure for gout. On the way home his gout, unaffected by the healing springs, caused him such agony that he decided he could travel no further. He stayed at the Castle for six weeks, playing host to friends, colleagues and placemen, and during his time there made the inn his home to such an extent that even the ostlers and waiters were ordered to wear his livery. In the 1820s the Castle passed to Thomas Cooper, who achieved the impossible by going bankrupt and ended his days as the station-master of Richmond, in the employ of the London & South Western Railway. The Castle flourished until 1840, when the Great Western Railway opened at Swindon, twelve miles away. The Castle's trade collapsed almost overnight, and it stood empty for two years until in 1843 it became the home of a boys' public school, Marlborough College. The old inn still forms an integral part of the school buildings.

The golden age of coaching was also an age of great rebuilding, during which the architectural face of the country was transformed. The wealth generated by the agricultural and industrial revolutions not only created townscapes such as Bath and Brighton and splendid piles such as Castle Howard, Osterley Park and Dodington House, it also left an indelible mark on the nation's inns. It is safe to say that in most market towns the principal inn, if not Georgian in origin, will have been largely rebuilt or extended at some time in the eighteenth or early nineteenth centuries. For while it may be an exaggeration to claim that there was a revulsion of taste against anything Gothic or Tudor which smacked of barbarism, it is certainly true that with the money now available, and with colonial expansion well under way, people wanted and could afford something more modern, more convenient and more in keeping with the imperial times than the rough stone or timber-framed relics of earlier epochs.

One of the first inns to be rebuilt was the Rose & Crown at Saffron Walden (once kept, some say, by the boyfriend of Shakespeare to whom the sonnets were addressed) in 1690, followed by the White Hart at Spalding on the Boston–Grimsby turnpike in 1714. The Cross Keys at St Neot's, the George at Rye, the Ferry at Tottenham, the Dolphin at Southampton with its enormous bow-windows, the Sun at Hitchin, the White Hart at Lewes and the Lion at Shrewsbury were among the dozens of inns which came in for massive rebuilding between 1730 and 1780. In the last two decades of the eighteenth century, an even grander style in coaching-inn architecture began to make itself felt. The Angel at Bury St Edmunds, the Swan at Bedford and the White Hart at Salisbury all boast great pillared porticoes which make them the equal of, or superior to, the important municipal buildings of the period.

The coaching age produced some of its finest monuments in its last thirty or forty years: the Royal Clarence at Bridgwater, the Mytton & Mermaid near Shrewsbury, dignified enough for an affluent country seat, the Grosvenor in Shaftesbury, built in 1826 to replace a monastic guest-house of Saxon origin, the Burford Bridge, originally the Hare & Hounds, at Box Hill in Surrey, the Verulam Arms at St Albans, made redundant by the railway within ten years of its opening, and the Bell at Saxmundham, built in 1842

The White Hart, Salisbury. An outstanding example of the classical coaching inn with its impressive portico, the White Hart replaced a medieval inn. The figure on top of the pediment was added in 1827, some twenty-five years after the building's completion

and ruined by steam just four years later. These inns, with their ostlers and fresh horses every-ready, with their coffee-rooms, kitchens, private parlours and bedrooms, catered in the main extremely well to commoner and aristocrat alike. But they could afford to be choosy about their clientele, as Pastor Karl Moritz, a German who made a tour of Britain on foot in 1782, found to his cost. Travellers on foot were treated with some suspicion, not to say outright hostility, and Moritz recorded:

> They showed me into a kitchen, and set me down to sup at table with some soldiers and the servants. . . . While I was eating, a post-chaise drove up; and in a moment both folding doors were thrown open, and the whole house set in motion to receive with all due respect these guests who, no doubt, were supposed to be persons of consequence.

Arriving at another inn, near Oxford, Moritz was permitted to buy a glass of ale but was refused food, and was curtly told to press on into the town itself, exhausted as he was. With justifiable indignation, he concluded:

In England, a person undertaking so long a journey on foot is sure to be looked upon and considered as either a beggar, or a vagabond, or some necessitous wretch. . . . It is impossible, even in theory, and much less so in practice, to approve of a system that confines all the pleasures and benefits of travel to the rich. A poor peripatetic is hardly allowed the humble merit of being honest.

And it was not only those who chose to go about on foot who found cause for complaint. John Byng, 5th Viscount Torrington, travelled widely between 1781 and 1794, and although he singled out some inns for praise, he found that in general:

The innkeepers are insolent, the hostlers are sulky, the chambermaids are pert, and the waiters are impertinent; the meat is tough, the wine is foul, the beer is hard, the sheets are wet, the linen is dirty, and the knives are never cleaned. . . . I look upon an inn as the seat of all roguery, profaneness, and debauchery; and sicken of them every day. . . . For the sake of hasty gain, innkeepers hire horrid servants and buy bad provisions and poisonous liquors.

Either the Viscount was unusually hard to please, or he had bad luck in his choice of inn, for his peers amongst the gentry rapidly took the greater inns to their hearts. The rigid social segregation of the outside world soon made itself felt inside the inn as well, for if richer travellers were to use public facilities, they did not expect to have to mix with the mere *hoi polloi*. The private rooms and coffee-room were the preserve of those who travelled inside the coach; those who endured the hardships of the roof made do with the kitchen. Among the many contemporary writers who remarked on this snobbery was Thomas de Quincey:

It was the fixed assumption of the four inside people that they, the illustrious quaternion, constituted a porcelain variety of the human race, whose dignity would have been compromised by exchanging one word of civility with the miserable delf-wares outside. What words then could express the horror and sense of treason in that case . . . where all three outsides, the trinity of pariahs, made a vain attempt to sit down at the same breakfast table as the consecrated four? The course taken with the infatuated outsides was that the waiter ... sang out: 'This way, my good men,' and then enticed these good men away to the kitchen.

The principal inns soon became a rallying point for polite local society, which did its best to emulate the high life of those centres of royal patronage, Bath and Brighton. The coaching inns were going up in the world, and soon they acquired apartments to match their new-found status. Most of the larger coaching inns possess an assembly room, ballroom, or 'long room' (either still intact or partitioned into bedrooms, for they were generally on the first floor), where took place the hunt ball, the winter assemblies, the concerts, the exhibitions and all the other events and functions at which local gentry congregated. Frequently these assembly rooms vie in elegance of proportion and ornament with the staterooms of the mansions of the rich: the Lion in Shrewsbury possesses a splendid assembly room which was long held to be the work of the brothers Adam themselves, and even an unassuming country inn like the White Lion at Eye in Norfolk possesses a beautifully adorned mid-eighteenth-century ballroom. The Lion in 1807 entertained no less a personage than the Duke of Clarence, later William IV; in 1830 Madame Tussaud exhibited her waxworks there; Paganini played there in 1831; and the Swedish Nightingale, Jenny Lind, was a firm favourite with local *cognoscenti* and performed at the Lion more than once. Jane Austen, David Garrick, Sir Joshua Reynolds and even George III were among the many luminaries entertained at the Bear at Devizes. The New Inn at Berkhamsted knew the exiled Louis XVIII of France so well that on his restoration he sent for the landlord's daughter, Mary Page, and returned her home from Paris laden with gifts. The subscription dances at the Dolphin, Southampton, were well-known: Jane Austen with her mother and sister spent the winter of 1808 there and were regular attenders, as were Clarence and the young Princess Victoria. 'Prinny', later George IV, celebrated his birthday in 1798 at the Old Ship in Brighton, and his morganatic wife, Mrs Fitzherbert, often presided over the festivities there.

The Lion, Shrewsbury. Another hall-mark of the climax of the coaching era, the Lion's elegant assembly room was built in the late eighteenth century in the style, if not the actual hand, of the Adam brothers

The end, when it came, was perhaps not as sudden as has been imagined. The railways took some years to spread their tentacles over the country, and though the major coach routes were killed off fairly swiftly, local services lingered on for forty or fifty years in some parts. As late as 1844 a new coach service started running between London and Cambridge, the Great White Horse in Ipswich was rebuilt and there were hourly coaches between London and Brighton. In 1851 the George at Shrewsbury ran coaches to and from Hereford and Aberystwyth, road mails were still calling at the Swan at Tewkesbury in 1864 and the Star at Lewes still ran coaches in 1874. Many of the crustier old reactionaries preferred coaches to trains, and from the 1850s on there was a small but viable tourist interest in the nostalgia (as it had already become) of coaching. Perhaps the last commercial coach in the country ran from the Crown at Amersham to London: the advent of the Metropolitan line in 1894 finally killed it off.

These survivals were, however, anachronisms. The railways took less than fifteen years to erode the greater part of the trade: the Verulam Arms went in 1837, the Castle at Marlborough in 1841, the Bell at Saxmundham in 1846. The George at Rye managed to survive the departure of its last London coach in 1845, but one of the better known casualties was the Chapel House Inn on the main Oxford to Birmingham road in 1850, where less than seventy years earlier Dr Johnson had told his faithful Boswell:

> There is no private house in which people can enjoy themselves so well as in a capital tavern. . . . There is nothing which has yet been contrived by man by which so much happiness is provided as by a good tavern or inn.

But when the author and cyclist Charles Harper visited the place in 1906, the outbuildings had long been labourers' cottages and the house itself was a bed and breakfast hotel.

The best chance of survival for many of the old coaching inns, now that their main source of business was gone, was to lease or sell part of their premises to those who could best make use of them. A wheelwright set up shop in the yard of the George at Dorchester-on-Thames, and a tent-maker was based at the White Hart Royal at Moreton-in-Marsh in the Cotswolds. Stables became dairies or warehouses while the inns themselves struggled on as mere village beerhouses. Deserted inn yards proved ideal depots for local carriers whose businesses had grown up to supplement the rail network, carting goods and passengers from the stations to outlying farms and villages. The revenue yielded by the carrying trade proved a life-saver for many once-glorious coaching inns, and in many towns carried on right into the 1920s. But even when an old inn managed to limp along in this fashion, the glitter had worn off. Those which survived as well-founded and reasonably affluent hotels could not continue as the favoured haunts of nobility and royalty, as Washington Irving discovered when he visited the Lion at Shrewsbury in 1855. A depressing and dingy place it was, compared with its former splendour, and the assembly room was being let as a warehouse. It was, Irving remarked:

An uncheerful old hotel, which takes upon itself to be in the best
class of English country hotels, and charges the best price; very dark
in the lower apartments; pervaded with a musty odour.

Some, particularly the town inns, did better: the Mitre at Oxford
survived on the strength of an excellent restaurant and a long association with the University, and continued to attract notables such
as Peel, Gladstone, Cecil Rhodes, Hilaire Belloc and Noël Coward.
In London, the great coaching termini became hotels: the Belle
Sauvage at Ludgate Hill became the Belle Sauvage Hotel and the
Golden Cross at Charing Cross became Morley's Hotel. The
railways even proved beneficial for trade in such picturesque areas
as the Lake District, which had always been praised by the poets
but which were for the first time accessible to greater numbers of
visitors.

But the Nimrod, the Old Blue, the Diligence, the Flying
Machine, the Quicksilver, the Rapid, the Triumph, the Emerald,
and the Union ran no more; the Haycock at Wansford, the Blue
Bell at Barnby Moor, the Bull's Head at Meriden, the Swan and the
Angel at Ferrybridge, the Old Angel at Basingstoke and the Talbot
at Atcham stood silent and empty. The coaches slowly rotted with
the straw in which they had been abandoned, until they were
broken up for firewood and their iron-rimmed wheels were sold
to trap and gig drivers. But many of the inns were only dormant:
either closed and slumbering, or eking out a painful existence on
whatever custom happened along and whatever shrift the landlord
could make. It was not to be many decades before the tinkle of a
bicycle-bell or the honk of a motor-horn sounding down the leafy
lanes heralded the coming of a new generation of road travellers,
and stirred up the old houses again into the life and vitality they
had once known.

6

PALACES AND PUBS
1830-1904

As expected, the Beer Act of 1830 provoked an explosion in the trade. With virtually all restrictions removed, beer prices fell by half to 2d (1p) or 1d a quart, while the number of beerhouses mushroomed—between 40–50,000 new ones opened in the two decades following the Act. But in all its other objectives the Act was a miserable failure. Tea imports, which the Government had hoped to curb, were unscathed. Gin consumption showed a brief decline in the 1830s, but by 1845 had climbed above the 1830 level.

The Act's biggest failure was in its main objective—the reversal of the trend towards tied houses. True, thousands of independent beerhouses were set up, many of them low dives in desperate slums, but the main beneficiaries of the Beer Act were the very people it had set out to tame: the big breweries. Like the distillers, they were in a strong position already; now they could deploy all their resources to exploit an expanding market on a scale no movement of independent traders could hope to match. Within ten years of the Act's passage, Bass had increased their output from 10,000 to 60,000 barrels a year; by the end of the century they were producing a million barrels a year. There was room, too, for new companies to establish themselves: Davenport's was founded in 1846, and Ansell's, now a subsidiary of Allied Breweries, in 1858.

The experience of Victorian England was on the one hand the triumphant growth of Empire, with all its economic advantages, and on the other the painful and sordid side-effects of that boom— horrific slums, appalling poverty and almost unmanageable crime.

Certainly the Beer Act was partly to blame for the fact that, by 1900, 10 deaths per 100,000 were the direct result of alcoholism (compared with 4 per 100,000 today), and many more were drink-related, but the Act must share the blame with a number of other factors.

The vast increase in population—in the first forty years of the nineteenth century, London's population more than doubled to over two million—created many problems: poor education, over-crowded and decaying housing, polluted water-supplies and non-existent sanitation. Added to this was the fact that there was not enough work to go round. Many of those in full-time employment were on starvation wages, and a great number had only part-time or seasonal work. Henry Mayhew devoted much of the first volume of *London Labour And The London Poor*, published in 1851, to a study of the capital's 30,000 costermongers and their families. Although not by a long chalk the worst-off of London's workers, the costers were largely illiterate, lived in overcrowded and un-hygienic mazes of courts and alleys, fell prey to typhus, cholera, smallpox, rickets and a hundred and one other diseases, and came near to starvation whenever a run of bad weather interrupted trade. They had to borrow heavily to equip themselves with barrow and stock, they faced persistent harrassment from the fledgling Metropolitan Police (founded in 1829), and their earnings fluctua-ted wildly with the season, so that although they were well-off at times, on other occasions they were virtually destitute.

For the very poor, things were much worse. Overcrowding was perhaps the main problem. A parliamentary report of the mid-nineteenth century revealed that an inspector found three women living in a room 9ft square; 200 lodgers were put up in a 40-room house in Borough; and in Manchester 200 people were crammed into 10 rooms in 4 labourers' cottages. Rooms were partitioned and sub-partitioned, let and sub-let; and in Manchester 7,000 people were reported to be sharing 33 privies. The staple diet in the slums was cheap fish, onions and potatoes, and at a time when 250oz of solid food a week was considered the minimum necessary to feed a single prisoner, whole families of slum-dwellers might subsist on 120oz. Death from malnutrition was not uncommon, and malnutrition-related diseases were endemic.

Small wonder that the 'dangerous classes' or 'surplus population' (Victorian euphemisms) chose to take refuge in the bottle. All the symptoms of the gin epidemic a century earlier were repeated, only this time it was the beerhouses that profited. The slum-dwellers packed them to the doors, old and young alike—for children made up a disproportionately large part of the slum population, and since they often had to earn a living from the age of seven or eight, and might take a mistress or turn prostitute at eleven or twelve, they might justifiably feel entitled to drink alongside their elders.

It took the Government until 1869 to relearn the lesson of the early eighteenth century and repeal the Act. Suddenly the proprietors of slum pot-houses found themselves having to apply for Justices' licences, and in many cases being turned down; so most of the more squalid drinking-dens soon disappeared. But those thirty-nine years proved very much a gestation period for the pub as we know it, for during that time a number of institutions were developed, all of them descendants of the town taverns of previous centuries. Undoubtedly the most important of these was the gin-palace, but there were a number of other variations on the theme.

Music-hall, for instance, was born in the large town beerhouse of the early part of the century, where a dramatic tradition dating back to the Middle Ages was continued. Even before Shakespeare's day, troupes of itinerant mummers had performed their mimes and miracle plays in the yard of the local inn, perhaps using a farm cart as a stage, and by the nineteenth century many beerhouses had halls and stages of their own. Mayhew's costers were very partial to blood-and-thunder melodrama, and even enjoyed Shakespeare's tragedies if the production was gory enough. These pub-theatres were also used for variety concerts, and they were able to improve their business enormously after the 1843 Theatres Act, when smoking and drinking were banned in the auditoria of legitimate theatres. The tavern concerts soon gave way to 'saloon theatres', where the show was as big a draw as the refreshment, and the separation of pub and music-hall was complete by the 1890s, when the capital's thirty-five main halls and numerous lesser ones entertained up to 45,000 people a night.

The wave of French immigrants which Steinmentz had noted, and disliked, also had a profound effect on the social life of the capital and, eventually, the whole country. Many of the refugees who fled the Terror and Napoleon were aristocrats, and many of them came over with quite enough jewellery and other portable wealth to set up in business for themselves. As so often with refugees, they tended to choose the catering trade. 'Hotel' is a French word rarely if ever heard in England before the nineteenth century, but it rapidly gained currency. At first, the refugees were able to make good money by billeting the officers of the wartime armed forces, and by the time the wars were over hotels had become an established part of the scene. One of the first purpose-built hotels was the Royal at Ross-on-Wye in 1837. By the 1850s those inns which had survived the decline of coaching were often describing themselves as hotels, and at the same time the expanding railway companies were building station hotels all over the country and on all scales, from the humblest Railway Inn to the great establishments of the main termini. The rising middle classes, seeking to escape the cities to holiday in some remote and picturesque spot hitherto inaccessible, gave the hotel trade a further boost, and in spa towns all over the country hydros and hotels made good profits right up to World War I.

Another French import was the café, although the original concept was somewhat different from the egg-and-chip joints we now know by the term. Then they were the heirs of the Parisian coffee-houses, more ornate and glittering than their English cousins. Perhaps it was the Englishman's distrust of French morality, as typified by Steinmentz, that soon gave these places the reputation of pick-up points for prostitutes. Certainly the cafés and the casinos (at that time dance-halls rather than gambling-dens) did their best not to disappoint. There were at the time more prostitutes available in London than at any time before or since, and clients from senior partner to humble clerk thronged the cafés—Sam's, Sally's, the Grand Turkish and, most famous of all, Kate Hamilton's Café Royal; and the casinos—Kellner's, Caudwell's, the Portland Rooms, the Argyll Rooms—where cheap bubbly, masquerading as champagne and sold at exorbitant prices, flowed like water, where a girl cost five or ten shillings and where the police looked the other way.

For the more lowly pleasure-seeker there was always the dangerous Ratcliffe Highway in London's East End, where in dozens of mean dives the girls 'waited for Jack', whose pockets would be bulging with back pay after a long voyage; the best known of these pubs was the White Swan, always called Paddy's Goose. But the well-heeled slumming it in rough districts had to be careful: 'bearing up' was the cant expression for mugging clients lured down alleyways by prostitutes into the arms of some 'Chokee Bill', who would be waiting with his neddy (cosh) or his garrotte.

Perhaps Victorian England was not so prim and proper as we imagine it. Certainly many of the pubs were not. A prosperous publican in a seedy area, such as Stunning Joe Banks, proprietor of the Hare & Hounds in St Giles (also known as the Holy Land, and without doubt the most dangerous slum in London), might be the biggest man in the community. His establishment might be a lumber, or favoured resort of criminals; he himself might be a fence, a smasher (distributor of counterfeit coins), or even a layer-on (organiser of major crimes). Ratting was one of the most popular sports in the country after bull- and bear-baiting were outlawed in 1835 and cock-fighting was banned in 1849. It was conducted almost exclusively in pubs, where there were often special pits constructed for it. A ratting-match was one of the few occasions when social rank could be forgotten. The dogs, usually mongrel terriers, competed to kill a given number of rats within a stated time, and it mattered nothing whether the owner was a doctor or a docker, a lawyer or a labourer. In a sizeable venue, 2,000 or more rats might be killed in a week, normally for a prize such as a silver dog-collar.

The landlord would charge sixpence or so for admission, and naturally sold plenty of drinks, but the real money lay in the fast, furious and quite illegal betting that accompanied each match. The fancy—the habitués of bare-knuckle prize-fighting (outlawed in the '60s)—were very much inhabitants of the pub world. The great Tom Cribb, on his retirement from the ring, was set up as the landlord of the Union in Panton Street off London's Haymarket (the pub now bears his name) by admirers who included Lord Byron. At such disreputable haunts as Jem Burns's Queen's Head in Windmill Street and Sambo Sutton's Black Bull in Drury Lane, daring young swells could hire gloves and spar a few rounds with some old pug. Burns himself was a noted fight promoter, being one of the backers of Tom Bendigo, who defeated Ben Caunt (himself landlord of the Coach & Horses in St Mártin's Lane) for the championship in April 1845.

The term 'public house' is another Victorian euphemism, and perhaps the more genteel people of the time were justified in the suspicion with which they regarded the pubs. However, not all pubs warranted this hostility. In respectable suburbs and the quiet cul-de-sacs of the more select areas, a number of restrained and well-managed establishments catered for the needs of the male servants of the upper and middle classes and for the menfolk of those classes themselves (working-class women were seen in pubs, but never middle- or upper-class women). Not all working-class beerhouses were the dens of vice that they were imagined to be. Then, as now, a well-managed pub found itself the focus of the local community, and many thoughtful and conscientious landlords became more and more sympathetic to the growing political consciousness of the working classes. Working men's benevolent and friendly associations often had their headquarters in the upstairs room of the local. The costers, for instance, whom Mayhew found to be anti-establishment republicans and socialists and 'Chartists to a man', set up a friendly society known as the House of Lords at the Roebuck, Holborn, and the Street Mechanics', Labourers' and Hawkers' Association had its home at the Lamb nearby. In the countryside and provincial cities, many pubs became 'houses of call', which functioned as hostels and employment exchanges for the many itinerant craftsmen who tramped the roads, offering credit, hiring out tools and helping to set men who were down on their luck back on their feet again. The best of these were often jointly organised by the landlord and local trade unionists, while the worst were often little better than 'padding kens' (doss houses) such as the Three Queens at Chelmsford, the Castle at Braintree, the Woolpack at Newmarket, the Cock at Bedford and a host of others where a penny or two would buy a tramp or moucher (professional beggar) a straw shake-down for the night in some leaky, overcrowded, cold and verminous lean-to.

But it is the gin-palaces which are perhaps the most solid legacy of Victorian days to the licensed trade. Originally, these palaces of the poor were the distillers' answer to the threat posed by the Beer Act; the first is generally reckoned to have been Thompson & Fearon's in Holborn Hill, opened in 1831 and variously attributed to the architects J. B. Papworth and Stephen Geary. However, within a few years, the term was no longer applied merely to highly ornate gin shops, and came to mean all pubs of a particular style of architecture and decor.

The main factors behind the rise of the gin-palace are threefold. The prime one was the Victorian love of ostentation, often quite ungoverned by good taste. Secondly, to compete with the new beerhouses that began to open after the 1830 Act, the distillers had to hit back with all their might. Many of these beerhouses were the most basic of establishments, so the gin-sellers went to the opposite extreme. They reasoned, and rightly, that an environment of opulence and extravagance would prove an irresistible temptation to those whose own surroundings were so miserable, and they spared no expense in creating at least an illusion of elegance and luxury. Indeed, many of the most lavish of the gin-palaces were to be found in the worst of the slums. Finally, the ever-increasing population further sharpened the already competitive instincts of the nation of shopkeepers. To stay in business something extra had to be offered, and soon, all over London and the big cities, new shop-fronts of ornately carved wood and brilliantly lit plate glass began to appear—like a contagious disease, according to Dickens. Where chandlers, druggists and grocers led, the licensed trade was not slow to follow.

The gin-palace continued its development from those early days right up to the beginning of this century, a late example being the recently restored Barton's Arms at Aston, Birmingham. Its debt to the nineteenth-century love of display is evident both in exteriors, which ranged from Swiss chalet to Gothic and Italianate and eventually to a chaotic mix of them all, and interiors, where the decor could reach truly absurd heights of fantasy. The Swiss Cottage in Hampstead (designed by P. F. Robinson, who was responsible for much of Brighton Pavilion) and its twin in Forest Hill, South London, both date back to the 1840s. They were followed in the 1850s by an Italian Renaissance style, which was also employed in the design of many railway stations and municipal buildings, and which in turn gave way to mock-Gothic. By the 1870s, when such pubs as the Old King Lud on Ludgate Circus were built, it is sometimes hard to know what the style is meant to be and from where it was borrowed.

Eccentric exteriors, however, are not unusual in Victorian and Edwardian buildings. The shops and offices on the south side of Oxford Street backing onto Soho, Sheffield Town Hall, Westminster Cathedral, Osborne House on the Isle of Wight—these are all examples of whimsy in an age when it was a highly valued commodity. Where the gin-palace is unique is in the treatment of its interior; and that owes much to the march of technology.

Perhaps the most important ingredient in the creation of the fairy-tale effect inside a gin-palace was the combination of gas illumination and plate glass. Carefully placed mirrors and great sheets of plate glass, breaking and reflecting the blaze of the gas-jets, could make a fairly small bar-room seem much larger than it really was. The earliest methods of decorating plate glass were grinding and acid-etching, but after the 1840s and '50s new techniques made possible great panels of richly ornamented glass, often 12ft square or more. Three significant events in the popularisation of glass were the repeal of the excise on it in 1845, the repeal of the window-tax in 1851 and, in the same year, the opening of the Great Exhibition in the glass Crystal Palace sited in Hyde Park. More than anything, this enormous structure (later moved to the area of South London which now bears its name) opened the eyes of the public, and the licensed trade, to the possibilities of glass. A machine patented in Bristol in 1850 enabled brilliant-cutting, hitherto only possible on a small scale, to be used for much larger patterns, and apart from the introduction of sand-blasting in 1870, these techniques remained in use almost unchanged until the gin-palace went out of style. The most favoured themes in glass decoration were taken from nature: vine, hop and acanthus foliage, the national flowers of the four countries of the United Kingdom and birds perched on branches. In later years it became possible to achieve different depths of cut, which meant that several tones could be used to break up the light still further. The illusion of space this created was heightened by stopping the partitions dividing the different bars a few feet short of the ceiling, so the drinker had a vista of unbroken relief patterns on the ceiling stretching away overhead apparently into the distance.

This glass revolution had an effect on the beer itself. Previously beer had been drunk out of pewter, earthenware or even wooden pots and piggins, and since these materials are opaque, the appearance of the drink hardly mattered. As glass mugs became more common, however, drinkers found they preferred the shining, amber bitter or pale ale to the murkier porter. By the end of the century, porter had lost its hold on the London market, sinking from around three-quarters to a quarter of all beer sold. Bottled beers, too, became more prevalent, and the old practice of taking a jug down to the pub to be filled became less common.

The first gin-palaces were generally long narrow rooms with a bar-counter stretching all down one side, the whole being divided by partitions into as many separate rooms as were considered

necessary. But not all sites were suitable for this sort of treatment, and in time the different bars—saloon, public, smoking-room, four-ale (so called because mild, favoured by manual workers, cost 4d [1½p]) and so on—came to be grouped round an island or waggon bar which might form a horseshoe or even a complete circle. A plethora of small rooms was often favoured: the Dun Cow in the Old Kent Road had no fewer than eleven, and in many Victorian pubs in the north of England there are still little rooms which will take no more than six or eight customers. The bar-counter itself was often a solid slab of mahogany, sometimes with a 'snob-screen' of louvred opaque glass at eye level so that respectable drinkers need not fear being recognised. In early days the main theme of decoration was the way in which barrels, bottles, and beer-pumps were arranged; later on, however, pillars, pediments and pinnacles rose up like some dream of Camelot. This woodwork, generally of oak, mahogany and rosewood, and often artificially grained, was as much a product of traditional craftsmanship as any medieval choir-stall or hammer-beam roof, and little expense was spared.

Keeping the whole place clean was vital work, for if the correct light-effects were to be created, every surface, even the wooden ones, had to be a sparkling reflector. The task of dusting and polishing was often carried out by maids working an eighteen-hour day for a few shillings a week, for staff was no problem in an era when over 10 per cent of the adult population was in service. Today, however, it is often hard to imagine how brilliant these interiors must originally have been, since age and tobacco darken wood and stain glass, and few landlords can afford the staff necessary to combat them.

The traditional colours for a pub interior were a combination of warm but sombre reds, different shades of brown and cream, all glowing with a subtle patina of nicotine. For its brighter splashes

---

The White Hart, Hull, Humberside. The White Hart's interior has been opened out and the original feel of the gin-palace is lost, but this magnificent ceramic horseshoe bar with its mahogany fittings, dating from the 1890s, is still in place

the bar-room relied on the lettering of advertisements, posters and bottle-labels. Wallpaper may have been acceptable in suburban saloon bars, but more favoured were moulded wall- and ceiling-coverings such as Tynecastle, made of leather and canvas, Lyncrusta, made of canvas and linseed pulp, Cameoid, or pressed paper, and Anaglypta, made of pressed paper pulp. These were perhaps the only examples of ersatz then in common use for they were meant to replace hand-moulded plaster, but, unlike the glass-work and joinery, could be stamped out by the yard in a mill.

Gin-palaces did attract patrons of every rank, but their chief appeal was to the poor. For the middle classes there was something immoral, something Babylonian, about their bright allure, so in business districts a better trade was done by the dining-rooms and luncheon rooms which flourished. One such was Short's in the Strand, converted from a hotel in 1833 to cater for Somerset House clerks. Short's still laid on a shilling ordinary, but the hearty fellowship this communal meal was supposed to engender was already giving way to the greater intimacy of separate tables. H. E. Popham, visiting Simpson's fish restaurant at Cheapside in 1926, believed it was the last place in the capital still running a one o'clock ordinary complete with chairman and a prize for guessing the weight of the cheese. Fish restaurants were particularly popular in Victorian London, stretching along the Thames from Richmond to Greenwich, for the river, despite the pollution, still provided eels, whitebait and oysters at four a penny. Foreign restaurants also came into vogue, eclipsing the native chop-houses: the Café Royal, Regent Street (not the same as Kate Hamilton's establishment of the same name) in 1863, Kettner's in 1867 and Pagani's in 1871. Thus the catering trade was no longer confined to inns and taverns, and eventually many victuallers did away with licences altogether—the first Lyons' tea shop opened in 1894.

Pubs were no longer respectable. Certainly the aristocracy were no longer in the habit of trading quips with the masses over a pot of ale, as many had done in the disreputable days of George IV. A mood of reform was gathering strength; for it was felt that the gin-palaces, for all their triumphs of design, were no more than cleverly baited traps for the vulnerable, who had to be protected by their moral superiors from their own worst instincts. The Queen herself was the patron of the Church of England's temperance society, although she and most of the middle classes believed rather in moderation than total abstinence, and were utterly opposed to the fervent prohibitionism of radical temperance crusaders, largely nonconformists, such as the British and Foreign Temperance Society. Such militants, after early successes, eventually alienated those who would have been their most influential allies, although they did have their effect on the licensed trade. The attempts at reform made by successive governments tended to the haphazard, and were often carried out as economic expedients rather than as a cogent programme aimed at drink-related problems. Many measures were clearly contradictory: Gladstone's Refreshment Houses Act of 1860, for instance, permitted the sale of wine without a Justices' licence and at the same time lowered the duty on wine. This came about partly because Gladstone wanted to popularise wine, believing it to be more wholesome than beer or spirits, but also because he wanted to foster trade with France. It had no effect on beer and spirit sales; in fact spirit consumption per head was twice the present figure in 1875. It did, however, encourage grocers and others to start selling liquor, and assisted the growth of off-licence chains. Another move was to ban under-sixteens from drinking spirits in the 1872 Licensing Act; yet at the same time the price of Scotch was being permitted to fall. It was Gladstone who, despite his peculiar beliefs about the wholesomeness of wine, repealed the malt tax in his 1880 Inland Revenue Act, thus lowering the price of beer. (This Act was an important boost to the big brewers, increasing their share of the market at the expense of the smaller fry, many of whom were driven to the wall. There were over 12,000 pubs brewing their own beer in 1880; in 1914 there were fewer than 1,500.)

If prohibitionists and governments alike were unable to effect any reform in the licensed trade, there were plenty of intelligent and practical bodies prepared to take concrete steps to achieve it, and who eventually inspired the big brewers to do likewise. One of these was the People's Refreshment House Association, who at their peak owned about seventy managed houses, mainly in the West Country, where, although liquor was available, managers received commission only on food and soft-drink sales.

This chapter ends in 1904 because of two significant reforms which took place in that year. One was Balfour's Licensing Act, in which many of the recommendations of the 1899 Royal Commission were embodied; the other was the foundation of another of those practical bodies like the PRHA. This was the Hertfordshire County Trust, formed after years of campaigning by Earl Grey. Both of these events were to have a profound effect on the development of the public house.

7

DECLINE AND FALL?

The most militant prohibitionists may have alienated their potential allies in high places, but they were too numerous and too strident to be ignored altogether, and both the 1904 Licensing Act and the formation of the County Public House Trusts owed much to their influence. H. P. Maskell and E. W. Gregory commented in *Old Country Inns*, published in 1910:

> Some temperance reformers have dreamt of a land without public houses, and even today it is not uncommon to hear a lecturer . . . express the wish that every drop of intoxicating liquor in the country could be run into the sewers tomorrow, and every public house at the same time have its shutters put up.

The temperance hotels set up by these crusaders, though many, did not last; there are a few left today, but they are not nearly as common as they were. Many of these were entirely new establishments, but some were old inns taken over by the temperance men. They failed partly because people did not like to be preached at, any more than they do now, particularly about their drinking habits, but largely because they were uncomfortable. Maskell and Gregory believed that

> The temperance hotel is only very rarely comparable to the fully-licensed house. Tradition may have something to do with the comfort of an old inn, and temperance hotels have no tradition whatsoever. Their inception was due to a protest, and even today . . . the hotels which advertise themselves as being dogmatically averse to a particular form of refreshment . . . seem unable adequately to provide comforts about which there can be no question whatever.

Nevertheless, by issuing a direct challenge to the licensed trade, the reformers had at least made a mark.

The People's Refreshment House Association was set up in 1899 and by 1910 was running about seventy pubs very successfully by permitting the sale of alcohol but allowing their managers commission only on food and soft drinks, a policy pursued by most of the County Trusts too. 'The trade has been forced, not without some grumbling, to recognise tea as a form of liquid refreshment which may be legitimately called for by the traveller', wrote Maskell and Gregory. In fact the trade was to be forced into a total re-evaluation not of its product, but of the way in which the product was retailed—of which more later.

The Government acted out of a kindred spirit of reform. Balfour's Licensing Act of 1904 sparked off the closure, with compensation, of thousands of pubs; in the decade following its passage something like a thousand were suppressed by the Justices of the Birmingham area alone. The number of beerhouses in many smaller towns was halved—ten or fifteen pubs is now the normal provision for a town of 7,000 people, whereas eighty years ago it was thirty or more.

Balfour's Act was only one in a series of laws designed to shift the pub's emphasis away from alcohol by restricting its market: the 1901 Child Messenger Act limited off-sales to children to one pint in a securely corked or sealed bottle; the 1902 Licensing Act raised the licence fee substantially; in 1921 the closing-hours concept was replaced by one of 'permitted hours' which allowed pubs to stay open throughout the day for sales of soft drinks and food; and Lady Astor's 1923 Act finally banned under-age drinking. Lloyd George's 1914 Defence of the Realm Act contained one very curious measure designed to curb drinking: it banned 'treating' (buying other people's drinks) altogether. As can be imagined, this was generally ignored, but 'DORA' had a more serious side to it: it restricted brewers' output, encouraged them to produce weaker beer, and established a board of control which, in 1916, began the Carlisle Brewery State Management Scheme. (This lasted until

1973, when the brewery was sold to Theakston's.)

These measures had a lasting effect, and the spirit which inspired them quickly percolated through to the Justices whose job it was to enforce them. They became very stern towards the licensed trade, and often did their best to make the opening of new pubs impossible by the imposition of impracticable conditions. In fact, when Welwyn Garden City was being planned it was seriously suggested and widely debated that it should be a wholly dry town. This was also the kind of thinking which inspired Earl Grey to campaign for the foundation of the Trusts.

Grey was an aristocrat, more used to string-pulling than rabble-rousing. His campaign took place not on the platforms of nonconformist chapels, but in the drawing-rooms of the country gentry. Many of the great old coaching inns had, after the advent of steam, dwindled to mere country beerhouses, many of them actually owned by local landowners and only leased to the breweries. It was not until the first bicycle bells were heard ringing down the lanes in the 1870s and '80s that they began hesitantly to shake off their torpor and revive. It was here that Grey saw his chance to improve the state of the licensed trade generally. In persuading respectable local dignitaries to raise capital and develop organisations to run these places themselves, he successfully appealed to three instincts: a sense of tradition, a desire for improvement and—never far below the surface—the urge to make money.

It took him three years of dropping quiet words in receptive ears before finally, in 1904 the Hertfordshire Trust was established, with the county's hart couchant, still the Trust Houses Forte trademark, as its badge. Its first pub, the Waggon & Horses at Ridge Hill, opened that year with an ex-policeman as its manager. Within a short time, the Trust had acquired a second, at Elstree, and Lord Rothschild built and donated a third, the Rose & Crown at Tring. By 1910 the Trust had climbed into the black, its first dividend being $2\frac{1}{2}$ per cent. Other counties had been following Hertfordshire's lead, and all the time there were amalgamations. In 1919 the County Trusts merged to form Trust Houses Ltd, with headquarters in London and over a hundred properties up and down the country. (In 1970 they became Trust Houses Forte.)

However improbable it may seem, cyclists were a key factor in the Trust House movement. For many people in the last thirty years of the nineteenth century—people like Mr Cummings in *Diary of a Nobody*—the bicycle provided a cheap way of escaping the city for a day or two in the fresh country air. Clubs were formed, and the roads around London were soon filled on balmy days with cheery throngs, a hundred or more strong, bent on pleasure. One of the pleasures they discovered was the country pub. The travel writer Charles Harper, writing in 1906, recalled how, in the early days, a cyclist was such a novelty that when he called at a pub he would be sat down to dine with the family, and charged 10d (4½p) for roast beef and whortleberry pie. But later commercialism crept in, and a less appetising meal in the public bar would come to 1/6d (7½p). Ripley in Surrey, a convenient 23 miles from London, soon became the cyclists' Mecca, with the humble Anchor, once a waggoners' stop, more popular than the old coaching house, the Talbot. Harper wrote:

> It was then the most popular place in the wheelman's world. On Saturdays and Sundays it was no uncommon thing to see two or three hundred machines stacked in front of the Anchor.

Cycling had its dangers, however, the worst being of practical jokers, as Harper painfully discovered:

> All the world regarded the cyclist as a pariah, and to knock him over with a brick, or by the simple expedient of inserting a stick between the spokes of his wheel, was a popular form of humour.

For thirty years before the first cyclist appeared, the roads of England had been empty of virtually any but farm traffic. Soon, however, the cyclists were succeeded by the first generation of motorists with their slow, uncomfortable and unreliable horseless carriages. Runs out to Brighton with the Road Club (later the RAC) became as popular with drivers as the Ripley Run had been with cyclists, and the half-forgotten coaching inns found, doubtless to their astonishment, that they were loved once more. Many which had gone out of business were reopened, and most of them had new signs to hang out: no longer 'Stabling and Fodder', but simply 'Petrol'. The first motorists were well-heeled pleasure-seekers, but soon the car crept into business use as well, particularly among commercial travellers who had always had their own hotels and their own customs. (Perhaps the most famous of these was the Red Horse at Stratford-on-Avon, now sadly defunct, where the boots kept a stock of carpet-slippers which he let out to residents by the night.) In the 1920s and '30s motor-borne custom became the rule rather than the exception: Trust Houses embarked on a huge modernisation programme, more former inns were re-opened and most of the larger hotels boasted garages.

If legislators, ideologues and a revival of demand exerted a great influence over the licensed trade, then the greatest movement for change came from the brewers themselves. They were especially sensitive to the pressures that came from the new laws. The wave of suppressions that followed the 1904 Act forced the industry to look seriously at the way its product was sold. The brewers felt keenly the opprobrium in which they were held by many—the Operative Brewers' Guild, founded in 1906, had as its main aim the raising of the brewers' professional status and thus infusing some respectability into the trade. They believed that the only way to shed their unfortunate image was to redesign the pub itself.

The 'improved' pub marks a big step away from the gin-palace mentality. The masculine exclusiveness of the bar gave way to an environment in which it was hoped women would feel just as much at home. Greater emphasis was placed on soft-drink and food sales; and amenities such as social centres, committee rooms, sports halls and even, in at least one case, a fully equipped theatre, were often provided. The design and layout had to be drastically altered to accommodate this sort of thinking, and for the first time the brewer's architect came into his own. He had always been there, of course, but previously his own tastes and instincts had been very much subordinated to those of the client; now for the first time he was given free rein.

His first act was to banish the trappings of the gin-palace: the opulent, and therefore seductive, gas-jets, wood-carvings and panes of brilliantly cut glass were too decadent to be permitted to survive. New pubs were to be built without them, and in many old pubs they were torn out and unceremoniously dumped. But the architect encountered a problem whose solution has eluded him ever since. He had destroyed, albeit in good faith, one tradition; he needed another to fill the gap. Bearing in mind both the redis-covery of the great old Tudor inns, and the popularity of mock-Tudor in the ever-spreading suburbs, it was back to the days of oak beams and ingle-nooks that his imagination led him.

It is claimed, notably by Gorham and Dunnett in *Inside the Pub*, that the 'Tudorbethan' phase marks the first break with the ver-nacular tradition in the pub's long history, and that the rustic, Georgian, and other 'pseudo' styles that followed widened the break still further. But this is not entirely fair. The 'pseudos' were not the first to look outside the very narrow confines of the ver-nacular for inspiration: we have seen how gin-palaces were often modelled on some notion of Italian, Swiss or Gothic styles; and for that matter the great classical coaching inns looked back to the Roman Empire. The difference between brewer's Tudor and a gin-palace is no greater than that between a gin-palace and the type of tavern that preceded it. Gorham and Dunnett add that the 'Tudorbethan' style 'embraced all the incongruities inevitable when sterilized medieval frills are draped round twentieth-century mass-production and amenities'.

Their verdict on the style, that it was a 'collection of theatrical shams bearing no relation to architectural honesty or the true functional pub tradition', is too severe. Two of these 'sham' pubs are the Langold Hotel, a Tudorbethan in a Nottinghamshire mining village, and the brewer's rustic Plough in the 1930s Middlesex suburb of Northolt. Their quirks of design are great fun, and they both have plenty of that indefinable quality, atmosphere, which is an intangible most clearly noticed when it is absent. Architectural honesty is at best chimerical, and as for the functional tradition, the decor of the gin-palace was hardly functional. Although the pseudo decor is somewhat contrived, these two pubs occupy their place in the community in much the same way as the medieval ale-kitchen.

Having said that, it cannot be denied that something has gone wrong with modern pubs; somewhere along the way the tradition has indeed broken down, but it seems over-puritanical to blame the pseudo styles. The breakdown is a later phenomenon which, ominously, coincides with the continuing rise of the mega-brewery. There is always a tendency to giantism in commerce: the successful concern expands, its rivals are bought out or go to the wall. This is nothing new in the brewing industry—there has been concern about the monopoly enjoyed by the big brewers ever since the Beer Act of 1830. As early as 1910 over 80 per cent of all pubs were tied houses. The State Management Scheme was created to block a threatened local monopoly. Ansell's swallowed up four rivals between 1923 and 1938, while in 1919 working men in many areas set up their own breweries because the big combines were weakening their beer. (Two of these, in Wales and the North East, survive to this day.) But it is since the war, particularly in the 1960s, that the mega-breweries, the 'big six', have taken over. It was in 1961 that Bass-Worthington took over Mitchell & Butler, for instance, and this group merged with Charrington United Breweries in 1967. There were over 6,000 breweries functioning in 1900; of the 164 still open in 1978, 50 were owned by the 'big six' (Bass, Courage, Allied, Watney's, Whitbread and Scottish & Newcastle).

How much can be blamed on them is still a subject for much argument; but size brings inevitable drawbacks to which smaller breweries are immune. One is that they are so far removed from their customers that they cannot really know what drinkers are thinking; they can only reach conclusions based on reactions to their products and open to many different interpretations. Then there is the inevitable, and indeed deliberate, standardisation of the product, with the ensuing lack of variety for the public. Finally, their operations are so vast and so expensive (despite the doctrine of economy of scale) that it is all but impossible to change them. Having spent millions on a great chemical works of a brewery, it is far cheaper to brainwash the public with a barrage of TV advertising than it is to alter the product. All the results of the monopoly are there: a lack of responsiveness to public needs, an isolation that makes it impossible to define those needs in the first place and the temptation to provide shoddy mouthwash because it comes easier and cheaper than quality.

Chilled, filtered, pasteurised, dead keg beer was developed independently of the growth of the 'big six'; but it dovetailed perfectly into their scheme of things. Easy to mass-produce, easy to transport, easy to serve, it seemed a godsend to an over-centralised industry, and throughout the 1960s and early '70s it was ruthlessly foisted on to a helpless public. The CAMRA revolt has not succeeded in chasing it away altogether, and never will, but at least the brewers now know that they can not fool all of the people all of the time. They have been forced to revive at least the names of the minnows they swallowed, such as Tamplin's and Wilson's, both now parts of the Watney empire. In the authors' view, Bass and Allied have always produced good beer; Watney's is beginning to, and so is Courage.

Perhaps they could have ignored CAMRA if two hard commercial factors had not turned up. One has been the upturn in the fortunes of the small independent breweries, such as Young's, Bateman's, Marston's and Ruddle's, which have always put quality first and found that quantity follows. The second has been the amazing resurgence of the home-brew pub.

This had been on the decline since the seventeenth century. At its low point in the 1960s there were only six; now there are over two dozen, and more are opening all the time. Perhaps the most startling example is Penhros Court, near Kington in Herefordshire, where brewing started almost accidentally. The Court is a complex of thirteenth- to seventeenth-century buildings which was once a

Penrhos Court, Kington, Herefordshire. The brewery buildings, where fifty barrels a week are produced, a matter of a few minutes' production for the huge 'keg factories' of the Big Six. But quite apart from the superior quality of the product, the smaller brewery can actually be more cost-effective than the giant stainless steel mega-brewery

prosperous farm, but was sadly decaying when Martin Griffiths stumbled across it in 1972. He decided to buy and restore it; but the project had to be self-financing. Selling antiques and teas failed to raise enough cash, so one of the barns was converted into a restaurant. Given the climate in the licensed trade, and the disgust felt by many at the products emanating from the 'big six', the establishment of a brewery seemed almost a natural next step. Penrhos Court now produces fifty barrels a week of the only locally made real ale available in the area, but the experience of the past few years has proved exactly the opposite of the 'economy of scale' doctrine. Naturally there are problems—handling the marketing, accounts and legal side of the business as well as the brewing, on top of running a restaurant and restoring the buildings—which do not leave the family and staff much time for leisure. But the small brewery is more cost-effective than the giant plant: the worker-per-pint ratio is lower, there are no labour relations problems and delivery to the brewery's twenty or so outlets is cheaper and easier than it is with several hundred outlets to cover. And the beer is much, much better—in fact one problem which Martin Griffiths is taking far more seriously than the big brewers do is that of expanding production without affecting the quality of the beer. Starting a brewery is a particularly difficult way of starting up in business. Not only is a great deal of highly specialised knowledge vital in turning out a consistently good product, but the marketing side is more hedged about with monopolies and legal restrictions than almost any other. That so many choose to try it, and that so many flourish despite the unfavourable odds, must be a clear sign to the giants that what they produce is only accepted because usually there is no alternative. Indeed, Whitbread have recently announced that a number of their tied houses are to be converted to 'home-brew' pubs, and the landlords to be given courses in brewing. If the experiment is to work, these pioneers will have to produce an improvement upon Trophy or Tankard.

The battle for real ale, given the resources with which it was waged, and the powers against which its combatants found themselves ranged, has been highly successful. Now perhaps it is time for a campaign for real pubs. On housing estates dating from the 1940s to the present, and anywhere from Rochester to Rochdale, are to be found pubs suffering from the 'barn syndrome'. They are great, bleak, barn-like boxes with strip lighting, lino floors and enormous picture windows commanding panoramic views of the car-park. In the public bar the bleakness of the interior is accentuated by the stark brutality of the decor; while the abysmal kitsch (red flock wallpaper, bright blue carpet, cheap fake brass lamps) of the lounge bar is, if possible, even nastier. The vast spaces are unbroken by any screen or feature; the total effect is horribly reminiscent of the common room of an old folks' home. Here, if anywhere, the pub tradition has been broken, for there is no human element whatsoever. The barn syndrome was originally a product of the 1930s, when it was called the Post Office style; nothing with less atmosphere can be imagined. They are usually furnished in job lots from a central warehouse, and, like keg beer, they emphasize that insensitive commercialism diminishes variety and results in a loss of quality.

Pub design is an area in which it is easier to criticise bad design than come up with something good. But the essential feature of a pub is that it is neutral ground, where friends can meet as equals without the exaggerated courtesy of the guest–host relationship. Anything overpowering, such as the 'theme pubs' (for example, the Stonehouse in Sheffield which represents an Elizabethan street scene) which blossomed in the 1960s, will not do. Traditional pub decor, until the arrival of the gin-palace, was therefore neutral: its basis was cream distemper and natural timber shades ranging from pine to dark oak, splashes of colour being provided by sporting prints on the wall, bottle labels and even the clothes of the customers. The accent should be on simplicity: the Horseshoe at Arddleen in Powys was completely redesigned and redecorated only very recently, but it looks much as a country pub would have two hundred years ago because the landlord has found that he does not need gimmicks to attract custom; quality and simplicity do the job better. In planning any alterations to pubs, the large brewers might reflect that the pub tradition has only been maintained because it has been found successful not over a few years, but over centuries.

Nevertheless, decor and design are matters of taste and subject to whim. The economic facts, on the other hand, are quite blunt, and they tell a depressing story. Pubs are disappearing at a rate of a thousand a year. Sales of beer are dropping fast, while prices rocket. This is not to say that there is any real danger of the pub vanishing entirely; but if the trend is to be towards fewer and larger pubs, then again the public is being deprived of variety. The foremost pressure on the pub stems from their being consistently undercut by supermarkets and clubs. Canned beers are not much cheaper than draught beers, and they are nastier so do not really compete. More dangerous is the threat from the clubs. They sell beer much cheaper because they have fewer overheads and because their beer is heavily subsidised. They have their subscriptions coming in; they have £200 jackpot machines while the pub's maximum jackpot is only £2; but principally they have large, cheap and easy loans from the breweries. These three sources of income can cut more than 10p off the price of a pint, which makes the beer in effect a loss-leader.

The enormous taxes levied on drink do not help. Statistics say that the price of drink has actually gone down in the last decade, for while consumption has increased by a third, the proportion of income spent on it has remained almost the same. But far less of this money has been spent in pubs: in fifteen years 10,000 new off-licences have been taken out (most of them in supermarkets), and clubs and licensed restaurants have increased from 50,000 to 75,000. At this rate the pub's share of the market will have dwindled to 30 per cent by the end of the century. Reducing the duty on beer and spirits (and something like 70 per cent of the price of a bottle of Scotch is either duty or Value Added Tax) would certainly help arrest this decline. There are those who say that alcoholic consumption should be curbed, and that ever-higher taxes should be levied as a deterrent. But Britain has the lowest rate of deaths from cirrhosis in the West: 4 per 100,000 as against 30 per 100,000 in Italy and 50 per 100,000 in France. Of heavy drinkers—those whose intake of pure alcohol is more than 6.3fl oz per day—Britain has 3 per cent, compared with 4 per cent of Australians and Americans, 8 per cent of Italians, and 9 per cent of Frenchmen. The attitude of those who see drink as a curse is a hangover from the temperance movement of the turn of the century; it is based not on factual evidence, but on the desire to be the guardians of other people's morals. The evidence of the American prohibition suggests that the harder it is to get alcohol, the more likely it is to be misused.

British licensing hours are another contentious area. They, too, date back to the temperance era, to the Defence of the Realm Act, in fact. The idea was to keep munitions workers out of the pub and in the factory. They have certainly outlived their usefulness in that respect, and foreign visitors are constantly amazed that when they are thirsty, the law denies them the opportunity to have an alcoholic drink. The English Tourist Board, the Brewers' Society and CAMRA would all like to see a change; but it is very much up to the licencees themselves and their organisations—the National Union of Licensed Victuallers and the National Association of Licensed House Managers—to press for change.

It is perhaps sad that the English pub needs to be fought for. An institution so central to our national identity should have been treated with more respect over the last eighty years. Its present difficulties can be put down to that curiously English mixture of vices: greed, sanctimoniousness and blindness. It will take that English mixture of virtues—determination, imagination and a sense of proportion—to set matters right.

8

THE MAN BEHIND THE BAR

In the preceding pages we have examined the history and development of the pub itself, but we have met only in passing what many would regard as its key element: the landlord. The host of the Tabard in *Canterbury Tales*, Skelton's unsavoury Elynour Rummyng, Shakespeare's motherly Mistress Quickly, the great entrepreneurs of the coaching age such as John Laurence of the Lion in Shrewsbury—these are famous figures. Behind them stand the thousands or even millions of everyday landlords and landladies, unsung and for the most part unknown.

Much is made of the uncommon skills needed to be a good licensee. In the words of a poster to be seen in pubs all over the country, the perfect landlord must possess:

> The dignity of an Archbishop; the geniality of a travelling salesman; the smile of a film star; the voice of a sergeant-major; and the hide of a rhinoceros. And if he can call Time in a tone that combines firmness, regret, condolences, hope for the future, gratitude for the past, and a suggestion that this hurts him more than it hurts you . . .

There are several versions of this; it is the sort of pub kitsch that ranks with 'In God we trust; all others pay cash', and 'We have an arrangements with the banks: if they won't sell beer, we won't cash cheques.' But the near-saintly qualities attributed to, or claimed by, the good licensee are often more seriously expressed. Maskell and Gregory wrote in 1910:

> Diverse and sundry are the concerns in which the village innkeeper is called upon to give advice. He is the arbitrator in disputes, he solves weighty problems of rural etiquette. He knows the inner secrets of every home and can weigh the respective merits of his clientele to a nicety.

An intelligent landlord would be the first to disown this sort of sentimental nonsense. It suggests, first of all, that he is expected to be all-wise, which is utterly unreasonable, and second, that he is all-knowing, which might be disastrous for trade. (After all, would you go drinking where the 'inner secrets' of your home were known?) But what are the virtues of the good publican?

Principally, he is a businessman. His pub is his living and his first task is to make it pay. But there is no particular magic in doing this. His technical knowledge is less than that of a motor mechanic. Physically, his labour is easier than that of a hod-carrier. His knowledge of the law is largely common sense and can be quickly learnt. His hours are no more anti-social than those of a postman or night-shift worker, and he is no more tied to his business than is the newsagent, who also runs a seven-day-a-week service, and who also faces the problem of finding a competent stand-in if he wants to take a holiday.

What sets him apart is this: his business is relaxation. The pub is a social institution and the landlord must be a social animal. He must be neither too awkward nor too obtrusive in company, for a shy landlord can be as off-putting as a raucous one. And in a sense, although not in the omniscient sense of Maskell and Gregory, he must be 'the arbitrator in disputes'. He has to see that the rowdy youths and the more contemplative old men don't disturb each other, and he has to spot trouble coming and head it off quickly—a trick managed very neatly by one of the landlords in George Borrow's *Lavengro*, who sees the arch-Conservative Borrow squaring up to a Radical:

> 'There shall be no fighting here,' said he. 'No-one shall fight in my house, except it be with myself; so if you two have anything to say to each other, you had better go into the field behind the house.'

But his intention is not merely to send them outside to fight; he wants no fighting at all, for, as he says, 'I keeps a decent kind of establishment.' This he manages by launching into a long and windy monologue touching first Borrow's own prowess as a fighter, gained in the battle with the Blazing Tinman a couple of days earlier, and then moving on to his own career as a pug. By the time he has finished his reminiscences, all thoughts of violence have fled, and Borrow and the Radical are almost friends. The same spirit of reconciliation is evident in the host of the Garter in the *Merry Wives Of Windsor*, who contrives to prevent the duel between Dr Caius and Sir Hugh Evans:

> Peace, I say! Hear mine host of the Garter. Am I politic? Am I subtle? Am I a Machiavel? Shall I lose my doctor? No: he gives me the potions and the motions. Shall I lose my parson? My priest? My Sir Hugh? No; he gives me proverbs and no-verbs. . . . Boys of art, I have deceived you both; I have directed you to wrong places. . . . Your skins are whole.

Perhaps the perfect example of the landlord as arbitrator is Mr Snell of the Rainbow at Raveloe, from George Eliot's *Silas Marner*; who is

> a man of neutral disposition, accustomed to stand aloof from human differences as those of beings who were all alike in need of liquor. . . . [He lived] under the habitual sense that he was bound to keep his house open to all company, confident in the protection of his unbroken neutrality.

Here George Eliot introduces another question which was of more importance in the past than it is today. The publican's place of work is also his home. Today the public areas and private accommodation of the pub are sharply delineated; only favoured customers ever cross that line, and then only by invitation. But in the past the inn kitchen and parlour were also the innkeeper's kitchen parlour, and inevitably the lack of privacy became at times frustrating. In *The Road To Wigan Pier*, George Orwell was writing of boarding-house keepers, but it might easily have applied to a small innkeeper of any time up to the beginning of this century:

> I have noticed that people who let lodgings nearly always hate their lodgers. They want their money but they look on them as intruders and have a curiously watchful, jealous attitude which is at bottom a

determination not to let the lodger make himself too much at home. It is an inevitable result of the bad system by which the lodger has to live in somebody else's house without being one of the family.

This frustration often manifested itself as a determination to cheat the intruding guest or customer if at all possible. Mine host of the Garter resolves to 'sauce' three German dukes who 'have had my house a week at command' and forced him to turn away other guests. (In the event they 'sauce' him, escaping without paying on some of his best horses.) Similarly the landlord in *Lavengro*, when he has lost £50 cock-fighting and still owes the brewers £70, proposes to arrange a prize-fight between Borrow and a woman, the result of which is to be fixed beforehand, and at which 'all the sour and unsaleable liquids he [the brewer] now has, which people wouldn't drink at any other time', are to be on sale. For, as he says:

> Confound the respectability of my house. . . . Will the respectability of my house pay the brewer, or keep the roof over my head? No, no! When respectability won't keep a man, do you see, the best thing is to let it go and wander.

Dr Johnson and Washington Irving both make the point that all customers must feel perfectly at ease and at home in an inn; and by and large they were well satisfied. The poet Shenstone also found little to complain of; practically the only lines of his that are widely remembered are:

> Whoe'er has travelled life's dull round,
> Where'er his stages may have been,
> May sigh to think he oft has found
> His warmest welcome at an inn.

And of course most innkeepers, whatever resentments they may have secretly nursed against their intrusive customers, were too hard-headed ever to let them show.

Shenstone's 'warmest welcome', however, could be taken too far, becoming mere fawning obsequiousness. In Ben Jonson's *New Inn*, when the guest says that necessity commands him to leave, the host's reaction is:

She shall command me first to fire my bush, then break up house. Or if that will not serve, to break with all the world; turn county bankrupt in mine own town, upon the market-day. And be protested by my butter and eggs, to the last bodge of oats and pottle of hay. Ere you shall leave me I will break my heart. I'll pull my sign down, convert mine inn into an alms-house, turn it to an academy of rogues, or give it way for a free school to bring up beggars in.

This may be exaggerated, but it is not so very far from the truth. Here is a genuine note written to Boswell by the landlady of the Green Man at Ashbourne in Derbyshire:

Mrs Kilingley's duty waits upon Mr Boswell; is exceedingly obliged to him for this favour; whenever he comes this way hopes for a continuance of the same. Would Mr Boswell name this house to his extensive acquaintance, it would be a singular favour conferred upon one who has it not in her power to make any other return but her most grateful thanks and sincerest prayers for his happiness in time and in blessed eternity.

Such insincere flattery masquerading as hospitality deserved censure; and in fact satire became the literary norm wherever innkeepers were mentioned. We have already seen how De Quincey and Pastor Moritz complained of the hypocrisy which they encountered in many inns; Henry Fielding also found the double standards prevalent among innkeepers a fruitful target for attack. Landladies (for some reason it was always landladies, never landlords) were always discovering they had treated Tom Jones as a gentleman when they should have treated him as a mere vagabond, and vice versa. On one occasion he and his female companion were physically assaulted by a landlady who thought they were tramps and afterwards found out her mistake:

I am sure, madam, if I had once suspected that your ladyship was your ladyship, I would sooner have burnt my tongue out than have said what I have said.

Another landlady was more cautious, but betrayed the same consciousness of rank:

Nay, if I thought he was a gentleman's son, though he was a bye-blow, I should behave to him in another-guess manner; for many of these bye-blows come to be great men, and as my poor first husband used to say, *never affront any customer that's a gentleman.* (Authors' italics)

Jonson, Fielding, De Quincey, Pastor Moritz, Samuel Bamford and many others were right to attack hypocrisy wherever they found it. But they were also participating in a literary tradition which insists that the innkeeper must be, even if honest, a figure of fun. We have to look no further than Dickens; here is John Willet, landlord of the Maypole at Chigwell in *Barnaby Rudge*:

A burly, large-headed man with a fat face which betokened profound obstinacy and slowness of appreciation, combined with a very strong reliance upon his own merits. . . . If he were slow he was sure. . . . He was in everything the reverse of fast, and withal one of the most dogged and positive fellows in existence—always sure that what he thought or did or said was right, and holding it as a thing quite settled . . . that anybody who said or did or thought otherwise was wrong.

Willet, who is 'fit to tackle a chief justice', is a bully who oppresses his customers as well as his own son, for he considers:

If, sir, Natur has fixed upon me the gift of argeyment, why should I not own it, and glory in the same?

This tradition percolates through to our own day; Barliman Butterbur, of the Prancing Pony at Bree in the *Lord Of The Rings*, is a 'short fat man with a bald head and a red face', who 'seemed capable of an endless stream of talk, however busy he might be'. And if the landlord is not a clown, he is as often as not a comic-opera villain: Long John Silver kept the Spyglass at Bristol in *Treasure Island*, and has provided a stereotype for comedians ever since; and Joss Merlin of the *Jamaica Inn* is equally preposterous, if less well known.

Meanwhile women in the licensed trade have also been badly treated in literature, being generally characterised as widows who are more or less helpless on their own. It is historically true that women licensees tended to be widows of publicans, although this is not so true today. But that they were helpless is a great distortion. More usually they were redoubtable women, with as firm a grip on their businesses as any man. Mrs Nelson managed the Bull in Whitechapel with its extensive West Country coach trade with perfect aplomb for many years; there was a Mrs Mountain who was both innkeeper and coach-builder; while the George at Southwark was inherited and run by a Miss Murray who was quite equal to the task of maintaining a fleet of Kent and Channel coaches. But these are not the women licensees of literature. Instead we have Jim Hawkins's mother in *Treasure Island*, who is brave enough to rifle the dead Billy Bones's sea-chest to recover the money he owes, but faints when the rest of the pirates approach the Admiral Benbow. Then we have the widow who runs that inn on the Marlborough Downs, actually modelled on the Waggon & Horses at Beckhampton, in the Bagman's Story in *Pickwick Papers*. For the purposes of the story she is merely marriage-fodder, to be fought over by the good Tom Smart and the wicked bigamist. (Dickens partly redeems himself later in the book with the realistic note struck by the advice given to Sam Weller by his father: 'Be wery careful o' widders all your life, specially if they kept a public house.') Shakespeare is the worst offender. In *Henry IV Part I* Mistress Quickly is still married, although her husband, the Vintner, makes only a brief appearance. But she is no more than Falstaff's dupe, and by *Henry IV Part II*, when she is widowed and therefore has no one to look after her interests, he has reduced her to pawning her tapestries and plate. In *Henry V* she marries Nym, who has no experience of running a tavern at all, but still presumes to advise her:

> Let senses rule; the word is Pitch and Pay.
> Trust none;
> For oaths are straws, men's faiths are wafer-cakes;
> And Hold-fast is the only dog, my duck:
> Therefore, Caveto be thy counsellor.

But if innkeepers have been consistently made mock of in literature, their standing among their local communities has always been assured. Epitaphs often reflect this: John Wigglesworth, who kept a pub in Whalley and died in 1813 aged seventy-seven, is recorded on his headstone as a pillar of the church who 'was bountiful to the poor in private as well as in public'. On the gravestone of Richard Philpots of the Bell, Bell End, near Kidderminster, who died in 1766, is written:

> To tell a merry wondrous tale
> O'er a cheerful glass of nappy ale
> In harmless mirth was his supreme delight;
> To please his guests and friends both day and night.

Not deathless verse, but sincere. On the death of a Stamford innkeeper named Pepper, it was written:

> Hot by name, but not by nature,
> He brewed good ale for every creature.
> He brewed good ale, and sold it too,
> And unto each man gave his due.

While the death of John Bucket of the King's Head, Stockbridge, in 1802 provoked the sorry wail:

> And is, alas, poor Bucket gone?
> Farewell! convivial, honest John.

Epitaphs, of course, are hardly impartial, since relatives write them. The testimony of travellers, on the other hand, is often a better guide to the regard in which an innkeeper is held. Dean Swift's lines to the landlord of the Three Crosses inn are well known:

> There are three crosses at your door;
> Hang up your wife and you'll count four.

As is James Quin's parting shot:

> The famous inn at Speenhamland, that stands beneath the hill,
> May well be called the Pelican from its enormous bill.

Flattery, however, is more usual. Charles Kingsley, Thomas Hughes and Tom Taylor all stayed together at the Penygwryd Hotel, Llanberis, and between them wrote twenty-eight stanzas in praise of the innkeepers, Mr and Mrs Henry Owen. Sir Walter Scott wrote of William Thompson, who kept the Saracen's Head at Newark from 1784 to 1819:

> Travellers who have visited Newark more lately will not fail to remember the remarkably civil and gentlemanly manners of the person who now keeps the principal inn there.

The Bishop of New York's promise to Mrs Jones of the King's Arms, Malmesbury, would have set Mrs Kilingley of Ashbourne all atremble:

> All blessings rest on hostess Jones
> And her good spouse as well;
> Of their kind thought for tired bones
> Our countrymen we'll tell.

That good innkeepers are often praised by grateful customers hardly needs further illustration. But more concrete evidence of the innkeeper's standing in the community is not hard to find. Richard Pope of the Angel, Andover, was the local Tithingman and Court Bailiff; Richard Nyrens of the Bat & Ball, Hambledon, was secretary of the famous Hambledonians Cricket XI; Michael Solomon of the Angel & Royal, Grantham, left £2 per annum for a sermon against drunkenness to be preached every Michaelmas. The Dolphin at Southampton produced a three-time Mayor in the fifteenth century, an MP in the sixteenth, and a knight in the seventeenth. The instances of bourgeois solidity are today more prosaic but equally respectable: in their travels the authors have met landlords who have been Magistrates, Mayors, local council- lors, board-members of local football teams and leagues, solid Rotarians, Round Tablers, members of chambers of trade and the like.

If this local honours system has not changed much over the

centuries, neither has the sort of person who becomes an innkeeper. A thousand years ago the ale-wife ran the pub while her husband toiled in the fields or at his forge or mill. Today the situation is not radically different: the authors have known women stand behind the bar while their husbands work in factories, on farms, or, in one case, as the personnel director of a large company of asset-strippers. A former soldier took over a pub at Stretton, in Leicestershire, and called it the Ram Jam after a drink he had discovered in India; and Long John Silver himself had served, or claimed to have served, 'under immortal Hawke'. The authors have met landlords who are ex-policemen and former naval Petty Officers. The big sporting entrepreneurs of the past, such as the prize-fight arranger Stunning Joe Banks of the Hare & Hounds in Seven Dials, have their modern counterparts in men like the landlord of the Swan at Yardley, where major darts championships are held; and for every innkeeper of the past who organised bear-baiting or cock-fighting shows, there is one today who runs a football or cricket team.

Keeping a pub is extremely hard work. The day starts at 9.00am or earlier with cleaning and bottling up for the midday session which lasts until 2.30–3.00pm. After that there are glasses and crocks to be washed up and, if it has been busy, more bottles to be brought up. A break of two hours at most precedes the evening session, which lasts from 5.30pm to 10.30 or 11.00pm; then there's more washing up and wiping down to be done before bed. It works out to a day of twelve hours or more six days a week, with a little less on Sunday. As we saw earlier, the work is not particularly taxing physically or mentally, and even when the pub is open there may be stretches of an hour when no one comes in. But it takes up the whole day, and there is plenty more to be done on top of it: licensing hearings to be prepared for and attended; VAT returns and other accounts to be sweated over; stock-taking to be done; orders to be made out and forwarded; deliveries to be supervised; buying expeditions to the cash-and-carry to be squeezed in. The result is that the licensee is firmly bound to the pub; those who cannot find a trustworthy relief manager often go without a holiday for years on end.

But we need not weep for the licensee. Those who don't take to it don't stick to it; those who do, enjoy their calling. The intelligent licensee must be aware, in his free moments, that of all the institutions around which community life has traditionally revolved—the church, the manor, the forge, the mill, the pub—his is the only one which has suffered no loss of status. The unceasing and unchanging nature of the work which deters us attracts him, and he might see much of himself in that creation of six hundred years ago, the landlord of the Tabard:

> Our Host gave us great welcome; everyone
> Was given a place, and supper was begun.
> He served the finest victuals you could think,
> The wine was strong and we were glad to drink.
> A very striking man our Host withal,
> And fit to be a marshal in a hall.
> His eyes were bright, his girth a little wide;
> There is no finer burgess in Cheapside.
>
> *The Canterbury Tales*

GAZETTEER

THE HOME COUNTIES AND THE SOUTH EAST

BEDFORDSHIRE

Bedford, The Swan, High Street

The Swan is one of the most handsome of the purpose-built coaching inns of the eighteenth century, but before it was constructed there had been an inn on the site for at least three hundred years. Records of the earlier Swan date back to 1507, and in the seventeenth century it was used as chambers by judges on circuit. In 1674 a warrant was issued for the arrest of 'one John Bunnyon of the towne, tynker', for preaching against the liturgy of the Church of England, and it was to the old Swan that his wife Elizabeth came to plead vainly with the Circuit Judges, Sir Matthew Hale and Judge Twisden, for his release. It was while he was in prison in Bedford that Bunyan wrote the *Pilgrim's Progress*.

The new Swan was commissioned in 1794 by Francis, 5th Duke of Bedford, with the express intention of taking the bulk of the coaching trade away from the nearby Red Lion. To this end he spared no expense. He hired one of the best architects of the day, Henry Holland, to design a splendid classical building in lovely mellow stone. The River Ouse is overlooked by its two large bow windows, and the frontage is graced by a fine porch with a balcony and a great pediment spanning the whole façade and resting on four Ionic pillars. Inside he

had installed an imposing staircase with twisted balusters, dating from 1688 and taken from the ruins of Houghton House, which had been built in 1615 as a home for Mary, Countess of Pembroke, Sir Philip Sidney's sister, and was used by Bunyan as the model for the House Beautiful. There is also a collection of eighteenth-century paintings.

The Swan quickly became the town's principal inn, and even after the railway came to Bedford in 1846, retained its position as the social centre for the well-to-do of the area.

BERKSHIRE

Binfield, The Stag & Hounds

The dead elm opposite the Stag & Hounds, fenced off from the public and with its great hollow branches lying fallen around it, is said to mark the very heart of Windsor Forest. This tree, called the Centre Elm, and the pub itself, must have witnessed many of the brutal and gruesome punishments by which the king's absolute right to the hunting in his forests was upheld. Any peasant found with bow or traps in the woods was liable to have his right hand struck off. Even dogs were not exempt: any found foraging within the purlieus of the royal forest had their claws wrenched out.

The fourteenth-century wing of the Stag & Hounds may well have been a barracks for the warreners and verderers charged with the execution of these punishments. Some offenders, it is said, used to hide in the hollow trunk of the Centre Elm, which has been ring-dated and is more than eight centuries old. In time the forest laws softened to the point where the warreners and verderers lost their function as secret policemen and became gamekeepers of a less blood-thirsty nature. Elizabeth I is said to have watched their merry maypoling from an upstairs window of the Stag & Hounds.

It did not actually become an inn, however, until 1727, when it began to attract some of the passing posting trade. Among its visitors was William Cobbett on one of his rural rides in 1822; he breakfasted here and described it as a 'nice country inn'. At about that time a new wing was added onto the earlier building; while the older part is divided into a number of tiny rooms with space for no more than a dozen or so customers each, the well-proportioned and rather more dignified Regency wing has the feel of a different pub altogether.

The Stag & Hounds boasts a few curios, including a fragment of stained glass rescued from Westminster Abbey during the blitz and now set into a door, although how it got to Binfield is a mystery. In an alcove, protected by a pane of glass, is some exposed wallpaper printed with a hunting scene. How old this might be is uncertain, but it may date back to the house's conversion to an inn.

Since the local hunt stopped meeting here, the Stag & Hounds has lost its long connection with the chase. But morris men dance on the green once or twice a year, as the verderers did for the Virgin Queen.

Sulhampstead, Three Kings–Jack's Booth

This is not the only example of a pub with two names, but it is one of the few cases, if not the only case, where both names appear on the licence.

The building is eighteenth-century, with a Victorian tiled porch, but there seems to have been an inn or alehouse on the site long before that. Both names are so ambiguous that they hinder rather than help the search for the pub's history. 'Three Kings' could refer to the union of the crowns of England, Scotland and Ireland by the accession of James I in 1603; but it could also indicate a religious past (the Magi), or a connection with the Mercers' Company. Both the latter interpretations would make the pub considerably older. 'Jack's Booth' is generally taken to mean that a booth, or tent licensed to sell alcohol at fairs, prize-fights, race-meetings and other great gatherings, was based here in the seventeenth or eighteenth centuries. On the other hand, an earlier map is claimed to show the pub as the 'Jack Boot', which suggests that it was used by drovers bringing herds from Wales or Scotland to Smithfield. The authors would suggest that it existed as the Jack Boot in the late sixteenth century, and took the additional 'Three Kings' in 1603.

A regular in the eighteenth century was the Reverend Thomas Stackhouse MA, who became vicar of nearby Beenham in 1737. A prolific writer, his works include the *History of the Bible from the Beginning of the World to the Establishment of Christianity*, a gorily illustrated bestseller in its day. A dirty, dishevelled, unkempt figure, Stackhouse was better known in his own parish for his fondness of the bottle than for his scholarship. He did much of his writing in the alehouse, and was frequently drunk in the pulpit. His downfall came about one day when he had forgotten that the Bishop was due to pay a visit. The unhappy vicar had to be dragged out, helplessly drunk, to face his superior, who cried out in horror: 'Who is this shabby old man?' 'I'm the Vicar of Beenham', replied an irritated Stackhouse, who perhaps did not realise whom it was he was addressing, 'and I wrote the History of the Bible, which is more than you could do'. He was, of course, expelled from his living; but the proceeds of his books kept him in comfort (and drink) until he died, aged 75. He was buried in the village churchyard.

One thing Stackhouse would recognise about his local alehouse is the water—if he ever drank any, that is. The pub is still not connected to the mains and is supplied by its own well.

BUCKINGHAMSHIRE

Aylesbury, The King's Head, Market Square

The King's Head was built either as the guest-house of a nearby friary or as a Guild-hall (accounts differ) in the reign of Henry VI (1422–61), whose portait adorns the inn-sign.

The chief feature of the inn, for which it is rightly famous, is its magnificent high-ceilinged hall, with its great oak timbers and a stone-mullioned window in which several original stained-glass panes survive. These include the arms of Henry VI and his wife, Margaret of Anjou, the arms of Queen's College, Cambridge, of which Margaret was a founder, the winged lion of St Mark, the chained swan of the de Bohuns and the covered cup of the Butlers, Earls of Ormonde, founders of Aylesbury Friary

and lords of the manor in the fourteenth and fifteenth centuries. In the sixteenth century the manor passed to the Boleyns, whose family home was Hever Castle in Kent. It is claimed that Henry VIII stayed at the King's Head while courting the younger of the two daughters, Anne.

With John Hampden as MP, Aylesbury was firmly Parliamentarian in the Civil War. It was the scene of one of the first outbreaks of fighting in November 1642 in which Hampden, whose statue is in the square, was involved. He died of wounds after Chalgrove Field in June 1643, but his colleague Oliver Cromwell found the King's Head a convenient resting-place on his many campaigns. It was here that he received the thanks of Parliament after his victory at Worcester in 1651; and the room he is said to have used can be seen, with its (allegedly) original bed.

At that time the innkeeper, William Dawnay, was issuing trade tokens. Later on the inn attracted much of the town's coaching trade, and its fine cobbled yard remains unaltered. The King's Head survived the decline of coaching, but it dwindled to the status of market pub, and in 1925 its licence was relinquished and it became a temperance hotel. This state of affairs lasted into the 1960s, when the King's Head was purchased by the National Trust and reopened as a licensed hotel.

The complex of buildings rambling eccentrically round the yard has come up with a few surprises. A priest's hole has been discovered, with a peep-hole into the hall. More recently a plumber trying to trace the course of some old piping stumbled across two whole rooms which had been boarded up and forgotten. One measures 8ft by 14ft, the other 8ft by 6ft. But any romantic or dramatic theories

The King's Head, Aylesbury, Buckinghamshire. The stone-mullioned window in the old great hall, containing five original fifteenth-century stained-glass panels

were ruled out by the discovery in one of the rooms of a Victorian bottle, so they were probably boarded up because they were surplus to requirements.

The inn also contains much fine furniture. In the bar is a carved chest, dated 1695 and bearing the name of the owner or maker, Robart Idris. There is also a gate-legged table of the same period, and one of the high, round-backed settles once common in country pubs.

HAMPSHIRE

Andover, The Angel, High Street

There has been an inn on this site since at least 1201 when King John visited the town to grant its charter as a borough. He probably stayed at the inn then, as did Edward I a hundred years later and Edward II after him. What it was called then is not known, but later in the fourteenth century it became the College Inn because it was part of the estate with which William of Wykham, Bishop of Winchester in the reign of Edward III, endowed his foundation, Winchester College.

In 1435 a great fire swept through Andover, and among the largely timber buildings to be burnt to the ground was the College Inn, but within ten years a new inn had risen from the ashes, built at a cost of £87 by the master carpenter of Eton College. (He had quoted £90 for the job, but came in at £3 under budget.) Much of his work is still visible in the internal timbers. The new inn's first royal visitor was Henry VII, and his double daughter-in-law, Catherine of Aragon, paused here for a night in 1501.

From 1582 to 1633 the landlord was one Richard Pope, grandfather of the satirical poet, Alexander Pope. The landlord of the Angel was an important citizen in those days: in 1597 he served as the Priory Tithingman, collecting the church taxes, and in 1622 he was the Borough Bailiff, responsible for collecting debts, enforcing court orders and apprehending defaulters. In his day the Angel was much larger than it is now: it had twenty-six rooms, bearing such names as the Cross Keys, the Crown, the Lion, the Boar, the Star, the Falcon, the Red Rose and the Squirrel rather than mere numbers. His grandson, author of *Rape Of The Lock* and the *Dunciad*, was born in 1688, the same year that the Angel entertained its last Royal visitor, James II, who was fleeing into exile in France. In the coaching era the Angel found itself strategically situated a good day's run from London on the Exeter road, and since it was already an important and well-founded inn, it succeeded in winning a large part of the coach trade. In the late eighteenth century the somewhat boring and undistinguished brick frontage was added. It was from

one of the upstairs windows that in 1830 Bethell Coxe, a local magistrate, attempted to address a mob of enraged farm workers demonstrating against the Corn Laws. Coxe failed utterly to pacify them, and after the reading of the Riot Act, the local militia were called to make his point more forcefully.

Soon afterwards the Angel's coach trade collapsed, a blow from which it never recovered. One whole side of the yard, including all the stables and coachhouses, had to be sold off as shops. Recently they have been demolished to make way for a modern shopping precinct. The Angel has therefore lost its status as the town's principal inn, but is still its oldest and most fascinating pub.

Hambledon, The Bat & Ball, Broadhalfpenny Down

If not the birthplace of cricket, this unexceptional tile-hung pub, standing high on a bare down some two miles from Hambledon, can certainly claim to be the game's nursery. Just across the lane from it is a green, with a granite obelisk recording that this was the very pitch used by the famous Hambledon XI from 1750 to 1787, when Richard Nyrens, who kept the Bat & Ball, was club secretary.

The Bat & Ball was in those days called the Broadhalfpenny Hut, 'hut' being once a common name for a wayside beerhouse, a usage which has almost completely died out. A good day's cricket was then, as now, most satisfactorily rounded off with a few drinks, of beer at 2d (1p) a pint or of Nyrens' own punch, which he swore would 'make a cat speak' and 'put the souls of three butchers into one weaver', at 6d (2½p) a bottle. Whether it was this punch which made the Hambledonians such fearsome cricketers is a matter for conjecture, but in 1770 the side immortalised itself by thrashing an all-England XI by 168 runs and an innings. The last survivor of this great team was John Small who died in 1826 and is buried at Petersfield, his epitaph being: 'Last of the Hambledonians, bowled out by Death's unerring ball.'

Hambledon Ladies' XI was as renowned as the men's side. When they beat Bramley Ladies by eight runs it was reported: 'They bowled, ran, batted and catched as well as most men—even those of Hambledon themselves—can do in this game.' In fact a member of Hambledon Ladies, Christina Willes, is accredited with the invention of overarm bowling in a match in 1807, when she found her skirts got in the way of the underarm style then current.

Nyrens' son John kept the inn after his father's death, and continued the pub's cricketing tradition when he published the *Young Cricketer's Tutor* in 1833. Understandably the place has become a Mecca for devotees of the game.

Minley, The Crown & Cushion

Local legend has it that the Crown & Cushion takes its name from the coronation of King Harold which was held nearby. But since Harold was the first King of England to be crowned at Westminster Abbey, the name is much likelier to hark back to 1671, when Colonel Thomas Blood, who lived on Minley Common, broke into the Tower and made off with the orb and one of the crowns from the coronation regalia. It is maintained locally that this daring deed was carried out as the result of a bet with Charles II himself, and that Blood was arrested while showing off his haul to a crowd of admiring friends in the Crown & Cushion. Be that as it may, the King pardoned the thief and, on the intercession of the Duke of Buckingham, restored him to his estates. Sadly, a splendid yew which was once trimmed into the shape of a crown resting on a cushion and is thought to date back to Blood's day has not been clipped for many a year and is now completely overgrown.

When Blood knew it, the building was already 150 years old, having been originally put up as a row of three cottages in the early sixteenth century and converted to an alehouse in about 1590. Since then it has passed through the hands of three breweries: Palmer's, Crowley & Co and finally Watneys. Today it is a St George's Tavern, and has had an enormous 'Mead Hall' built on at the back, which rather dominates the older parts. It is surrounded by a collection of half-a-dozen or so old farm carts, and in summer there is morris dancing and cricket on the green. The neighbouring heaths are the preserve of the Army, and the Camberley & Sandhurst Drag Hunt meets at the pub.

The Crown & Cushion is a popular resort on a fine day, and deservedly so— but not only with the living, for it has no fewer than five ghosts, all of whom the landlord and his staff have come to know well. One, seen in the bar, is the spectre of the old shepherd said to have been the first landlord; then there are the two children upstairs who can be heard bouncing a ball and who also touch people on the shoulder and 'mislay' objects, a cloaked and hatted man and an old lady with a club-foot who can be seen climbing the stairs at the dead of night. The old monastic Angelus bell which hangs in the bar and is used to call time has also been known to ring by itself, for no apparent reason.

The Bat and Ball, Hambledon, Hampshire. As its name suggests, the Bat and Ball is inextricably linked with the history of cricket

Odiham, The George, High Street

Odiham is an extremely old town, but one would hardly guess it from the Georgian and Regency frontages which line the High Street. Take a look behind those frontages, however, and the true age of most of the buildings becomes clear.

The George is no exception. Its neat façade conceals a rambling Tudor inn which has been licensed since 1547. Its frontage and those of its neighbours are evidence of the prosperity which came to the town during the coaching era, when it was an important stop on the London–Southampton road. The former assembly room at the rear, now a bar, was added in about 1820.

But much that is considerably older did survive the remodelling of the coaching period: during recent renovations in an upstairs room, for instance, a rare example of Tudor wall-painting has been uncovered, dating back to about 1550, so it may well have been commissioned by the inn's first landlord. The painting is a cartoon, in black and silver on a pink wash, of six birds: an owl which says 'tewet tohw', a rook or crow cawing 'knave knave', a magpie, a wren, a dove and a robin, all underlined with a floral motif.

In the seventeenth century, the present dining-room served as the local courtroom, and the dignity of judicial proceedings was enhanced after the Civil War with panelling taken from nearby Basing House, which endured a prolonged siege by Parliamentary forces. The Royalist defence did not collapse until the very end of the war, whereupon the house was destroyed on the orders of the Protector. Scavengers salvaged everything usable from the ruins, and much of the panelling found its way to the George. An upright post in a bedroom is reputed to have a grisly connection with the inn's days as a court: it is said to have been the whipping-post where chastisements prescribed by the Justices were carried out. Whether this is true or not, the George's cellars were certainly used as cells, and during the Napoleonic Wars they were home to a small number of French prisoners who exercised in the inn yard and planted the tulip tree which blossoms to this day.

Later in the nineteenth century, the same yard was a regular venue for prize-fights. In the bar hangs a poem, supposedly by Tom Sayer, the Muhammad Ali of the bare-knuckle game, about his own career, entitled *Farewell To The Ring*. One of the country's last prize-fights was held here in the 1860s.

Southampton, The Dolphin, High Street
The Red Lion, High Street

The first record of a building on the site of the Dolphin was in 1200, when a couple called Simon and Celia paid eight shillings a year rent for it. By 1220 it was two dwellings, one of them probably an alehouse, but by 1454, when the name 'le Dolphyn' was first used, it had become one large house, possibly belonging to a wealthy merchant, for its owner, William Gunter, was Mayor three times—in 1477, 1485 and 1493. By 1506 it had become a prominent inn. In 1588 the landlord, Edward Wilmott, became an MP, and his successor, John Jefferies, was knighted by James I.

Names and dates, however, are almost all that survive of the Dolphin's distant past. There are a few fragments of fifteenth-century stonework to be seen, but its true fame belongs to the coaching era. Even before then it had had its share of prominent guests: Sir Humphrey Gilbert, explorer of the New World, in 1582, the Moroccan Ambassador in 1635 and Charles I in 1646. But in the age of coaching such visitations became the rule rather than the exception.

Being already the town's principal inn, and conveniently near one of the country's busiest harbours, the Dolphin became not only Southampton's, but one of England's, most important termini. The present building, completed in 1760, has the country's largest bow-windows, a magnificent ballroom which was added in 1785 and a newly discovered moulded plaster ceiling in what is now the County Room and was originally one of a number of private parlours for influential guests. Among the many notable guests who used these facilities were Jane Austen, a regular attender at the assemblies, the novelist Thackeray, who wrote much of *Pendennis* while a guest at the hotel, and William IV. The collapse of coaching made no difference to business since the railway and the docks still brought many wealthy travellers who required a luxury inn. Queen Victoria herself was one: she often passed through Southampton on her way to Osborne, the house designed by Prince Albert on the Isle of Wight, and would break her journey at the Dolphin. Finally, it was used by Field Marshal Sir Douglas Haig as the headquarters of the British Expeditionary Force prior to its embarkation for Flanders in 1914.

The Red Lion, further down the High Street, could not be more different. Its bland frontage conceals one of the treasures of our surviving medieval inns: a fourteenth-century great hall, timbered, galleried, of two stories and practically untouched.

Known as the Court Room, in 1415 this hall was the scene of the trial and condemnation by Henry V, who was about to embark for Harfleur and ultimately Agincourt, of the rebel Earl of Cambridge along with Lord Scrope of Masham and Sir Thomas Grey of Heton. The trial is recorded in Shakespeare's *Henry V* (Act II, Scene 2). Around the Court Room walls are the arms of Henry's co-judges: the Duke of York, the Duke of Bedford, the Earl of Warwick, the Duke of Exeter, the Earl of Westmorland and Baron Camoys. The tattered remains of an Elizabethan militia flag and an original Tudor fireplace are also to be seen.

Fortunately the Red Lion never rose to great prominence, or the hall would doubtless have been divided and partitioned. But it never became more than a town pub and still has a curiously depressed atmosphere. It is nevertheless spectacular.

HERTFORDSHIRE

St Albans, The Fighting Cocks, Abbey Mill Lane

The Fighting Cocks occupies the site of one of the gates of the abbey founded by King Offa of Mercia in 793 in honour of the English protomartyr St Alban. The widening of the little River Ver here to provide the abbey with a fishing pond and a mill-race was also Offa's work.

The octagonal eleventh-century building which forms the centre of the inn was originally a dovecote, which once stood elsewhere and was moved to the site in the fifteenth century. (In fact the Fighting Cocks boasts that it is the oldest inhabited licensed house in Britain, and was 'built before the flood'—the

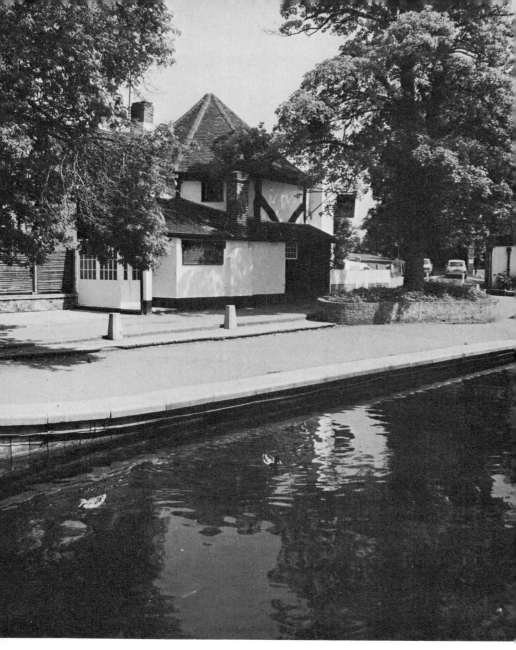

The Fighting Cocks, St Albans, Hertfordshire. An eleventh-century building surrounded by history—the Abbey of St Alban the Protomartyr on one side, the ruins of Roman Verulamium on the other

flooding, that is, of the Ver at the end of the sixteenth century.) This half-timbered dovecote is one of the few buildings in the neighbourhood not built of flint; the Cathedral up on the hill with the surviving abbey buildings, the remains of old Verulamium across the river and several rows of cottages are all of flint.

The inn was first recorded as a licensed house in 1599, when it was called the Rounde House. Oliver Cromwell stayed briefly in 1648, when what is now a curious sunken bar was the stable. Not long after, the inn became a centre for the barbarous sport from which it takes it name, and part of the main bar was a brick cockpit with stepped sides for the spectators. In 1849 the sport was banned and the inn became respectable, taking the name the Fisherman and flooring over the cockpit, but it soon reverted to its better known name.

A regular in recent years according to the landlord was the former Bishop of St Albans, Dr Robert Runcie, whose palace is just round the corner. But Dr Runcie is now the Archbishop of Canterbury and he probably finds it a little more difficult to slip out for a quick half without causing something of a stir.

KENT

Cranbrook, The George, South Street

Now a small and peaceful village, Cranbrook was the economic centre of south-west Kent for over five centuries. Its market was granted in 1290, and in the later Middle Ages it became an important weaving town. But from the beginning of the Iron Age right up to the Industrial Revolution, its principal im-portance was its status as capital of the Kentish Weald, whose abundant timber made it a major centre of iron-smelting and a vital source of raw materials for shipbuilding.

Edward I is supposed to have stayed here in 1299, but the earliest concrete evidence for the inn's existence is a mention in a 1464 rent-roll of the Corner Place and the late fourteenth-/early fifteenth-century stonework in the cellars. Later in the reign of Edward IV (1461–83) it is first recorded as the George. At the time it belonged to the Guildford family: Sir John was comptroller of Edward IV's household, while his son Richard was an opponent of Richard III who fled the country during his brief reign but returned with Henry VII and probably fought at Bosworth. When he was appointed Master of the Ordnance and made a Knight of the Garter, he disposed of the inn to the Henleys, a wealthy family of local clothiers.

Under the Henleys the George became a very important inn. They supervised its rebuilding and played host to Elizabeth I in 1573 when she made a progress through the South (the same progress that brought her to the Mermaid at Rye). She did not actually sleep at the George, but she did stay long enough to receive a deputation of local worthies who presented her with a silver cup weighing 68oz. At the same time the Court Leet of the Hundred of Cranbrook began to hold its meetings at the inn—the oldest surviving court record being the trial of Sir Thomas Moyle for heresy in 1554. Thomas Plume, the licensee in the days of Cromwell, held witch-trials here, and French prisoners were held in the cells during the Seven Years' War in the eighteenth century. It lost its status as a court in 1877, when the

Vestry Hall was adapted for the use of the magistrates; but the Magistrates' Dining Club, founded in 1817, continued to meet at the George until it was wound up in 1912.

In the eighteenth century, when so many inns were gaining business from the coaching boom, things did not run smoothly at the George. On the face of it, it was a prosperous time: many coaches stopped there, and the frontage was rebuilt in tiles and brick with a balcony of local ironwork. When a company of the Buffs was stationed in the town in 1736 and 1748, the officers were billeted here (one trooper succeeded in falling down the inn's well and breaking his neck); and when the Hampshire Militia succeeded them in 1760, their officers too (amongst them Edward Gibbon, author of the *History of the Decline and Fall Of The Roman Empire*) put up at the George. But the town was losing its status, thanks to the decline of the wool trade and of charcoal smelting. In 1765 the landlord went bankrupt with debts of £400, and in 1795 part of the George had to be sold off to become a grocer's shop. But in 1856 the George still had the facilities to provide a banquet for the Enniskillens on their return from the Crimea at which 5,000 turned up to cheer. As a Trust House it still retains its position as the district's principal hotel.

Elham, The Abbot's Fireside

When Ulaham was granted its charter in 855, it was already sacred ground, the site of a mythical battle between St Augustine and the pagan gods Thor and Woden. St Augustine, by prayer, caused the River Nailbourne to appear; his jealous rivals for the worship of the Kentish Jutes promptly blocked it up with boulders and trees. The battle ended in a compromise which makes it seem unclear as to which side the chronicler thought he should support for now, according to legend, the Nailbourne runs clear only once every seven years.

The Abbot's Fireside is not quite that ancient. It dates from about 1480 or 1485 and is a magnificent example of the architecture of its period. Originally a hall-house, it has a jettied first floor which leans outwards slightly but is well supported on an enormous timber transom running the length of the house. The ground-floor timbers are plastered over, but the beams of the first floor are exposed, and the rafter-ends which project between the lead-lighted windows are carved with angels and gargoyles.

It was first known as an alehouse in 1614 when Richard Hayes was the landlord. At that time it was known as the Smithies Arms, and a plaque over the fireplace bears the arms of the Smiths' Company. This is an early example of a pub being known by such a name; had it been any earlier it would certainly have been identified by some easily recognisable feature of the company's coat of arms—for instance, the Adam & Eve from the arms of the Fruiterers' Company, or the Three Crowns from the Mercers' Company arms.

Hayes was probably responsible for rescuing the great fireplace, which gives the house its modern name, from the ruins of the Archbishop of Canterbury's Palace at Lyminge. Its stone uprights support a carved wooden lintel, mantelpiece and overmantel. Charles II is said to have hidden in the chimney while fleeing the Roundheads in 1651, but this is not true. From Worcester, where he was defeated, he fled north to Boscobel, south again to Stratford and then to Lyme Regis in Dorset, where he failed to find a boat to take him to France, then to

The Abbot's Fireside, Elham, Kent, a magnificent example of fifteenth-century architecture

Salisbury and finally to Shoreham, where Captain Tattersall of the coal brig *Surprise* evacuated him. The nearest he came to Kent in his 45 days on the run was Brighton.

At some time in the eighteenth century, the Smithies Arms ran into financial difficulties and gave up its licence. It was divided into three cottages known as Keeler's Mansions, but was eventually reopened under its present name. One of its chief treasures is a sixteenth-century free-standing clock in black oak with a big octagonal dial. The body is intricately carved and painted, apparently by two different artists, with scenes from the Bible.

Sarre, The Crown

The little village of Sarre and its pub stand today in broad acres of rich farmland. But when the Crown was built in about 1500, it was a waterfront alehouse in a busy inland port, for in those days the Isle of Thanet was cut off from the mainland by the River Stour, which was a navigable waterway even for large ships. Evidently Sarre was a harbour well-known to the Huguenot corsairs of La Rochelle who were subsidised by Elizabeth I in their fight against the French. When their Protestant champion Henri Quatre was assassinated in 1610, it became a port of entry for Huguenot refugees. In fact a Huguenot landlord kept the Crown for a while in the seventeenth century, and is credited with introducing the liquor which gives the Crown its nickname 'Cherry Brandy House'. For centuries the cherry brandy was made at the pub itself to the original recipe; today it is made for the Crown at Faversham, still to the same recipe. It is a good deal less syrupy and more fiery than most commercial brands.

In 1784 the Crown became a halting-place for the newly introduced mail-coaches, and the frontage was rebuilt. But the interior still keeps its Tudor character of small, low rooms with exposed beams; one of its treasures is a fireback from the Sussex Weald, bearing the royal crown and the rose of England and dated 1650.

The show business photographs, mostly autographed, which adorn the bar are the legacy of a landlord named Linder who had previously been in vaudeville and maintained his contacts with the theatre world. Before his day, Cruikshank, Kipling and Dan Leno had all patronised the Crown; he attracted visitors like George Robey, Marie Lloyd, Mary Pickford and Douglas Fairbanks, Tommy Handley, Charlie Chester, Jack Warner and Jack Payne. Charles Dickens is supposed to have written much of *Bleak House* in a room overlooking the garden.

The Crown has a second nickname: the Halfway House. It is exactly $8\frac{1}{2}$ miles between Canterbury, Ramsgate and Margate. Doubtless many of the showbiz visitors were in summer season at the last two when they came to call.

MIDDLESEX

Uxbridge, The Crown & Treaty, Oxford Road

Rural Middlesex largely vanished beneath the suburban development that followed the extension of the Underground in the 1920s and '30s, and there is little left to remind the visitor of the county's bucolic past. But amidst the by-passes, shopping precincts, housing estates and factories, there are a few hints of what the area must once have looked like.

One such is the Crown & Treaty, a Wethered's house since 1819 which, with its small bricks and big chimneys, was built as a home for the Bennet family in 1576. In those days it had an extra wing and large gardens running down to the River Colne, but they were sacrificed when the new coach road to Oxford went through in 1785.

It came by its name in 1645 when it was the scene of talks between the Royalists and Parliament. Each side appointed sixteen commissioners for the negotiations, including Sir Edward Hyde for the King and Denzil Holles and Sir Harry Vane the younger for Parliament. The talks were in session for twenty days, and the town had to be divided into two camps so that the retinues of the commissioners could be lodged without coming to blows. Although Prince Rupert had just been crushingly defeated by Cromwell and Fairfax at Marston Moor, the King had won what he believed was an equally important victory over the Earl of Essex at Lostwithiel. Neither side was disposed to compromise, and mutual intransigence meant that the talks collapsed without a settlement being reached.

However, the room where the talks were held (called the Treaty Room although nothing was signed) is still to be seen, along with its original dark oak panelling and some contemporary furniture. The panelling was in fact all sold in 1931 to America, where it graced the office of oil mogul Dr Armand Hammer on the 78th floor of the Empire State Building. Now it is all back where it belongs, thanks to the personal intervention of the Queen. Visiting America before her accession, she expressed such interest in the panelling that Dr Hammer gave it to her as a Coronation present. She then insisted on returning it to its proper setting.

The inn also boasts a Parliament clock, dating from 1797 when clocks were taxed to pay for the Napoleonic War and few people could afford one of their own. The landlord's clock therefore became a valuable source of revenue to him, since anyone slipping in to see the time would feel obliged to buy a drink as well. In the bar is a stone fireplace, probably original, with an overmantel of ten panels representing ten of the twelve apostles— two are mysteriously missing.

When the house became an inn is not known, although it had become well-known by the height of the coaching era.

OXFORDSHIRE

Dorchester-on-Thames, The George, High Street

A busy main street cuts the village of Dorchester in two, and all the motorist sees as he speeds through is a ribbon of shops and cottages, a leavening of black-and-white buildings, and a disproportionately large church tower. But in fact Dorchester was an important centre for hundreds of years: the museum is full of finds from the pre-Roman sites which dot the area; for the Romans it was the administrative capital of the region; and for the Saxons it controlled the crossings of the Thames and the smaller Thame, was the scene of the conversion of King Cynegils by St Birinus in 635 and became the seat of a large diocese.

The great church was a cathedral until 1070 when the see was transferred to Lincoln. After that it was an abbey, and during the Dissolution became the parish church. Only three buildings out of what had been a great abbey survived the Dissolution. One was the church, the second was the monks' private guest-house, now the museum, and the third was the common hospice, built in 1450 and today the George Inn.

It was opened as an inn by Richard Bewfforest, who purchased the abbey and its estate and donated the church to the parish in 1540. Its big courtyard and open gallery have provided for travellers ever since. In the Civil War it flourished on the custom of a 1,000-strong Royalist garrison posted in the village to cover the approaches to the King's capital, Oxford. When war ended and the troops left, the busy road continued to be the inn's, and the village's, fortune: for a hundred and fifty years the coaches that clattered through Dorchester made the George their halt. But when they stopped coming in the 1840s, the inn fell on hard times: part of it had to be sold off as a private house, and a wheelwright rented the yard as a workshop.

The coming of the motor car spared the George any further loss of dignity and quickly restored its fortunes, but the road has now become a menace to the ancient buildings fronting it. Heavy lorries pounding through are shaking old foundations until they crumble, and much of the High Street, which is Grade II listed, is in danger of collapse unless Dorchester is bypassed.

One of the bedrooms is known as the Vicar's Room, and is equipped with an enormous four-poster bed. But who the Vicar was, what he did, and how the bed came into it, have sadly been forgotten.

A custom kept up at the George began in 1972 when the landlord pinned up a bounced cheque behind the bar. Now half the ceiling is covered with cheques, stamps, foreign banknotes, coins and anything else that takes the landlord's fancy. The collection is still growing, and already some of these items are so smoke-blackened that they bear a resemblance to nothing so much as ancient manuscripts.

Godstow, The Trout

Just 3 miles down the Thames from Oxford is Godstow where, since students discovered boats, the Trout has been a popular resort on a warm day. It was on the river-bank here on a sunny July afternoon in 1862 that Charles Luttwidge Dodgson began telling the story of *Alice In Wonderland* to three little girls, one of whom was Alice Liddell, upon whom he modelled the heroine of his story.

Just across the river are the remains of a Benedictine nunnery founded by Dame Ediva of Winchester in 1138 after she had experienced a holy vision. It was here that Fair Rosamund Clifford, the mistress of Henry II, span out her last days and died peacefully in 1176. The Trout was originally the nunnery guest-house, where male visitors could stay at a discreet distance from the chaste sisters. The nunnery itself survived the Dissolution as a private house, and was not reduced to its present ruins until after the Civil War. When the old guest-house first became an inn is not clear; but the present building is largely seventeenth-century and was constructed of stone pillaged from the remains of its former mother-house.

The long wharf along the river-bank in front of the Trout is today used as a beer-garden, and there is a footbridge, now blocked off, crossing the water to an islet on which there is a garden. Of the many Thames-side pubs, this is one of the loveliest and best-situated, but it has become so popular because of the proximity of Oxford that it can hardly cope with its summer custom. Even in May queues develop at the bar and often

(*below*) The Rose Revived, Newbridge, Oxfordshire. The bridge is thought to be the oldest surviving across the Thames

stretch right out of the door. The best thing is either to emulate Dodgson and his little girls and bring a picnic, or go in winter when the bar is warmed by a great blazing log-fire.

Newbridge, The Rose Revived

The Rose Revived hides its great age beneath a rather bland exterior. What you notice chiefly about it, after you have admired its setting on the banks of the Thames, with the fifteenth-century bridge beside it, is its unusual name.

The explanation offered locally is that Cromwell, as a Colonel of Horse in the early years of the Civil War, was engaged in a battle nearby. At the time he was wearing a rose, which seemed a trifle wilted by the end of a hot, tiring and dangerous day, so he took it to the inn and put it in a tankard of ale, whereupon it recovered its bloom. Such pleasant whimsy seems hardly consistent with the Protector's stern image; nevertheless, it is commemorated on the inn-sign which shows the rose in a pot of beer.

In fact the Rose is first mentioned by that name in 1753; in documents covering the next 150 years it is referred to either as the Rose or as the Rose & Crown. Until the 1920s the pub was the property of the Manor of Northmoor, whose lords were the Harcourts. In 1919 the poet Edmund Goss and the sculptor Sir William Hamo Thornycroft persuaded the then Lord Harcourt that they had seen the Rose called the Rose Revived while out rambling in 1878, when they were both Oxford undergraduates. If their story was true, it would indicate that the inn had been closed for a while and then reopened; but true or not, the name they suggested was finally adopted in 1926.

The exterior, thanks to rebuilding in the 1930s, gives few hints as to the Rose Revived's real age; but it is revealed by the low ceilings and heavy beams inside. It was already an inn called the Chequers in the reign of Edward IV (1461–83) when the landlord, Thomas Briggs, undertook to rebuild the old bridge in return for tolls and wharfage rights. His six-arch New Bridge, thought to be the oldest over the Thames, survives to this day and still carries a good deal of traffic.

Anthony Woods, the Oxford historian, wrote of the Chequers in 1659; but in a lease of 1700 it is referred to as the Fair House, after a horse fair that was held every September in an adjoining field. The value of the trade brought by the fair is demonstrated by the sharp increase in rent between 1700 and 1716. Briggs in the fifteenth century paid 3/4d per annum, and by 1700 this had risen to 4/-. But in a lease of 1716 the annual rent had risen to £5—a colossal leap. Another factor behind this increase was the growing value of the wharfage; until 1861, when the railway came to Witney, the Rose Revived was an important coal depot, the coal being brought up the Thames by barge. Landlords in the eighteenth and nineteenth centuries were referred to as 'victuallers and wharfingers', so the coal must have been as important a part of their business as the inn. It may have been in the middle nineteenth century, when the wharfage side eclipsed the licensed trade, that the

(*opposite*) The Golden Cross, Oxford, one of the country's most beautiful pubs despite the garish trappings of the Schooner Inns group

Rose suffered its temporary closure—if this ever happened. There are no records to prove that it did.

It was purchased by the Abingdon brewery of Morland's in 1935 and has been one of their tied houses ever since.

Oxford: The Mitre, High Street
The Golden Cross, Cornmarket Street

Unfortunately it cannot be said that Oxford's pubs match the colleges in splendour; the city has no inns of the calibre of the George at Stamford or the Angel & Royal at Grantham. But the Mitre can be traced back to 1230, when the site was occupied by a building known as Burwaldsaft Hall, whose barrel-vaulted cellars still remain. During the Reformation these cellars were a centre for persecuted Catholics, where Mass could be heard in relative safety. They contained a priest's-hole which sadly vanished during rebuilding work in the 1920s.

It became a tavern in 1285, and was known as Croxford's. From the first it was a base for the undergraduates, and became one of their strongholds in the 'Town versus Gown' riots of the thirteenth and fourteenth centuries, when disputes between the civic and academic authorities over status often burst into full-scale riots. During one such outbreak, the landlord of Croxford's, Thomas Peake, woke up to find himself besieged by a gang of his young regulars who were demanding to be let in and given weapons. Before he consented they had torn down his lamp-bracket and inn-sign. They then stripped the place of anything remotely offensive—table-legs, chair-legs, brooms, spits, even a rolling pin.

In 1605 Croxford's was divided into two, which were named Dagville's and Gill's. This arrangement continued until 1631 when the halves were reunited, rebuilt and renamed. The sign of the Mitre was chosen in honour of Bishop Fleming of Lincoln, founder in 1427 of Lincoln College. The street frontage was replaced in the eighteenth century, but in the courtyard a row of seventeenth-century dormers survives. For two centuries the Mitre was the city's leading coaching inn, and afterwards survived on the strength of a famous restaurant which attracted Peel, Gladstone, Cecil Rhodes, Hilaire Belloc and Noël Coward. In 1926 the old stables were replaced by a mock-Tudor edifice, and much of the yard has since been built over. The Mitre is now a Berni Inn.

The Golden Cross has also been severely altered, but it is still a fascinating old inn. It has no street frontage, but through the seventeenth-century carriage arch is a spacious courtyard flanked by ancient buildings. The oldest part is on the left: originally built by the Augustinian Canons of Osney in about 1190, it was quickly sold to raise money for Richard I's crusades. The purchaser was a vintner named Mauger, who turned it into a tavern. It was rebuilt in 1430 and named Gyngyver's Inn, and apart from the eighteenth-century bays on the ground floor, the 1430 building with its steep-pitched roof and oriel windows survives untouched.

Gyngyver's was acquired by William of Wykeham for New College in 1390. In the sixteenth century the college also purchased the half-timbered Bull across the yard and made one inn out of them, naming it the Golden Cross. Latimer, Ridley and Cranmer, condemned to burn by Bloody Mary, spent their last nights on earth at the newly formed inn;

The Burford Bridge Hotel nestles at the foot of Box Hill, Surrey (*see page 132*)

and in 1685 the county's Lord Lieutenant proclaimed the death of Charles II and the succession of James II from its yard. Three years later one William Lovelace with an escort of 400 dragoons proclaimed the deposition of James from the very same yard.

Later on the Golden Cross shared some of the coaching trade, and its metamorphosis into the group of buildings standing today was completed by the addition of the eighteenth-century stables and forge.

SURREY

Box Hill, The Burford Bridge Hotel

Picturesquely sited at the foot of Box Hill's steep and wooded slopes, the Burford Bridge Hotel got off to a flying start in life and has maintained a position well up in the market ever since.

Originally a seventeenth-century private house (although only the stone-mullioned rear windows are left as evidence), it was converted to an inn in the 1770s when a new bridge was built over the River Mole to carry the London-to-Brighton coach road. Being a convenient distance from London, the Hare & Hounds, as it was first called, soon became a regular halt for travellers and quickly found favour with many great personages. Lord Nelson and Emma Hamilton dallied here for a few days in 1801 and again in 1802; other visitors included the poets Wordsworth and Southey, the literary critic William Hazlitt and Princess Victoria, who before her accession seems to have stayed at even more inns than Elizabeth I. Keats completed *Endymion* in a room overlooking the gardens, dating it 'Burford Bridge, November 28th 1817'. Robert Louis Stevenson wrote much of his *New Arabian Nights* at the Burford Bridge Hotel, as it had by then become, in 1878, and returned in 1882 to visit his friend George Meredith who lived in a cottage nearby.

Most of the rambling complex of buildings making up the hotel dates from the nineteenth century, but it is still being extended. In 1935 a seventeenth-century tithe barn was removed here from Abinger, and now forms a banqueting suite complete with minstrel gallery. On a small bracket in this gallery stands a Victorian terracotta Mr Punch, and although he is not very decorative, the staff believe it is bad luck to move him—chairs collapse under their occupants and stair-carpets shoot out underfoot, sending people tumbling to the bottom, whenever he is tampered with.

Chiddingfold, The Crown

Rightly revered as one of the finest examples of medieval timber-framing in the country, the Crown is the architect's or domestic building researcher's dream of home. Built about 1285 as a guesthouse for pilgrims travelling between Winchester and Canterbury, and as an occasional rest-home for Cistercian monks, it is a hall-house of the Wealden type. A hall-house consists of a great hall open to the roof with storied wings at either end. The Wealden type represents an early attempt at formal composition in domestic architecture by the use of bays (six in the case of the Crown) and a central recess.

It was probably first let as an inn in 1383, when it was leased to one Richard Godfayre for fifty years at 4/- per annum. Godfayre was either an unscrupulous man, or someone in authority had

The Crown, Chiddingfold, Surrey. Built in the late thirteenth century as a pilgrim's guest-house, it represents the best of medieval half-timbering

it in for him, for he was prosecuted four times: twice for overcharging, once for selling short measure and once for failing to display a sign.

The inn is first mentioned as the Crown in a deed of 1548, and at about this time it was largely remodelled. The hall was divided into two floors, a great stone fireplace was installed (later inscribed JHON KNIGHT 1584) and a painted panel of about that date has been found in an upstairs passage when some whitewash flaked away. For the expert, as well as the leaded lights and King-post roof, there are examples of plank, singlefold, linenfold and multiple linenfold panelling to be seen, and coins left by craftsmen as their 'signature' in the reign of Elizabeth I have been found in the woodwork and plastering.

Chiddingfold was a major centre for the stained-glass and iron-smelting industries from the fourteenth to the seventeenth centuries, thanks to an abundance of fuel and deposits of the firestone and malmstone needed to build furnaces. The village church contains a window made of over 400 fragments of stained glass dug out of ancient refuse pits. Perhaps it was because of the town's importance that the 14-year-old Edward VI chose the Crown to stay at during his southern progress of 1552. His 4,000-strong retinue included such figures as the Lord Treasurer, the Lord Privy Seal, the Lord High Admiral and the Lord Chamberlain, who camped on the village green. But they took so much feeding that local supplies ran out, and the young king was forced to dismiss all but 140 of them.

Although the Crown is timber-framed, it was tile-hung in the eighteenth century to keep out the damp. This piece of sacrilege occurred just in the nick of time, for it preserved the timbers from enthusiastically wielded Victorian pitch-pot which transformed into black-and-white hundreds of buildings that ought to be gold-and-white—gold being the natural colour of oak. The Crown's tiles were stripped off in 1951, and the exposed timbers shine, as they should, a mellow tawny.

SUSSEX

Alfriston, The Star

The Cuckmere Valley in which Alfriston stands was one of the first parts of Britain to be overrun by the Saxons, possibly as early as 450. The village itself has been there since at least the ninth century, and is mentioned in the Domesday Book. But the exact age of the Star is something that experts like to quarrel about, some saying about 1450, others saying about 1520.

Whoever is right, there is no disputing that the Star is one of the finest of the later pilgrims' inns. Originally called the Star of Bethlehem, it possesses a splendid timber frame, so solid that although there are no upper cross-braces, the

The Star, Alfriston, Sussex, is one of many of the country's oldest inns now in the hands of Trust House Forte

beam supporting the projecting floor has not sagged in the least, despite the immense weight of the Horsham stone roof. The beams are also remarkable for their carvings. They include St Julian, St George or St Michael fighting a Wyvern, the fret or heraldic knot of the de Echyngham family, St Giles, a greyhound, two serpents, Jack o' the Green, and a bear and a lion climbing a heraldic mace. The grotesquely carved figurehead, painted a bright red, was probably found by wreckers who were active in the area, and is thought to have been washed ashore from one of the Dutch warships sunk in 1672 at the Battle of Solebay by the Duke of York. Inside the old inn, once the property of Battle Abbey and now a Trust House, are a fine oak staircase and a Tudor fireplace. Unfortunately the extension at the rear, built in the 1920s, is unsympathetic to say the least.

In the late eighteenth century the Star attracted some of the local coach trade, and also drew custom from the nearby racecourse. But it was best known as the haunt of a notorious gang of smugglers led by Stanton Collins, who lived at Market Cross House, now the Smugglers' or Market Cross Inn, and was transported for sheep-stealing.

Dell Quay, The Crown & Anchor

The Crown & Anchor stands right on the water's edge in a harbour which has seen intensive maritime activity since Vespasian invaded the Isle of Wight nearly 2,000 years ago. Only two miles away is the Romano-British villa at Fishbourne, and there may have been some sort of building on the site of the pub even then; there are thought to be traces of Roman foundations in the cellar, but if so they have been covered up.

The Crown & Anchor's story really starts at the end of the sixteenth century, or the beginning of the seventeenth, when it was converted from two fishermen's cottages. At the time, the harbour was much busier than now: apart from the fishing, there was a corn mill, wharfage for barges and a customs-warehouse. It was also a nest of smugglers. Revenue cutters were docked at Dell Quay from 1753 to 1800, and the coast was often the scene of grim fights between the free-traders and officials. In 1749 an excise man named Galley and an informer named Chater were tortured and killed, and their bodies hidden in a well; seven men hanged at Chichester for the crime. Legend has it that six excise men were captured and hanged by smugglers at about the same time, and buried in the cellar of the Crown & Anchor itself, where the gang often hid and where their contraband was stored. Today the channel is too silted for commercial use, but Dell Quay still has a busy marina, and in keeping with tradition a light is kept burning in a seaward window of the pub (actually the window of the Gents).

The old game of Ringing the Bull is still played in the public bar, the bull being an earthenware bull's head on the wall with a hook in its nose. The object is to swing a quoit hung from the ceiling over the hook—considerably more difficult than it sounds.

Lewes, The White Hart, High Street

Behind a rather ordinary classical frontage is hidden the rambling timber-framed home of the Pelham family, built for them in the sixteenth century. But the Pelhams were destined for higher things. In 1653 they moved out of their house, and in 1717, the year that they were elevated to the Duchy of Newcastle, the house became an inn. The name was inherited from an earlier tavern some way down the street, from which the licence, and probably much of the custom, was transferred.

The first landlord, Richard Verrall, was one of the pioneers of the coaching trade, and the White Hart quickly became the town's principal inn, much in demand for assemblies, balls and election dinners. His son William, author of *The Compleat System of Cookerie*, inherited it in 1737 and remained landlord until his death in 1761, upon which the inn was sold to Thomas Scrace. Under Scrace the business continued to flourish: the County Court was held in a panelled room upstairs, and the Flying Machine left at 6.00am every Monday and Thursday for the Golden Cross at Charing Cross, returning on Tuesdays and Saturdays. But Scrace was evidently not wholly an establishment figure; at any rate, he tolerated the antics of a group of young radicals calling themselves the Headstrong Club. Their shining star was a young Customs officer called Tom Paine, who was later to write *The Rights of Man*; looking back on his youthful days there he was to remark that the White Hart was the 'cradle of the American Revolution'.

In 1820 another well-known radical, William Cobbett, passed a night on his rural rides; and in 1929 the Labour Foreign Secretary, Arthur Henderson, chose the White Hart for his meeting with the Soviet envoy Mr Dorgalevski. After the meeting, diplomatic relations between the two countries were resumed, much to the disgust of the Conservatives. Referring to the White Hart's long association with Sussex county cricketers, Stanley Baldwin remarked: 'I think the Foreign Secretary was playing a straight bat very carefully, but after lunching with the Soviet representative he collapsed.' He added: 'To those whom it may interest, you get the best of ale there.'

Those enjoying their ale, however, might have their pleasure somewhat tempered by the knowledge that in 1555 seventeen Protestant martyrs who were burned during the Marian persecution were buried under the cellar floor, although this story is also told of the Star, which since 1893 has been the Town Hall.

Edward VII made a balcony appearance to a cheering crowd on a visit to the White Hart in 1880, when he was Prince of Wales. The novelist Jeffrey Farnol was a regular in the 1930s.

The bar across the courtyard was, in the coaching era, a separate tavern called the White Hart Shades, reserved for servants of the more prosperous travellers. A Parliament clock dated 1797 hangs in the main hall.

Midhurst, The Spread Eagle, South Street

'That old and most revered of all prime inns of this world', as Hilaire Belloc described the Spread Eagle in 1912, dates back to about 1430 when the older part, with its jettied first floor, was built. Midhurst had been in the hands of the de Bohuns since 1190 when it was granted, or more probably sold, to them by Richard I, and they had a hunting-lodge on the site before the inn was built.

In its earliest days it accommodated a row of shops on the West Street frontage, and was one of the sixty-one taverns in Sussex licensed to sell wine. It was, unusually, an inn as well as a tavern; Elizabeth I came to stay in 1591.

The Spread Eagle, Midhurst, Sussex. The sixteenth-century Old Market House is now The Tavern, a bar separate from the hotel itself

In the seventeenth century the inn flourished and expanded. In the 1640s and '50s the Spread Eagle issued trading tokens, and in about 1650 the brick and stone wing and the stables (now called the Jacobean Hall, although Carolean would be more accurate) were added. By 1730 the property's insurance value was £1,000, a very substantial sum in those days, and it had begun to capture much of the coaching trade on the London to Chichester Road. It maintained this trade for 150 years, and was one of the country's last operational coaching inns, for Midhurst was not connected to the rail network until the 1880s.

After the final collapse of its coaching trade, the Spread Eagle had to wait a mere twenty years for the motoring boom to restore its fortunes. In 1907 it was one of the first of the old coaching inns to open a garage, which was demolished in 1966 to enlarge the car-park. An old and ailing Edward VII paid a call in 1909; thirty years later the visitors were Goering and Ribbentrop, who had spent a day racing at Goodwood and going over the Leonardslee estate at Horsham, which Goering remarked would make a nice country seat for him once Britain was conquered. Prince Charles visited in 1968, and the novelist Anya Seton stayed in 1972 while researching *Green Darkness*, in which the Spread Eagle figures. There are visitors from beyond the grave, too: a coachman in one of the bedrooms, a 'golden lady' in the residents' lounge and a girl in a green Tudor dress in one of the bars.

A curious custom preserved at the Spread Eagle is that of 'booking a pudding'. Those who want to stay at Christmas have a personal plum duff, with their name painted on the bowl, hung from the dining-room rafters. Also in the room are two old painted windows.

Rye, The Mermaid, Mermaid Street

The Mermaid remains much the same as it was when built some five hundred years ago. But even then it was not the first inn on the site in this largely unspoilt, walled town. The original was a wattle-and-daub building of about 1300, when Mermaid Street was Middle Street and when at the bottom of Middle Street there was the sea and a harbour for two hundred ships. It was thanks to the importance of the harbour that the French raided Rye in 1377, leaving much of the town, including the old Mermaid, a smoking ruin.

It was not rebuilt until about 1420, the new building being raised on the foundations and barrel-vaulted stone cellars of the old. A century later one of Rye's exports was Popish priests fleeing Henry VIII's Reformation; above the great fireplace in what is now the Lounge Bar is the priest's-hole where they hid, and amongst the panelling the initials IHS, Iesus Hominum Salvator, are carved. But by the middle of the sixteenth century, a change of management had brought a change of politics, and from being a centre of subversion the Mermaid became a pillar of the establishment. The Quarter Sessions dinner, Mayor-making and the Herring Feast were all held here, and in 1573 Queen Elizabeth herself made a visit.

This period of comfortable conformity was not to last long, for in the next

---

(*opposite*) The Mermaid, Rye, Sussex. When an inn first stood on this site, Mermaid Street dropped steeply down to the sea, now two miles away

The Mermaid

Re-built 1420

century the wool exports on which the south coast ports depended began to dry up, and many seamen turned to smuggling for a living. The inn became the headquarters of the Rye smugglers, who were known as the Hawkhurst Gang. Under their leader, George Gray, they practically ran Sussex for many years, threatening witnesses and defying the magistrates and revenue men. In 1735 Thomas Moore, a gang-member out on bail, set upon a man, who was to testify against him, in broad daylight in the street outside the inn, and would have murdered him if the captain of a revenue cutter tied up in the harbour had not witnessed the attack and rushed to the rescue. One trio, Fairall, Kingsmill and Perrin, were particularly notorious for their ferocity, and nobody could be found to give evidence against them. The Mermaid is supposed to be connected by a tunnel to another inn used by smugglers, the Bell in the High Street; and another secret compartment to match the priest's-hole is to be found in one of the bedrooms. Russell Thorndyke used the inn as the setting for his stories of Dr Syn, the smuggling parson; Dr Syn's Bedroom and Dr Syn's Lounge recall the connection.

The silting up of the harbour, which began after a series of particularly savage storms in the 1780s, spelled the beginning of the end for the smugglers of Rye, but they were not finished off until the 1830s, when the coastguards engaged them in a number of running sea-fights. But the Mermaid has banked heavily on its association with the old 'free-traders' ever since, and it has attracted visitors such as Ford Madox Ford, Henry James, Ellen Terry, Hilaire Belloc and Rupert Brooke. In 1913 the Mermaid was bought by the mother of the novelist Richard Aldington and became a servicemen's club during World War I. It is now such a tourist attraction that in 1973 it even won a Queen's Award for Export.

THE WEST COUNTRY

AVON

Bristol, The Llandoger Trow, King Street

Bristol was Britain's second seaport until the emergence of Liverpool in the nineteenth century, but the bombings of World War II wiped out much of its heart, and insensitive post-war development has largely destroyed the character of what remains. There are still corners where it is possible to recapture something of the city's former atmosphere, though, and King Street is one.

King Street was laid out in the seventeenth century as a thoroughfare leading down to the wharf from which most of the Welsh coal and wool trade was conducted. The Llandoger Trow was built as a row of five houses in 1664, and some time later became a waterfront inn of somewhat dubious character. The man who gave the house its name and possibly turned it into an inn was one Captain Hawkins, who had plied his trow, or flat-bottomed river-barge, between Bristol and Llandogo on the Wye for many years before retiring. Certainly the house was known as the Llandoger Trow in 1775, when the licensee was one John Jones, although in 1740 it appears to have been leased by a gunsmith.

Looking at the half-timbered building with its three tall gables (there were five, but two were badly bomb-damaged and had to be pulled down), with the waters of the Welsh Back lapping beside it, it is impossible to resist a mental picture of carousing deck-hands and villainous pirates. Indeed, it has been suggested as the model for the Spyglass in *Treasure Island*, and is traditionally supposed to have been the place where Daniel Defoe first met the Scottish sailor Alexander Selkirk, on whom he based the character of Robinson Crusoe. One of the ceilings is quite black; the legend is that it was painted with female nudes, which so offended the widow who ran the place that she had them painted over. Some say that the widow was hoping for a husband from amongst her clientele and painted the nudes over because she was fed up with all the men looking at them instead of her.

Another noteworthy building in King Street is the Theatre Royal, and the Llandoger Trow for many years provided a convenient local for actors and stagehands. Playbills dating from 1806 are preserved in the inn, and visitors have included Henry Irving and Beerbohm Tree.

The Trow was restored by its present owners, Berni Inns, in 1962.

(*overleaf*) Llandoger Trow, Bristol. Two further gables at the far end of the building were destroyed by wartime bombing

The Jamaica Inn, Bolventor, Cornwall, immortalised by Daphne du Maurier and now a popular haunt of coach parties

CORNWALL

Bolventor, The Jamaica Inn

The Jamaica Inn's fame springs largely from Daphne du Maurier's novel of nineteenth-century wreckers, which the management naturally exploits to the full. There is a Mary Yellan's Bar, named after the novel's heroine, and a Joss Marlin's Bar, named after the villain, who also figures on the signboard, while the gift shop attached to the inn trades heavily on souvenirs and even country wines bearing the names of the book's principal characters. The gimmickry is perhaps excusable since there is almost no local trade, and the Jamaica Inn relies entirely on tourism for its living.

This has not always been the case. The inn itself may have changed little since it was built in 1547, but the area has. John Burton, a china-and-glass salesman from Falmouth, spent Christ-mas Eve at the Jamaica in 1853 and found the taproom full of 'a lot of old boozers, principally moor men', includ-ing the gipsy fiddler Billy Lee, Boswell the rat-catcher, Billy Pepper-mint, a local drunk and 'a doggish cove who was wearing a waggoner's braided smock frock' and who sang a song of Brannen the Highwayman. Shepherds were always welcome to warm them-selves by the Jamaica's enormous log fire (which is still kept burning the year round even though the logs have to be brought long distances), and passengers on the coaches plying between Launces-ton and Bodmin rubbed shoulders with the many smugglers, wreckers and high-waymen who frequented the district.

All that changed in the late nineteenth century when the coaches stopped com-ing through, when effective law enforce-ment rounded up the criminal elements and when Methodism began to exert a stronger influence over the moor men. In fact the Jamaica became a temperance inn in 1893 when it was bought by a temperance body which had three other inns in the area, and only regained its licence in 1947.

Although it is undeniably a tourist pub, and although it trades heavily on Daphne du Maurier's novel, the inn's setting on the bleakest part of Bodmin Moor, and its sombre exterior of granite and slate, create an atmosphere almost impossible to dispel. Seeing the place on a dull and cloudy day, or on a wild night in winter, it is easy to believe those people who claim to have seen, sitting on the low wall outside, the ghost of a customer who was called away while halfway through his pint and who never returned. His body was found out on the moor next day, but his murderer was never discovered.

Lanreath, The Punch Bowl

Although it has only held a licence since 1620, the Punch Bowl is a place of extreme antiquity. The well on which it relied for water until it was connected to the mains, and which has now been covered over, was widely known in the area as a healing spring with miraculous properties. It was known as St Monarch's Well, possibly from the Latin 'monachus', meaning monk, but as the veneration of wells and springs was a feature of Celtic culture, St Monarch's may have been a place of

The Punch Bowl, Lanreath, Cornwall, built on the site of a healing spring which was perhaps a place of Celtic worship in pre-Christian times

worship before the Romans came.

The oldest part of the building, at the rear, was a longhouse of two rooms, one for the family and one for their livestock, divided by a central passageway, and may date from the thirteenth century. The front is sixteenth-century. For many years the Punch Bowl served as the local court-house, as did many other inns throughout the country. Two waiting-rooms were set aside in the building for the use of plaintiffs and witnesses, one of them being for commoners and the other for gentry. While they were waiting for their cases to be heard, they could refresh themselves with ale, mead and cider, and it is this side of the building's function which has survived. The two rooms are still in use as bars, and are known as the Farmers' Kitchen and the Men's Kitchen.

In coaching days the village stood on the main road between Looe and Fowey, and the Punch Bowl enjoyed a certain amount of the coaching trade. What is now a passage was the carriage arch leading to the cobbled stable-yard, and let into one wall is a window made of a coach wheel.

Morwenstow, The Bush

Like the Punch Bowl, the Bush is a pub with echoes of Cornwall's Celtic past. The site has certainly been settled since the fifth century, when St Morwenna established a small oratory here, and the oldest part of the Bush itself is thought to date back to about 950 when it was a hermit's cell. This is now the Kitchen Bar, and at one time it was a chapel, for a piscina, in which the communion vessels were washed, an ambry or niche in which they were stored and a squint through which the sacrament could be administered to lepers and others with infectious diseases, are still to be seen.

What is now the dining room was added, probably by the Cistercians, in about 1275. Like the Celtic hermits whom they succeeded at Morwenstow, the Cistercians tended to select the remotest sites to inhabit, believing that the further they were from men, the closer they were to God. Morwenstow, Cornwall's most northerly parish, must have been bleak enough for them, exposed as it is to gales coming in from the Atlantic. The Bush itself stands at the head of a combe running down to the sea which has the effect of funnelling the ocean wind directly at it, and the walls have had to be built very thick to withstand the force of it. This combe was also the route by which certain customers made their way from the sea to the inn which was their hide-out and warehouse; for the Bush was one of literally hundreds of coastal inns throughout the south which were the haunt of smugglers in the eighteenth century. Whether the ghost which haunts the pub harks back to those days, or even earlier, when the Bush was briefly a cobbler's workshop, is not known. But spectral footsteps have been heard, locked doors found mysteriously opened and vague figures seen.

Hard by the pub are the church and vicarage, which are also reputed to be haunted. The best-known incumbent here was the Reverend Robert Hawker, an eccentric antiquarian who helped Tennyson research his poem 'Idylls of the King' and was himself the author of the Cornish protest-song 'And Shall Trelawney Die?' about the execution of Bishop Trelawney by Henry VIII. Hawker was also responsible for the curious vicarage chimneys, each one being fashioned in the likeness of the towers of churches where he had been curate before coming to Morwenstow.

DEVON

Harberton, The Church House

Harberton's Church House is one of a family of inns in south-west Devon which were originally built to house masons working on church buildings. There has been a church in Harberton since perhaps the tenth century, and the foundations of the present St Andrew's were laid by Roger de Nonant who was granted the manor by Henry I in 1104. But the Church House dates back to the rebuilding during the fourteenth century which transformed the Norman church into the magnificent Perpendicular edifice that stands today.

The Church House itself, although only intended as a temporary lodging for workmen, was endowed as a separate chantry after the completion of St Andrew's and became for a while the home of a group of monks. Built of stone and Devon cob, the principal apartments of the building were originally a great hall in which the monks ate and slept, a chapel in which they prayed for the soul of their benefactor (this being the principal concern of a chantry) and a small workshop. It is likely that the small community also taught the village children to read and write, a task frequently undertaken by chantry priests to supplement their income. Although the great hall has now been divided up into different bars, it still retains the spaciousness of those times and contains an oak screen unearthed a few years ago during restoration work and some magnificently carved beams in the ceiling. A small window in an inner wall also contains some medieval stained glass which may be thirteenth-century.

Chantries were dissolved in the 1530s, at the same time as their parent monasteries, and the monks of Harberton—there were probably no more than half-a-dozen of them—went their separate ways. Probably at this point the vicar decided to put the now-redundant building to good and profitable use by brewing and selling church ales, which would have helped to eke out his living. Certainly the church and the pub, which are side by side, remained together until the 1950s, when the Church House was sold to become a free house.

South Zeal, The Oxenham Arms

The noble Tudor façade, with its stone porch and mullions, conceals a very much older building, for the Oxenham Arms was originally a canonry or lay monastery built in the late twelfth century.

One feature of the pub, however, is very much older than that and indeed is older than Christianity itself. For when the canons came to build their new home they found that the megalith on the site—put there as long ago as 3000BC—was too deep-rooted to budge, so they simply built the house round it. There it remains today, surely unique, a pre-historic standing stone supporting one end of the lintel of the dining-room fireplace. The megalith stands out a foot or so from the wall, and visitors can walk right round it; more recent attempts to dig down to its foundations have failed. Another fine stone fireplace is to be found in the residents' lounge. In this case it is the lintel that attracts attention: 8ft long and 2ft thick, its weight is incalculable. It stands on two sturdy granite pillars, and the whole structure is reminiscent of a prehistoric burial-place, although it is probably no earlier than fifteenth-century.

The pub's claim to have been licensed

since 1477 is certainly false, since it was a canonry until the Dissolution and was then purchased by the Burgoyne family, from whom it passed to the Oxenhams whose name it bears today, and whose family legends feature in *Westward Ho!* by Charles Kingsley. It probably became an inn when the family moved to a grander dwelling, but it retains the atmosphere of the homes of the lesser gentry. In the days of coaching it was a major stop on the Exeter to Okehampton road, although the village has now been bypassed and the pub's old stables have vanished.

The village of South Zeal and the Oxenham Arms itself figure large in two novels, Sabine Baring-Gould's *John Herring* and Eden Phillpotts' *The Beacon*, in the latter of which the heroine Elizabeth Densham arrives in the village as the Oxenham's new barmaid. Phillpotts called the pub 'the stateliest and most ancient abode in the hamlet', and with good reason, for it is a fine building which would merit attention even without its megalithic curio. Among the furniture there is an oak armchair dated 1599.

DORSET

Langton Herring, The Elm Tree

A pub that was once principally used by the village's fishermen, the Elm Tree does not seem particularly ancient. In fact it is some four hundred years old and has, as befits any self-respecting south coast inn, a history of violence and intrigue.

Being on the south coast, it is smugglers who tend to crop up first in any discussion, and the Elm Tree possesses under its flagged floor what appears to have been the beginning of a tunnel leading either to the beach where contraband was landed or to the church through which the smugglers could, if necessary, make an escape.

Stories of mysterious tunnels leading to and from pubs are common, but detailed explorations of these tunnels are so rare that one has to be sceptical. The effort of constructing a tunnel long enough to be useful involves the carting away of a great deal of spoil, the bringing in of bricks and props to line the walls and hold up the ceilings, and a gang of labourers besides. Former prisoners of war know how difficult it is to construct even a rudimentary one secretly; the tunnels we hear about in pubs are always represented as highly sophisticated means of mass communication. Any revenue man (or agent of the Reformation, if the tunnel in question is ascribed to fleeing monks) would know all the secret tunnels on his beat if he was even half-competent. In general, what appears to be the bricked-up entrance to a tunnel represents either repairs to the cellar wall, or access to further cellarage filled in long ago. The most that can be allowed is that a cupboard or niche once existed either to conceal regulars from the press-gang or small purchases of contraband from casual inspection.

At the same time as the smugglers were conducting their mining operations, a more plausible rogue was attempting to cheat the village fishermen out of their hard-earned wages. Exactly what con he was working is no longer remembered, but justice was short and harsh in the eighteenth century. When he tried to flee he was caught, taken back to the pub, and lynched in the bar. The beam from which he hanged, a former ship's mast, is still visible.

More recently, in the 1950s, the Elm

Tree was once again involved in the shadier side of life when it was used as a rendezvous by Harry Houghton and his girlfriend Ethel Gee. Houghton only came to the notice of the authorities because of his free-spending ways, but when he was checked out it was found that the source of his funds was one Gordon Arnold Lonsdale, a Canadian resident in England since 1955. Lonsdale turned out not to be Canadian at all. His real name was Konon Molody, and he was an employee of the KGB. Houghton and the Russian were both jailed, but after a few years 'Lonsdale' (who was also known as Vasily Pakhomov) was exchanged for Greville Wynne.

Shaftesbury, The Grosvenor Hotel

When Shaftesbury Abbey surrendered to Henry VIII's commissioners in 1540, it was already over seven centuries old, and the guest-house belonging to it, which was to evolve into today's Grosvenor, may have been equally ancient.

However, by the time of the Dissolution, this guest-house seems to have parted company with its parent institution, for we find a mention of it in 1533 operating under the name New Inn. By 1626 it had become the Red Lion, and in the eighteenth century this became the town's principal inn, attracting the bulk of the coaches using the road to the West Country originally laid out by King Alfred in 882 (now the A30). From 1785 to 1822, the quarter sessions were held in a specially constructed hall at the back of the inn. In 1826 the owner, the Marquis of Westminster, decided to carry out a major rebuilding programme. What, if anything, was left of the original Saxon inn was utterly swept away and replaced by a fairly typical, classical building incorporating a large and well-proportioned assembly room on the first floor overlooking the front. Even after the last coaches had departed, the Grosvenor, as it was now renamed, continued to flourish to the point of buying up and incorporating in 1878 both of its previous rivals, the Cock and the Star, which had belonged to Eton.

Perhaps what attracted the visitors to the Grosvenor, apart from Shaftesbury itself, which is a very picturesque old town, was the Chevy Chase sideboard. This famous piece, which is still to be seen in the old assembly room, was commissioned by the Duke of Northumberland in 1857 and was completed by Gerrard Robinson of Newcastle in 1863. It is 12ft long, 10ft high and covered with hundreds of hand-carved figures which represent the Ballad of Chevy Chase, a song which tells of the fourteenth-century battle at Otterburn between 1,500 Northumbrians led by Harry Percy (Hotspur of Shakespeare's *Henry IV*) and 2,000 Scots led by the Douglases. According to the ballad, the battle was caused by Harry Percy's poaching of Douglas deer. Only 53 Englishmen and 55 Scots are supposed to have survived the battle, and the sideboard shows Percy himself expiring shortly afterwards in the arms of his wife at Bamburgh, the family stronghold. In fact, both Hotspur and Douglas survived the battle, and even fought on the same side, later leading the rebel army against Henry IV at Shrewsbury, in 1402. Be that as it may, the sideboard is an object of breath-taking intricacy. Unfortunately it is constantly being vandalised by 'souvenir-hunters' who snap off whole figures and pieces of figures to take home with them, thus wrecking the pleasure of everyone else.

The Grosvenor Hotel, Shaftesbury, Dorset. Detail from the Chevy Chase sideboard, a masterpiece of Victorian craftsmanship

GLOUCESTERSHIRE

Coleford, The Speech House

Standing a few miles outside Coleford, the Speech House marks the traditional centre of the Forest of Dean. Even if this were not geographically true, it would be metaphorically so, for the hotel and its predecessors on the site have been at the heart of the Forest's affairs for centuries.

Built in the 1670s, the King's Lodge, as it was then known, replaced an older house called Kenesley Lodge as the home of the Court of Attachment. By the seventeenth century this Court had al-

ready lost much of its importance, but in the Middle Ages, when hunting meant much more to the economy of the royal household, it was a very important body indeed. It protected both the forest itself, by checking encroachment and punishing anyone found damaging trees, and the game by trying poachers who operated in the forest. Mutilation was the punishment for any of these offences in 1261, when the verderers of the Forest of Dean are first recorded (although traditionally they are supposed to have been founded by King Canute over two centuries before); but when the King's Lodge was built the

The New Inn, Gloucester. The open gallery surrounds all four sides of the courtyard and is the most impressive surviving example in the country

penalty had been lessened to mere transportation to the American colonies. Dock, witness box and bench have now vanished from the court-room, although the Court of Attachment still meets there four or five times a year. Poaching is now tried by the magistrates, and encroachment is a matter for the planning authorities, but the four verderers and the representatives of the Crown Agents and Forestry Commission who make up the Court still play a part in policy-making. They also protect the rights of the commoners, whose sheep graze in the forest, and of the Free Miners, who are entitled to dig for coal anywhere in the forest without permission.

The Speech House acquired its present name when it was first let as a hotel in the 1860s, by which time it had been found to be too large for the Court's diminished stature. The hotel was enlarged and restored in 1883.

Gloucester, The New Inn, Northgate Street

Edward II was murdered at Berkeley Castle in September 1327 and was buried in Gloucester Abbey. Almost immediately his tomb became a focus for pilgrimage, since it was believed that the person of an anointed king was sacred, and his body had miraculous healing powers (the laying-on of the royal hands was held to cure scrofula, known as the king's evil), and a number of hospices and inns were built to cope with the pilgrims.

The New Inn was designed and built by a monk of Gloucester, John Twyning, in 1445 as a guest-house for pilgrims, and is chiefly remarkable for its galleried courtyard, certainly the largest and most impressive of its type now surviving, and unusual in that much of the timber used in the framing is not oak, but chestnut. The gallery surrounds all four sides of the yard, and many of the bedrooms open off it as they have always done. Thus today's hotel guest has a chance to experience at least something of the atmosphere of a medieval inn (although with slightly more modern facilities). Originally the inn was constructed with an extra gallery on the top floor on one side of the yard, which looks as though it had been enclosed in Georgian times. A drawing of 1926 shows this upper gallery still open, although this may be a fanciful reconstruction rather than a faithful contemporary portrayal.

A courtyard of this size was such a convenient place of assembly that it eventually became an important place in the life of the town. Throughout the Tudor period it was used as a theatre where wandering players performed (Shakespeare himself probably among them) and on 9 July 1552, tradition has it, the Earl of Northumberland proclaimed his daughter-in-law, Lady Jane Grey, queen here. This Protestant attempt to prevent the return of Roman Catholicism under Mary Tudor failed. Jane's rule lasted ten days, and two years later she followed her father-in-law and husband to the block.

In the eighteenth century the New Inn was a centre for the coaching trade; luckily not many alterations were made. Chimneys, doorcases and windows were renewed, and the residents' lounge on the first floor seems to have been a small assembly room or a large private parlour at that time. Beyond that little has changed over the centuries.

Tewkesbury, The Gupshill Manor Hotel, Gloucester Road
The Berkeley Arms, High Street
The Bell, High Street

Tewkesbury is an ancient town with many ancient inns, but Gupshill Manor, although possibly a fifteenth-century building, is not one of them. It has only been a pub since 1951, when the licence of the Railway Inn was transferred to it; before that it was a bed and breakfast hotel, and before that a farm.

It is, however, an extremely good conversion, being comfortable and without gimmickry, although some of the reproduction weaponry and armour is a little unfortunate. The bars have been divided up so that they are neither too big and barn-like nor too small and claustrophobic, and the colour scheme relies largely on the traditional mixture of cream plasterwork and different kinds of timber. The sensitivity of the work is vindicated by the fact that the Gupshill Manor has been a commercial success— a fact which the designers of the garish and ghastly 'theme pubs' of the 1960s and '70s ought to have taken into account.

Perhaps the designers of the Gupshill Manor were luckier than those who have to create entirely new pubs from scratch in that the property came to them with a distinctive character and history. Originally built in the middle of the fifteenth century, it stood on the edge of the field where, in 1471, one of the most decisive battles of the Wars of the Roses was fought, when Edward IV trounced the forces of Henry VI and established a Yorkist regime which lasted until the battle of Bosworth in 1485. However, the whole house was rebuilt in the seventeenth century, when stonework from the ruins of Tewkesbury Abbey (the

abbey church survives) was incorporated. Visible in the bar is a corbel from a screen in the form of a crowned head, too worn now to tell whether it was a king or a queen. Much of the woodwork is also from the seventeenth century. Carved on one beam above the bar itself is a tiny mouse, the 'signature' of one of the joiners. At that time Gupshill Manor was the home of the Rainford family, whose genealogy is displayed in the entrance hall. The Manor was very much larger than it is today; half of it was burnt down in a fire in 1707.

Naturally, the pub has a ghost: staff and customers have all heard footsteps in empty rooms and seen a formless haze on the stairs, and a medium has confirmed (insofar as mediums can) that the house has a non-paying guest of the spectral kind.

The Berkeley Arms dates from about 1600, or possibly slightly earlier, and has always been a pub. Originally it was a tavern selling only wine, before the difference between taverns, beerhouses and inns became too blurred to have any meaning. However, there was a building on the site before this, for the layout of the rear part of the pub suggests a large medieval hall-house.

The Berkeley is first recorded as such in 1869; before then it was probably called the Queen's Arms. Until 1940 it

---

(*opposite above*) Gupshill Manor Hotel, Tewkesbury, Gloucestershire. In 1471 the Battle of Tewkesbury raged around the original building; the story of the battle is told on a map in the hall
(*below*) The Bell, Tewkesbury, Gloucestershire, from the grounds of the abbey church

was a complex of tiny snugs and parlours, but the glass partitions have all now been removed. Until that date, also, hot faggots and cold cuts were always available—a hang-over from the seventeenth century when the owner of the premises combined the trades of licensee and butcher.

The Bell stands just across the street from the magnificent abbey church and was at one time the monastery guest-house. After the Dissolution it was briefly a tannery, and was entirely rebuilt as an inn, the Angel, in the late sixteenth or early seventeenth century. The date 1697 above the door applies to a rebuilding. In the dining-room there are traces of a wall-painting, probably Elizabethan, and some of the panelling appears to have come from the old monastery. The Bell became a coaching inn, although it was at the Hop Pole that Mr Pickwick and his companions stopped to dine. But in 1857 it gained a long-lasting popularity and even became something of a tourist attraction when Mrs Craik (Dinah Mulock) made it the model for the home of Abel Fletcher in her novel *John Halifax, Gentleman*. The bowling-green which figures in the book gave the pub its name at the time, the Bell & Bowling Green, and until the regatta wound up in 1921 it was always the scene of the Regatta Ball. Since then the old stone coach-house has been pulled down, the coach-yard has been extended and, in 1971, an extension at the rear was built around an eighteenth-century frame.

SOMERSET

Dunster, The Luttrell Arms

The fifteenth-century hall which is the centre-piece of the Luttrell Arms was originally built either as a guest-house or a personal residence by the abbot of Cleeve, and replaced a row of three houses which are known to have existed in 1443. The splendid, original hammer-beam roof, fireplace and twelve-light window, which make the pub something of a showplace, are still intact, and along with the seventeenth-century yarn market and largely Victorian castle, make Dunster a popular place to spend a day with the many tourists who flock to nearby Minehead in summer.

The Luttrell's stone exterior was begun in 1622 and finished probably in 1629, the year in which George Luttrell, lord of the manor, died. Many of the rooms contain exquisite plasterwork commissioned by him.

The Luttrells have been lords of the manor of Dunster since 1404, and probably acquired the abbot's old house during the Dissolution. At that time, the village, now 2 miles inland, was a thriving little seaport, and the inn was first christened the Ship. Under this name it endured a brief siege at the end of the Civil War, when Parliamentary forces were sweeping the West Country clear of Royalists. The Georgian windows and new roof were probably added in or around 1779, when the Ship changed its name to honour its owners. At the same time the Georgian wing at the rear was built, and the Luttrell Arms enjoyed a fair amount of trade from coaches using the coast road.

The plasterwork on which George Luttrell lavished so much money was probably executed by Dutch craftsmen attracted to the town by the prosperity of its weaving industry. One overmantel bears the arms of England and France, a representation of Actæon being torn to pieces by his own hounds on Mt Cithaeron, and a figure of either James II or George Luttrell himself. The pub remained in the hands of the Luttrell family until 1949, when it became a Trust House.

Glastonbury, The George & Pilgrims

Glastonbury, with its mysterious tor rising steeply out of the flat Isle of Avalon, is one of England's most historic towns. Here ancient Britons lived in stilted houses in the marshes and constructed timber causeways that were miles long. Here Joseph of Arimethaea is said to have brought the boy Jesus, and planted his staff which took root to become the abbey's strange Christmas-flowering thorn. Here King Arthur was carried, wounded by his treacherous son Mordred at the battle of Camlann, to lie hidden in the Isle of Glass until Britain's direst hour of need, and here King Alfred hid from the Danes, waging guerilla warfare until his final triumph and the conversion of the Danish king.

It is entirely fitting, therefore, that Glastonbury's principal inn should be one of the best monastic hostelries of the fifteenth century. Built by the abbot, John Selwood, in 1475 to replace an earlier inn on the site, the George & Pilgrims was designed to accommodate the wealthier of the thousands of visitors who came to the abbey. The frontage, which survives unchanged, is as cleverly designed and elaborately executed as the west front of any great church of the period.

The principal difficulty faced by the inn's designer was the narrowness of the site—only 34ft wide. With the tall, narrow, arched windows with their heavy stone mullions, the upward thrust of the bay to the left of the entrance arch, and the square columns at each end of the building all giving a strong vertical emphasis, the façade would have looked much narrower than it really was. It was therefore decided to incorporate equally strong horizontal string courses at each of the three floors, and a horizontal panel containing three shields bearing the arms of the abbey and the initials of the abbot over the arch. The result is that, although the effect of height much prized by ecclesiastic architects is not lost, it is offset by an illusion of width. The whole is one of the most impressive fronts of its type.

Although the abbey itself was destroyed in the Reformation, its former guest-house survived as a flourishing business; in fact Henry VIII is traditionally supposed to have watched the abbey burn from an upstairs room which now bears his name. However, the stone statuary which once graced the frontage was removed and smashed, and today the many niches are empty.

It is perhaps fortunate that the George & Pilgrims never became a major coaching inn, and has therefore never been rebuilt as have so many other monastic inns. Nevertheless, there was a lively posting trade, and, incredible as it may seem, the narrow arch was once the access for post-chaises to the stables (now demolished) at the rear.

Inside the inn there are many moulded oak beams, a bedroom known as the Monk's Cell which is supposed to be haunted, and a fireplace surrounded by Delft tiles, all of which are eighteenth-century except one, which the visitor can amuse himself by trying to detect.

The George and Pilgrims, Glastonbury, Somerset. The inn was built at the same time as the tower of St John's Church in the background

The George, Norton St Philip, Somerset. The differing architectural styles, over a century apart, and the stone steps leading to a waggon loading platform can be clearly seen

Norton St Philip, The George

The George is another of the outstanding monastic hospices which have survived almost intact. A barn was built on the site in about 1230 by the Carthusians of the newly founded priory of Hinton Charterhouse, but it was entirely rebuilt in 1397 as a wool-exchange and guest-house for the wool merchants with whom the monks did business. The village was the home of an important wool-fair throughout the fourteenth and fifteenth centuries, and the Carthusians were major producers. A large hall for

the storage of baled fleeces was approached by an exterior flight of stone steps which also served as a loading platform for waggons. The upper storeys were gutted by fire and rebuilt in half-timbering in about 1500; evidence of more formal ecclesiastic architecture, including a stone stair-turret, is visible in the tiny courtyard at the back. The courtyard also contains an open gallery, perhaps the earliest to survive.

The Dissolution caught up with Hinton Charterhouse on 31 March 1539, when the prior, Edmund Horde, signed the deed of surrender. The priory's

157

estate passed to the crown, and with it went the George, which rapidly became a flourishing inn. In June 1685 it was briefly the headquarters of the Duke of Monmouth during his ill-fated rebellion against James II. After an unsuccessful attack on Bristol, the Duke and his enthusiastic but untrained followers fell back southwards and camped around the village. An attack by James's troops was bloodily repulsed; but after the fight an assassin entered the village and tried to shoot Monmouth as he stood at an upstairs window of the George. The next day the rebels moved westward to be annihilated at Sedgemoor, after which Monmouth was captured hiding in a ditch; his hair had turned grey overnight. The area around Norton St Philip was considered to be a centre of disaffection with the king and support for Monmouth, and Judge Jeffries stayed at the George for a few days during the Bloody Assizes.

After the excitement of 1685, the village and its inn sank back into undisturbed bucolic calm. The George never became a major coaching inn, although it did possess some stabling. Charles Harper, visiting in 1926, found that:

> The vast building is now no more than a village alehouse, and with a modern bar fitted in pitch-pine! The greater part of the interior is in a dismantled condition, and the inn does not presume to offer accommodation for the traveller ... The long ranges of the upper floors [are] now dilapidated.

(*opposite*) The Crown, Wells, Somerset, built virtually on the doorstep of the Cathedral

However, business has certainly improved since Harper's visit, and the George now has an extensive tourist trade as well as its purely local custom.

Wells, The Crown

The Crown, which stands in the market-place within 200yd of the Cathedral and moated Bishop's Palace, is supposed to have been built in about 1450, but if this is true no traces of the original work are visible. The street frontage, which has three bays and three storeys, and the large cobbled inn yard, which includes a number of timber oriel windows, are thought to have been built in about 1590.

The inn was used by William Penn, the Quaker who went on to found the state of Pennsylvania, in 1695. While visiting the town with some of his followers, he preached from an upstairs window to a crowd of more than three thousand who had assembled in the market-place to hear him. For this he was arrested and imprisoned on a number of vague charges by the civil authorities. Perhaps surprisingly it was the Bishop of Bath and Wells, Bishop Kidder, who intervened and had the notorious nonconformist set free.

A few years later the management of the inn set up a coffee-house, an imitation of the establishments which were popular in the London of Boswell and Johnson. The gentlefolk of Wells took to it in great numbers, meeting there not only for a drink and a chat, but also to do business. A town doctor, one Claver Morris, even held consultations there.

The Crown never became as popular a coaching inn as its rival, the Swan. However, the management did run several purely local services, and as late as 1850 a coach left the Crown every day for Bristol.

Today, equipped with four-posters in the bedrooms and even a couple of squash-courts, the Crown has a flourishing tourist trade and has succeeded in keeping its regular local custom too.

Winsford, The Royal Oak

Winsford, in the very heart of Exmoor, is a village with plenty to boast about. With its green, on which there is an open-air skittle-alley, its church, its medieval pack-horse bridge and its thatched houses, it is one of Somerset's most picturesque spots. The village pub, the Royal Oak, matches its surroundings.

Thatched, like several of its neighbours, and half-timbered with many great beams to be seen inside, the Royal Oak was originally a twelfth-century cottage which grew into a farm. A sideline for the farmer's wife, as with so many others in the Middle Ages and even later, was brewing beer for the villagers and for the jaggers or packmen who carried Irish yarn from Minehead to the markets at Tiverton and Exeter. Many of these doubtless fell victim to the seventeenth-century highwayman Tom Faggus, whose hideout was in the hills around Winsford, and who was probably a dispossessed Royalist soldier. He is immortalised in R. D. Blackmore's *Lorna Doone*.

The lonely road across the moor became a little busier in 1813, when it was widened and resurfaced to become the Minehead and Tiverton turnpike. Coaches paused at the Royal Oak to change horses, and the increased income enabled the landlord to insert the dormers, with their little arched windows, in the roof.

Winsford's most famous son in recent years was Ernest Bevin, who went on to lead the Transport & General Workers' Union and became Attlee's Foreign Secretary. But the Royal Oak itself has also done a certain amount of work for Britain overseas: some years ago it was chosen as the typical English inn (if only that were true), and a model of it was sent to New York to feature in a British trade exhibition there.

WILTSHIRE

Beckhampton, The Waggon & Horses

Originally Tudor, the Waggon & Horses was built with the materials that came readiest to hand—in this case the sarsens from the stone circle and avenue at Avebury nearby. These are not the only ancient remains in the area: there is Silbury Hill looming in the background, and Stonehenge itself is a mere 12 miles away. But any magical powers they may have possessed did not trouble those who plundered them.

The pub is strategically sited at the crossing of two ancient routes, and throughout its history the location has ensured it a busy trade. Now it is mainly tourists, and at one time coaches on the London–Bath road used to call in. But what makes the Waggon & Horses rare is that it was principally used by the juggernauts of the seventeenth century, the great freight waggons with their 8ft wheels. Not much freight travelled by waggon before the nineteenth century; conditions were too bad. But the

---

(*opposite*) The Royal Oak, Winsford, Somerset. A picturesque pub in a picturesque village

Waggon & Horses was equipped with a smithy where the great lumbering cart-horses could be shod, and at one time there were enormous stables across the road to house them for the night, with lofts above where the carters slept in the hay.

Before banks became widely trust-worthy, waggoners and the merchants who employed them were often forced to travel with large quantities of money. Not surprisingly, therefore, the lonely roads around Beckhampton were in-fested with highwaymen for nearly two hundred years. When they were caught, the law was ruthless, and the gibbet where their bodies hung in chains, often for months, stood beside the inn almost within living memory. Another stood on the top of Inkpen Beacon, not far away.

The stone-mullioned windows and the overhanging thatched roof which appeal to modern tourists appealed also to Charles Dickens: the Waggon & Horses is the original for the inn in 'The Bagman's Tale' in *Pickwick Papers*.

Devizes, The Bear

The Bear, now the principal inn of Devizes, owes much of its rise to the very same highwaymen who plagued the downs around Beckhampton. The gib-bets proved so inadequate a deterrent that in the 1780s the authorities were left with but one alternative—to adopt a new route for the London–Bath road. Conse-quently the old road through Devizes was upgraded and the downs road largely abandoned, and before long as many as thirty coaches a day were stopping at the Bear.

Even before the coach trade arrived the Bear had been the town's main inn. First recorded in 1599, the Bear had beside it (where the Corn Exchange now stands) a large public hall where func-tions were held and where elections took place, a big yard known in 1654 as the Queen's Stables, which had once been the earthwork dividing town from castle, and a bear garden used for bear- and bull-baiting which in 1664 passed to the

Waggon and Horses, Beckhampton, Wiltshire, built with stones from nearby Avebury

owners of the castle. In the 1750s and '60s the landlord, John Watley, was one of the most eminent innkeepers in the West Country, and it was under his auspices that the Bear Club, originally a dining club for the gentlemen of the town but later a charitable trust providing scholarship places for local children, was established.

Watley's successor was even better known, although Thomas Lawrence, who came to the Bear from the American Coffee House in Bristol, was more famous for his son's achievements than for his own. Lawrence was responsible for marking the road over Salisbury Plain with conspicuous posts at half-mile intervals—a boon in winter—but it was Thomas Lawrence junior who attracted the custom of such famous people as David Garrick, Fanny Burney and Mrs Siddons. Not only would the five-year-old recite great chunks of Milton, he also drew remarkable portraits. By 1820 he was president of the Royal Academy.

Thanks to his son, the Bear was already a well-known inn by the time Lawrence left in about 1780. Under the Halcombe family who succeeded him it became even more prosperous and a new wing was built; for the new coach road brought with it patrons of great rank, including George III and Queen Charlotte in 1789. The Queen came again in 1817, recording that she had had a most elegant repast and that the inn had put at her disposal ten pairs of horses as fine as any ever put in harness. Since 1758 the Bear had been virtually the officers' mess of the county militia, and it was here that the officers of the regiment entertained the Prince of Wales, Prince Arthur of Connaught and Prince Edward of Saxe-Coburg when they reviewed the troops in 1893.

One of the regular dishes on the Bear's menu is Devizes Pie, taken from a recipe of 1836 but believed to be a much older delicacy. Served cold, it includes calf's head and brains, pickled tongue, sweetbreads, lamb, veal, bacon and boiled eggs served in a jelly and spiced with cayenne.

Salisbury, The White Hart, St John Street

The ancient town of Salisbury boasts many historic inns: the George, built in 1314 and rebuilt in 1453, closed down long ago, although the building may still be seen fronting a shopping arcade, the splendid half-timbered Haunch of Venison, built in 1320, the King's Arms, the Chough and the Red Lion.

The White Hart, while not so ancient as these, is certainly as interesting. It is a fine example of the way the Georgians, when they could afford to, tore down older inns and replaced them with fashionable classical styles. The White Hart replaced a building first recorded in the reign of Henry VII (1485–1509), in which Walter Raleigh met James I after his disastrous 1618 expedition to Guyana. The knight was not looking forward to the interview; so much so that he feigned leprosy and took to his room, apparently fasting but being secretly supplied with bread and mutton from the White Hart kitchen. The angry sovereign was not mollified, and sent Raleigh first to the Tower, then to the block.

By 1755 the old White Hart had become a prosperous coaching inn, the home of the Salisbury Stage Coach and running 'neat four-wheeled chaises' at 9d (4p) per mile. By 1800 the inn was doing well enough for the owners to decide it would be worthwhile to rebuild, and so they did, in grand style. All that remains of the earlier inn is a piece of timber to which is tacked a piece of hessian some four inches long painted with gold acanthus foliage on a blue background. Found in an attic and now kept locked up by the management, this has not yet been dated but is likely to be a remnant of a Tudor wall-painting of about 1560.

The new building is easily imposing enough to be a town hall or medium-sized country house. The centre-piece, and the hotel's pride, is the portico of four Ionic pillars topped by a pediment which gives the building its imposing and severe tone, and illustrates how differently the Georgians regarded their inns. They were not content, like earlier generations, to put up with the rustic eccentricity, the almost accidental quality, of earlier timberframed buildings. Wealthy travellers were not prepared to rough it while travelling, any more than they were at home; they wanted the best money could buy, and many an astute innkeeper was willing to invest large sums to ensure he could provide it. In the White Hart, and in many other similar inns, we can see an architectural example of how the acute class-sensitivity of the Victorian era evolved.

After the new building was complete, the White Hart became an even more important place in the social and even in the administrative life of the region. Balls and banquets were held there, and in 1810 a Commission of Bankruptcy held a hearing there into the collapse of a bank founded by three local men. Thomas Ogden, William Bowles and George Wyndham were the directors of the Salisbury and Shaftesbury Bank; the inn still keeps a number of their bank-notes.

Coaching continued well into the nineteenth century at the White Hart. The moulded figure of a hart above the pediment was added in the late 1820s to compete with a rival, the Antelope. But even after the trade's collapse, the inn continued to flourish as a country hotel. Visitors' books of the turn of the century show how many Americans came to stay, perhaps to revisit the place where the President of Congress, Henry Laurens, spent a night in 1780. He had been captured at sea and stopped for a night with his escort on his way to fourteen months' imprisonment in London.

EAST ANGLIA

CAMBRIDGESHIRE

Buckden, The Lion

Originally built about 1490, the Lion served for many years as the guest-house for the palace of the bishops of Lincoln, the ruins of which still stand in the village. Now a smart hotel, it would then have been a pretty rough and ready place; more attention was paid to such details as the timber ceiling boss, which is carved with a lamb and the legend 'Ecce Agnus Dei', than to the comforts of guests who bedded down in the rushes as near the fire as rank allowed.

At some time in the sixteenth century—probably not until well after the Dissolution—the old guest-house became an inn and since then it has held a variety of names. At first it was the Lamb & Flag, then just the Lamb. A lion from the See of Lincoln's coat of arms was then added, becoming the Lion & Lamb, until about fifty years ago it dropped the Lamb altogether and was merely the Lion.

The village's main street was, until recently bypassed, the Great North Road, down which great numbers of coaches and chaises began to move in the early eighteenth century. Some years after this, when trade had grown substantially, the Lion underwent rebuilding operations. The old great hall was partitioned, a section of it becoming the inn kitchen, the open hearth with its 10ft

carved and chamfered lintel became the cooking range, both the wings at the rear were extended (although one still retains some original work) and a new frontage was added.

At the same time the red-brick George across the road was built, and the two inns shared the traffic, the Lion taking the 'up' or London-bound coaches while the George catered for the 'down', northbound travellers.

Cambridge: The Eagle, Benet Street
The Blue Boar, Trinity Street

Built in the early seventeenth century as a posting-house, the Eagle takes its name from the arms of the Stanley family and was originally called the Eagle & Child. (It is still sometimes nicknamed the Bird & Bantling.)

The Eagle evolved into a small but flourishing coaching inn during the eighteenth century, and one side of the courtyard is still overlooked by the original open gallery. However, the oak balustrade and pillars were removed, probably in the Regency period, and replaced in cast iron. At the time this was not unusual—some of the main London coaching termini boasted the same feature—but the rest have all been pulled down, with the exception of the George in Southwark, and the Eagle's iron gallery is now unique.

In the 1770s the Eagle was the headquarters of the town's Whigs. It was the home of the Rutland Club, established by John Mortlock, MP, when the Duke of Rutland, a leading Whig, was MP for the University. But it is remembered now for its clientele during World War II, when East Anglia was crowded with RAF and USAAF bomber bases. The Eagle became a favourite rendezvous for the bomber-crews, who left their names written on the ceiling of the bar in soot from candles and the ubiquitous American Zippo lighters. Among the dozens of names are 'Wild Hare', 'Bob and Tommy', and 'Bert's Boys of 196 Squadron' (Bert being Bomber Harris' other nickname). Many of those who survived German flak and night fighters return regularly to the pub.

A more important coaching inn was the Blue Boar, which is first mentioned in 1693, when the churchwardens of All Saints' held a party here to celebrate Queen Mary's birthday. According to parish records they spent the princely sum of 2/- (10p), which was probably enough to get them all pleasantly maudlin, if not roaring drunk. The inn had

---

(*opposite above*) The Lion, Buckden, Cambridgeshire, one of a string of large coaching inns along the Great North Road. The road which passes the building, now by-passed and quiet, was for hundreds of years one of the busiest and most important routes in the country

(*below*) The Eagle, Cambridge. The tourists flock here in season to see one of the town's prettiest inns. The iron gallery, once common, is now unique

probably inherited its name from another across the street, which had been recorded in 1552.

The coaching trade began in the eighteenth century; at its height the landlord (John Mound, a former butler to the Bishop of Ely) advertised services to London, Sheffield, Birmingham, Norwich and Ipswich. Early in the nineteenth century there was a major rebuilding, and a somewhat bland frontage was added. After the collapse of coaching, the Blue Boar declined, eventually to be rescued by Trust Houses; it has recently been modernised in a characterless style by THF.

Huntingdon, The George, George Street

Sitting astride the old Great North Road as it does, Huntingdon has always been strategically placed, and its principal inn, the George, was well known even before the age of coaching as a stopping-place on the road from London to Yorkshire and Scotland. It is first recorded in the reign of Henry VIII, and in 1574 became the property of a brewer called Henry Cromwell, whose grandson Oliver was a gentleman farmer until called to higher things.

The building Henry Cromwell knew has gone without trace, although Charles I might recognise some elements of the George in which he stayed for a few days in 1645. Two sides of the inn yard are overlooked by original timber-framed seventeenth-century wings, one of them possessing an open gallery, a carriage entrance with carved wooden pillars and a much later dormer containing a clock; the other, possibly a little older, having a jettied upper floor and external staircase. These wings are, unfortunately, the only survivors of a

The George, Huntingdon, Cambridgeshire. The coach-yard with open gallery

disastrous fire in 1870 which destroyed the other two sides of what was the largest inn yard in the country. (These two wings have been rather replaced.)

Like most of the larger inns on the Great North Road, the George became an important post in coaching days. At a convenient 60 miles from London, it became an overnight halt for many coach services, and as late as 1839 there were seven services calling here.

Even after the age of coaching, the George played an important part in the development of road transport: it became the base for an out-of-work coach-driver named Thomas Hennessey, whose cousin William was landlord, and who started one of the country's first bus services, between Huntingdon and Cambridge.

Wansford, The Haycock

Wansford has for centuries been the place where the Great North Road crossed the Nene; the earliest mention of its bridge is 1221 when indulgences were granted to those who helped pay for its upkeep. It may be that the Haycock started its long and chequered career at about this time, for the lintel beam in the open hearth of the Smoke Room is thought to date back to the reign of King John (1199–1216). But the first record of it comes only from 1571, when there was a three-storey inn called the Swan on the site, which was flooded when the river rose and swept away three arches of the bridge.

The present building, according to a date-stone found in the garden, was

The Haycock, Wansford, Cambridgeshire. Another major stop along the Great North Road, at the point where it crossed the Nene

erected in 1632. It was clearly a posting-station of major importance even then, for the stabling accommodated 150 horses (probably more pack-animals and riding-horses than coaches in those days), and the area of the Collyweston slate roof is more than an acre.

The last mention of it as the Swan was in 1706; by 1712 it had become the Haycock, and the village had become known as Wansford-in-England. The story behind these changes relates to a mythical character, one Drunken Barnaby. The first version, by the Water Poet, John Taylor, says that Barnaby was sleeping off a binge on a hay-stack when the Nene was flooded by the Collyweston quarrymen to carry their slate-barges. Barnaby awoke to find that he and his stack were being washed:

Down the current; people cried
As along the stream I hied
'Where away,' quoth they, 'from Greenland?'
'No, from Wansford bridge, in England!'

Celia Fiennes' version, written in 1698, largely agrees until Barnaby wakes up, demanding to know what country he is in—which the villagers evidently found amusing enough to warrant commemoration both on their inn-sign and in the name of their village. Viscount Torrington, in his journeys round the country in the 1780s and '90s, recorded that the original Barnaby sign was still in existence, and was most impressed by the Norton family who kept the inn at that time.

169

The innkeeper in 1808, Jeremiah Mallatratt, lost the Haycock in a card game to Anthony Percival who died in 1826. In 1841 his widow handed the inn over to their son Thomas, a legendary figure in coaching days who became proprietor of White's Club in 1859. After his death in 1878, his widow, Elizabeth, carried on the inn along with its 625 acres and ten labourers until 1887 when the Haycock became a farm. She retained the beer-licence, however, and ran the old inn as a village pub until 1893, and on her death in 1898 the whole property was bought by Lord Chesham.

For the next five years the building served as a hunting-box; among the Cheshams' many guests there were the Duke and Duchess of Teck, parents of Queen Mary, the wife of George V. Afterwards, the distinguished stone building, with its pedimented porch and matching window above, had a variety of tenants until 1928, when it was re-opened as a first-class country hotel. The inn still contains a cock-fighting loft, brew-house and Elizabethan granary.

ESSEX

Chigwell, The King's Head

Famous as the meeting-place of Sir John Chester and Geoffrey Haredale in Dickens' *Barnaby Rudge*, the King's Head was originally built in the reign of Henry VIII as an administrative centre for Epping Forest. Like the Speech House in the Forest of Dean, it was home to the Court of Attachment (known as the Forty-Day Court because of the intervals at which it sat) and was also a guest-house for government officials. Elizabeth I stayed here on a hunting expedition to the forest.

The last record of the Court's sitting there is in 1713, and after that it seems to have served as the village school for a while before becoming an important posting house on a new London–Norwich road which bypassed the most dangerous and remote parts of the forest where highwaymen (including Turpin) were a constant menace.

Dickens first stayed at the King's Head in 1841. It was, he wrote, 'such a delicious old inn'; but when he decided to use it in a book he made it rather more delicious than it actually was. He endowed it with 'more gable-ends than a lazy man would care to count', and 'huge zig-zag chimneys, out of which it seemed that even smoke could not choose to come in more than naturally fantastic shapes imparted to it in its tortuous progress.' In fact the King's Head has four gables, one of which was at the time the White Inn which has since been incorporated. But its heavily timbered frontage with the big bay windows, and the even better view of the back from the pub garden, are impressive enough without the need for glorification. In the book, Dickens calls the King's Head the Maypole, which has confused some commentators because there used to be a genuine Maypole in Chigwell Row. But it is clear that Dickens used the King's Head as his jumping-off point and let his imagination do the rest.

Chigwell's best-known resident was Admiral Hardy, the same man who kissed the dying Nelson at Trafalgar. He held a commemorative ball every year on the anniversary of the battle, which always well-attended, although he was not liked. A number of letters preserved by the local history society say that he was disagreeable, insane, once attacked a young woman and received abusive Valentine cards.

Colchester, The Red Lion, High Street

Colchester was already a major settlement when the Romans captured it, and it became the first Roman town in Britain. The Red Lion stands on a Roman site: fragments of mosaic were uncovered during the excavations of 1857 and 1882, so it is likely that a building has been standing here for nearly two thousand years.

The existing house, however, was built as a home for a wealthy burgess in the fifteenth century. There is fifteenth-century masonry in the cellar, and the wattle-and-daub infill between the timbers has been dated to around 1470. The frontage, with its projecting upper floors, is richly timbered with wooden panels carved in the Perpendicular style, quite as elaborate as any church traceries.

The earliest mention of the Red Lion is in 1529, although at that time it was the White Lion, and it was probably converted from a private house to a tavern selling wine in about 1500. By 1625 the lion had changed colour, probably to mark the accession of James I in 1603, a red lion being one of the supporters of the arms of Scotland. In the Civil War, East Anglia was a Parliament stronghold—Cromwell himself was an East Anglian—but in the short second Civil War of 1648 the town fell into the hands of Royalists led by Sir George Lisle and Sir Charles Lucas. After a siege of several weeks, Colchester fell to General Fairfax. The beaten defenders were rounded up and held in the Red Lion yard while their leaders were hastily tried and then shot, Lisle's last words being: 'Your shot, your shame; our fall, our fame.'

During the siege the town had been in desperate straits, with starving citizens eating dogs, cats, rats and anything else they could find. It rapidly recovered, however, and in 1656 and 1668 we hear of the Red Lion issuing its own trade tokens when coinage was scarce—the mark of a prosperous concern. Some rebuilding was carried out at the dawn of the coaching era (a lead gutter in the yard bears the date 1716) and in 1756 the inn was the terminus for an express service to London, although its rival, the Cups, was the more prominent of the two in coaching terms.

The Red Lion became a Trust House in 1913 and subsequent renovations uncovered several finely carved interior beams which had probably been plastered over for two hundred years. The old inn yard is now roofed over.

Hempstead, The Rose & Crown

The Rose & Crown was built between 1578, when William Harvey, the physician who discovered the circulation of blood, was born in a cottage on the site, and 1598, when the landlord of the Bell, as it was first called, was summonsed for keeping a disorderly house. It has served as the village alehouse ever since, although at the end of the last century, for reasons nobody can remember, it changed its name.

Harvey is buried in the village churchyard, but Hempstead's most famous son was born in the Bell in 1705. He was Dick Turpin, and his father was not only brewer and alehouse-keeper, but smallholder and village butcher as well, and the blood-runnels and meat-hooks with which he plied his trade are still to be seen in the pub's bar—as is a copy of the registration of Dick's birth from the parish archives.

Young Turpin was first apprenticed to a butcher in Whitechapel, but he

The Rose and Crown, Hempstead, Essex, birthplace of Dick Turpin

never took to honest work. First it was cattle-rustling, then smuggling, poaching, house-breaking and finally highway robbery. In 1739 he was arrested and hanged for horse-stealing at York, and all the efforts of his father, who still ran the Bell, failed to save him.

Dick Turpin was not a gallant or romantic man—he once sat a woman on a fire until she told him where her money was hidden—and his utter indifference to suffering was probably instilled into him during his childhood at the Bell. The village butcher in those days was also the village slaughterman, and when trade was brisk the house must have fairly reeked with blood. Successive landlords of the Bell also profited handsomely from the cockfights held in the arena across the lane, where they sold refreshments and held money for the furious betting which always accompanied a 'main'. Acting as pot-boy for his father, young Dick Turpin became used to cruelty while still a child.

There is nothing cruel about the Rose & Crown today, and the arena has become an innocent place with trees planted where once a ring of posts and boards prevented the steel-spurred fighting cocks from escaping. An enviable peace has settled over the village and its alehouse, which has already been serving pints for four centuries and looks set to continue for another four.

North Weald Bassett, The King's Head

Like Hempstead's Rose & Crown, the King's Head has served as the village alehouse since the sixteenth century; but in this case a record of the first licence ever taken out on the property survives. This was in 1592, but the building appears to be some forty or fifty years older, and tradition has it that it was built of ships' timbers salvaged from Tilbury docks. This is a story that is often told of half-timbered pubs, usually to make them seem romantic, but in the King's Head's case it could easily be true. Pre-fabrication marks on the beams could well be shipwrights' marks. In the reigns of Edward VI and Mary Tudor, the mighty navy built up by their father Henry VIII fell into decay; many ships were laid up and scrapped, and builders near naval dockyards found it cheaper to salvage old ships' timbers than to make new ones.

The King's Head also helps foster the myth that our ancestors were very much smaller than us. Doors on the ground floor are barely 5ft high, and the ceiling clearance is no more than 6ft in places. But of course, the house was not built like that; in fact the ground level appears to be steadily rising, as a comparison with old prints will show. A look into the magnificent Squire's Room, where the ground-floor ceiling was taken out to create a noble two-storey parlour for any quality who might happen to call, shows that door-cases on the upper floors are a more normal size.

If the ground level is not rising, the pub is sinking. The King's Head is a crooked house, with beams leaning and sagging in all directions. It suffered some bomb-damage in the war (there is an airfield in the village) and comparison with old photographs, combined with regular surveys, indicates that the crookedness is getting worse. A stream runs near the foundations, and the ground is possibly a little spongy. A well-built timber frame is supposed to

be resilient enough to give in all directions at once without falling over; one can only hope this is true.

The King's Head stands on the old London–Colchester coach road, and in the eighteenth century it made an effort to attract some of the posting trade. It was at this time that the Squire's Room was made, and the whole front was stuccoed over to persuade passing travellers of the pub's modernity. It does not seem to have been a very successful effort, for no more substantial alterations were made. The stucco came off in 1927, and apart from some reasonable new buildings at the back, the King's Head is much as it ever was.

LINCOLNSHIRE

Grantham, The Angel & Royal, High Street

Simply the Angel until 1866, this is one of the most important inns, both culturally and historically, in the country. The land belonged to the Knights Templar until the order was suppressed in 1312, and there had been an inn on the site for at least a hundred years before that—King John and his retinue stayed at the inn in February 1213 during the Barons' War.

That John, and later Richard III, stayed at the inn presents something of a mystery. Normally they would have sheltered at a castle, but Grantham has none. However, the layout and style of the frontage of the Angel & Royal is strongly reminiscent of a castle gatehouse, and one or two street names indicate the existence of a castle. Certainly the inn is at the highest point of the town, where one would expect to find the castle: perhaps it was planned but never completed, and the Angel really was intended as its gatehouse. But the only remnant of the twelfth- or thirteenth-century building is the masonry in the cellar.

The oldest visible portion of the inn is the gateway. This dates back to the reign of Edward III (1327–77) who, with his queen, Phillipa of Hainault, adorns its hood mouldings. The rest of the frontage is fifteenth-century; but the wall itself is a yard thick and may be contemporary with the arch, while the bay and oriel windows, the carved angel, the buttresses and the parapet tracery are later additions.

Above the arch is the state room known as the Chambre du Roi where Richard III in October 1483 wrote the letter (a photograph of which is now on show) instructing his Lord Chamberlain to send him the Great Seal so that he could endorse the death warrant made out for the Duke of Buckingham, who was in rebellion against him. Now a restaurant, this room is the hotel's showpiece. The fan-vaulting in the oriel and two bay windows is worth travelling some distance to see. There are two more examples of the same vaulting on the ground floor, as well as a carving of the pelican in piety feeding her young with her own blood. (This is one of many religious symbols supporting the view that the Angel was used principally by pilgrims visiting the shrine of St Wulfram, to whom the parish church is dedicated.) Two fourteenth-century fireplaces, discovered since World War II, have now been exposed and restored.

The Angel and Royal, Grantham, Lincolnshire. The building resembles more a medieval castle than an inn; was it originally intended as a gatehouse?

Not only pilgrims, but also merchants, took advantage of the Angel, and after the Reformation it continued to be used by the wealthier travellers, including Charles I in 1633. In 1706 the landlord, Michael Soloman, died, leaving £2 a year for a sermon to be preached against drunkenness every Michaelmas—this custom is still observed. It was in Soloman's day that the Great North Road (which now bypasses the town) came into use as a major coach-route: at its height the Angel was a stopping-place for the York, Edinburgh and Aberdeen Mail, the Royal Charlotte, which served London and Edinburgh, the York and Leeds Post Coach and the York Highflyer. The untiring Viscount Torrington stopped by on his travels in 1791; and it was at this time that the old leaded windows were replaced by Georgian sashes.

The decline of coaching hardly affected the Angel, principally because it was situated in the Belvoir Hunt's country, and visiting nobility and royalty, including the Prince of Wales, used the old coach buildings as stables. It continues today to defy the best efforts of Trust Houses Forte to rob it of atmosphere.

Lincoln, The Green Dragon, Broadgate

Standing in Lincoln's low town, with the bulk of the great Cathedral looming on the hill above, the Green Dragon was originally built as a guest-house for St Catherine's Priory in the fourteenth century. The Priory's estates were purchased during the Dissolution by Charles Brandon, Duke of Suffolk, but since rents were falling and wages and prices were rising, he recouped as much of his outlay as possible by selling off the guest-house as soon as he could.

At first it was not licensed. The purchaser was a merchant named Thomas Grantham, who made it his home for nearly thirty years before selling it to the city authorities to be rented out. The first tenant was a weaver named Peter Gollande; the next, Hugh Moxon, carried out much rebuilding and, at some time between 1590 and 1620, added the extra floor of attics which earned the old guest-house the name 'Great Garret'.

For the next eighty or so years Great Garret was a bakery, but by 1702, when the property changed hands again, part of it was in use as a beerhouse. The lease of 1702 describes it as 'The Great Garrattes, the garth thereto adjoining, the Tower garth, the Tower, and a piece of ground paled in on the west side'. The Great Garret itself became the home of Alderman Benjamin Harris, so it was probably the Tower which was the beerhouse.

This beerhouse was known as the Green Dragon by 1750, when the historian Thomas Sympson recorded it. About a century later it was pulled down and replaced. The Victorian pub was itself pulled down in 1955 to make way for road-widening, and the licence was transferred to the Great Garret itself, which has been restored.

Stamford, The George

Another of the aristocrats of English inns, the George is one of more than four hundred listed buildings in the town. The story of the George begins in 947, when King Edred granted the land to Croyland Abbey. Whether or not the monks built a hostelry here is not known, but shortly after the Conquest much of their land, including this site, was granted to the Abbey of Peterborough.

The Green Dragon, Lincoln, with the spire of St Swithins rising above it and the mighty Cathedral sitting atop its hill in the background

The George, Stamford, Lincolnshire, one of the most impressive and remarkable of all English inns

The present inn incorporates traces of three medieval buildings: on the south side was the House of the Holy Sepulchre, a guest-house for pilgrims starting their journeys to the Holy Land, originally owned by the Knights of St John; a church in what is now the garden; and on the north side the Hospital of St John and St Thomas, founded in 1174 for the poor by Peterborough Abbey. In 1188 a George Inn was given to the Abbey by one Richard Humez, though whether it was the same George is not known; and in the following year a charter of Richard I confirmed all three buildings in the possession of the Abbey.

We next hear of the George in the early fifteenth century, when a chapel of St Mary Magdalene was added, but apart from the chancel and crypt this was completely destroyed in a Lancastrian attack in 1461. Shortly afterwards the whole property came into the possession of a substantial citizen named John Dickens, who was an alderman of the town in 1476, 1483 and 1493. His daughter Alice, who inherited the inn from him, married a townsman named David Cissell or Sicillt, who was one of Henry VII's sergeants-at-arms; in 1539 their son Richard was wealthy enough to purchase the Priory of St Martin's and 300 acres; his son William Cecil became the first Baron Burghley, was Elizabeth I's chief minister and ordered the execution of Mary Queen of Scots. He was also the builder of Burghley House; in 1597, a year before his death, he had the George completely reconstructed, granting the landlord a right, which is still exercised, to nominate one inmate of the town almshouses.

It was in the days of coaching that the George came to prominence. Situated

on the Great North Road, on a crossing of the River Welland, Stamford attracted a heavy volume of traffic, and the George was the town's principal inn. As early as 1714 it had a George Tap for the servants of wealthy travellers; in that year the landlord, one Bolton, was sabred to death by a German dragoon who suspected him of being a Jacobite. A lynch-mob assembled, but the killer escaped. At a time when the George serviced 20 'up' and 20 'down' coaches every day, the frontage was rebuilt, the gallows sign was added, an assembly room, ballroom and minstrel gallery were installed and two large parlours, still called York and London, were set aside for travellers. London was 9 hours and 20 minutes away: the full fare from London to York was 25/- (£1.25) inside and 15/- (75p) outside. Guests could also regale themselves at the inn's cockpit, built of local freestone in 1725. It was 40ft across and could seat 500 spectators; after cock-fighting was banned in 1849 it served as a schoolhouse for a while, but was eventually demolished.

Guests at the George have included Charles I in 1641 and 1645, William III in 1696, 'Butcher' Cumberland in 1745 and the King of Denmark in 1768. The George also played host to Daniel Lambert, who died in Stamford in 1809 aged 32 and weighing 52st 11lb. In the lobby is a portrait of him and his enormous walking-stick.

(*opposite*) Duke's Head, King's Lynn, Norfolk, a building almost too good to be an inn

NORFOLK

King's Lynn, The Duke's Head, Tuesday Market Place

Built between 1685 and 1689 by a local architect, Henry Bell, the Duke's Head is a splendid classical building almost too good to be an inn. In fact it was not at first an ordinary inn; it was more of a private guest-house for merchants arriving at the port. It belonged to a wealthy wine importer of the town, Sir John Turner, who also financed the building of the Corn Exchange. (The Exchange was also designed by Henry Bell, who was three times mayor.)

The Duke's Head stands on the site of a Tudor inn, the Griffin, whose staircase, with its turned baluster and oaken rail, was incorporated into Sir John's new house. At a time when much of the heavy import and export trade between the Midlands and the Continent flowed through King's Lynn, merchants from all over Europe came to stay at the Duke's Head, where they were entertained with lavish banquets. Later it became the town's main coach terminus; it played host to Princess Victoria, and no admittance was granted to anyone arriving on foot or on horseback (although as class divisions became more sharply marked in the nineteenth century that rule was not at all uncommon).

With the advent of the railways, the Duke's Head declined somewhat, but it always retained its status as Lynn's principal hotel. It became the home of Norfolk's first Masonic Lodge, which once entertained the Prince of Wales (later Edward VII) to dinner while he was staying at Sandringham. It was at about this time that Bell's brick front was stuccoed over.

It is often said that the Duke's Head

The Adam and Eve, Norwich, a startling hotch-potch of brick and flint

Maid's Head Hotel, Norwich, one of the many inns across the country which claims to have played host to Elizabeth I

was named after the Duke of York, who reigned as James II from 1685 to 1688. This is highly unlikely. After the Glorious Revolution of 1688 in which James was usurped, it was considered extremely unwise to commemorate him in any way—especially as his son (the Old Pretender) and grandson (Bonny Prince Charlie) kept their own hopes of restoration alive until 1745 and the battle of Culloden. William III's Dutch Dragoons and the Hessian Guards of the Hanoverians had been known to butcher on the spot anyone suspected of being Jacobites. The Duke's Head was possibly named after some Hanoverian prince or even perhaps after John Churchill, Duke of Marlborough, hero of the French wars of Queen Anne's reign.

Norwich, The Adam & Eve, Bishopsgate
The Maid's Head, Wensum Street
The Blue Bell, Orford Hill

A riverside pub, the Adam & Eve takes its name from the arms of the Fruiterers'

Company and claims a date of 1249. The oldest part of this flint building is, however, no earlier than fifteenth-century, and most of it dates from about 1720.

In the nineteenth century the Adam & Eve was particularly popular with the wherry-men who plied up and down the county's rivers and carried as much freight as the railways and roads. From 1845 to 1880, the pub belonged to the Howes family who had a wherry themselves and used to carry chalk for cement up to Yarmouth and return with sand. In those days a wherry-man invested something like £300 in buying his vessel, and as often as not he and his family lived in it permanently. A gaff from the Howes' boat is built into the bar.

The Maid's Head was known as the Mold Fish or Murtel Fish Tavern as long ago as the fourteenth century, when it sold wine to the more genteel citizens. By 1472 it was the Maid's Head. There is a Tudor inglenook and hearth, and Elizabeth I is reputed to have stayed on one of her many royal progresses. The gables and timbers have been replaced in this century. As a coaching inn, the Maid's Head became more and more a centre for the social life of the city's gentry; it was the venue for many balls, exhibitions and concerts, and the City's first Masonic Lodge was founded here, at a time when the Norwich Machine went to the Green Dragon in Bishopsgate, London, thrice weekly, taking just over a day.

The Bell was also a tavern in the sixteenth century; it was known as the Blue Bell until about 1600 when it became colourless. The interior contains many of the original beams, and the roof timbers are all intact, but the present undistinguished frontage is eighteenth-century. The inn contains a good Georgian staircase. Although it possessed a large yard and generous stabling, the Bell never became a coaching inn or attracted the cream of the city's society. It was known as a centre of cock-fighting and the haunt of ne'er-do-wells, including a Hell Fire Club which specialised in breaking up Wesleyan and Quaker meetings and generally harassing all nonconformists. Reactionaries of a slightly more dignified nature founded the Loyal and Constitutional Club at the Bell in 1831; Wellington himself was a founder member.

Thetford, The Bell, King Street

Built in 1493, the Bell was originally part of a seminary, the College of the Blessed Virgin Mary, and became an inn only after the Dissolution.

The oldest part of this L-shaped, timber-framed building is the block fronting onto King Street. The corner of King Street and Bridge Street was known as Bell Corner, and it was the wooden beams here that were used as the town's official notice-board where various decrees and promulgations were displayed. Many of the beams are still studded with rusted nails, some of them dating back to the sixteenth century. The wing running out at the rear once looked out over the inn yard, now the car-park, and had an open gallery which has been closed in but can still be traced as a corridor passing rooms 10 and 16. Both of these contain wall-paintings dating to the mid-sixteenth century, discovered in 1938 when decades of wallpaper were stripped away. (The bottom layer was not paper but cloth, and might have been seventeenth-century.) The mural in room 10, protected by a glass panel, consists of a repeated floral motif which may represent a Tudòr rose. The mural in room 16 is even more charming; it consists of a series of arched windows with trees in full blossom peeping through. In the same gallery, also protected under glass, is a panel of wattle and daub which was exposed in 1948.

In Georgian times the Bell became a posting house on the Newmarket–Norwich road; it was at this time that the sash windows were inserted in the King Street frontage and the timbers of the projecting upper floor were plastered over. The stables and brewhouse which served the Bell at that time have been pulled down, and a rather anonymous modern structure has been erected in their place.

Bedroom 10, the honeymoon suite, has a rather mournful ghost. She is Betty

(opposite) The Bell, Thetford, Norfolk. The statue commemorates Thomas Paine, advocate of 'the rights of man' and American revolutionary, who was born in the town

Radcliffe, a seventeenth-century land-lady who was done to death in that room by a discarded lover. Not only have guests complained of sharp drops in temperature accompanied by the over-powering smell of a woman's scent, but poor Betty has been known to pace up and down the room at night wailing loudly.

SUFFOLK

Bury St Edmunds, The Angel

Of all the great coaching inns that sur-vive (all the main London termini hav-ing been demolished), this must surely be the largest. The present enormous four-storey building with its grand por-tico and balcony was completed in 1779, the architect being a Mr Redgrave; the Angel it replaced was, in the fifteenth century, a group of three inns: these were the Castle, first mentioned in 1418; the Angel, built in 1452 as a monastery guest-house on the site of a much earlier monastic building, whose vaulted cellars still survive; and the White Bear, later called the Boar's Head. The Castle and the Angel were sold as one property in 1553; four years later they and the Boar's Head were presented to the Guild-hall feoffees to pay for repairs to two local churches and for the curates' stipends. In 1582 the feoffees sold the whole property as one inn called the Angel; thirty-five years later it was given back to them by Katherine Potter, the grand-daughter of the original purchaser. It remained in their possession until 1917, the rent (£24 a year in 1620, £40 in 1723) being used for local charitable work.

Until 1871 the square in front of the Angel was the venue for the annual Bury Fair, and the inn provided ordinaries, or communal set meals, for those attend-ing. The Bury Fair was an important event: it was patronised by Henry VIII's sister Mary, the widowed Queen of France who married Charles Brandon, Duke of Suffolk, and in 1689 Thomas Shadwell wrote a comedy about it.

The major rebuilding decade of the 1770s was inspired by the coaching trade, which had begun in 1739 and steadily expanded. Mail coaches, light flies and post-chaises all stopped at the Angel between London and Norwich, and managed to survive for many years after the advent of steam. A new service, the Surprise, was started in 1840; it took six hours to London from Bury and cost 14/- (70p) inside, 8/- (40p) on top. This coach, along with the Old Bury and the Hope, was still running forty years later when the writer James Hissey stayed. The London termini for these services were the Bull in Bishopsgate and the Spread Eagle, Regent's Circus.

Dickens knew the place well from his forays as a reporter covering the 1835 general election. It was at the Angel that Mr Pickwick, confined to bed with rheu-matism, learnt that Mrs Bardell was suing him for breach of promise; here, too, Pickwick and Sam Weller had their meeting with Job Trotter. Dickens returned in 1859 and 1861 to give read-ings and recalled that 'not a word—not to say an idea—was lost'. His audience he commended as 'very fine'.

The Angel is another place sup-posedly riddled with mysterious tun-nels. A story told in the town is that in the nineteenth century a local man set out to explore them, keeping in touch with his friends by playing the fiddle. The music grew gradually farther and farther away, and finally died altogether. The explorer, needless to say, was never seen again.

The Angel, Bury St Edmunds, Suffolk. The portcullis once guarded the grounds of the now-ruined abbey

Clare, The Bell

There may well have been an alehouse on the site of the Bell shortly after 1078 when Richard de Clare, a baron of the Conquest, built his castle here. Twelfth-century records speak of a building backing onto the outer bailey being used by the garrison as a watering-place, and the Bell seems to fit the frame. Certainly the oldest part of the pub—the narrow block fronting Cavendish Road—is early medieval and might easily have been an alehouse, but there is no conclusive evidence.

However old it may be, the Bell owes its fame and fortune to the expansion of the wool trade. In the fifteenth century, Clare became an important market town, and the Bell became a market pub. Today that merely means staying open all afternoon, but in those days it meant accommodating the merchants and their pack-trains, and by 1580 the Bell (at that time known as the Green Dragon) was ready to expand.

When the extension came to be built, there was a ready source of lumber close at hand. This was Clare Priory, which had slowly been decaying since the Dis-

The Bell, Clare, Suffolk, built on the prosperity of the wool and coaching industries

solution forty years before, and naturally it was cheaper to plunder it for building materials than it was to buy new timbers. The result of this sound business sense is the ceiling in the Tudor Bar, lifted complete from one of the rooms in the Priory.

With good stabling ready-built, the Bell was well placed to exploit the coaching boom when it came along. It became a prosperous posting-house, and even the coming of the railway in 1850 left its trade unaffected. The commercial travellers who came on the train would put up at the inn and hire one of its horse-and-buggies to tour the neighbouring villages. This trade lasted until after World War I: the last pony was turned out to grass and the last trap broken up for kindling in 1927. At the same time the Bell was still doing well out of the town's market: in Victorian times cattle auctions were held in the inn yard, and a one o'clock ordinary was still being served in 1928.

The pub has changed considerably since those times, when there was a mania for privacy. It seems hard to believe that the lounge, which is not exactly enormous, was three tiny parlours until after World War II, and the bow window on the corner was once the fireplace of a little snug. It all made hard work for the pot-boys and serving-maids, and a place like the Bell could have had ten or a dozen staff, including cellarman and ostlers.

The change of name is a minor mystery. Nobody knows when or why it happened. One theory is that the green dragon was the emblem of a noble family which fell from grace, and that the sign of the bell was selected to replace the dragon in honour of the village's fine wool-church.

Lavenham, The Swan

Suffolk is wool country: Kersey, Worsted, Lindsey are East Anglian names. The Flemish weavers who migrated to eastern England in the fourteenth century can hardly have regretted leaving their homeland, for in England they became enormously wealthy.

Lavenham, with its splendid Perpendicular church and half-timbered Guild-hall, was one of the boom-towns of that time, and the Swan, first recorded in 1425, started life as a row of three houses which were both the homes and workshops of prosperous weavers, producing textiles which clothed half of Christendom.

The wool trade declined, but the story of the Swan is one of almost uninterrupted growth. It is thought that the earliest part to become an inn was the building on the corner of High Street and Water Street, probably in the reign of Elizabeth I or James I. By 1667 all three houses on the High Street frontage had united as one inn, prosperous enough for the landlord, John Girling, to issue trade tokens. The inn was endowed with generous stabling, used by the packmen who toured the district collecting finished cloth woven by cottagers who worked at home.

A hundred years later the same stabling had enabled the Swan to become an important coaching inn. The Lavenham Machine made the journey to London and back thrice weekly, at 11/- (55p) per passenger, and the inn was also a port of call for post-chaises plying between London and Bury St Edmunds. A bill of sale of 1830 reveals that the Swan possessed 6 parlours, 2 kitchens, 4 cellars, 12 bedrooms, a brewery and stabling for 50 horses.

The inn experienced a major setback

The Swan, Lavenham, Suffolk. The medieval Wool Hall which forms the rearmost part of the hotel

when railways killed the coach trade, and for nearly a century the Swan languished as a mere country pub, its yard used only by local carriers and its frontage covered up with ugly Victorian brick. Motor-borne trade rescued the inn, and in 1933 it became a Trust House. The brick frontage was removed to expose the ancient timbers, old flues were unblocked, guest-rooms reopened and the former carriage arch became the new main entrance. During the war it was a revived Swan which played host to the American and British bomber crews stationed in the district who wrote their names on the bar walls and left their squadron flashes and cap badges as mementoes. Many of them, aged only nineteen or twenty, never returned; but their badges are faithfully preserved.

The most recent phase of expansion came in the 1960s, when Trust Houses acquired a row of shops in Water Street and the medieval Wool Hall in Lady Street at the back of the hotel. The Wool Hall was actually dismantled in 1911 and sold to Princess Louise to be re-erected at Ascot, but the vicar, the Reverend Henry Taylor, a keen conservationist, persuaded her to give it back, whereupon it became for a time a hostel for women railway workers. The conversion of the Hall and the shops into bedrooms and lounges was carried out by Trust Houses' architect James Hopwood, who also designed the new dining-room and cloister garden which stand on the old inn yard, using local craftsmen and largely traditional materials. These buildings were executed before Trust Houses became Trust Houses Forte; there was still some idealism behind the commercialism then, and the new work blends surprisingly well with the old.

Long Melford, The Bull

Like Lavenham, Long Melford was a wool town, and like the Swan, the Bull started life earning its keep in the weaving trade. The Bull is slightly later than the Swan, though—it was probably built in the reign of Edward IV (1461–83), since a black bull was one of the supporters of his coat of arms—and it has always been one house whereas the Swan was originally three. Like the Swan, the Bull probably became in inn in the late sixteenth century when the wool trade was on the decline, and, again in common, it was given a brick frontage by the Victorians which was removed by Trust Houses in the 1930s.

The main part of the Bull was originally a large hall-house with a weavers' gallery and a smoke-hole in the roof. A wing reached back at either end, and a smaller storehouse at the rear completed the square. This arrangement was altered when the house became an inn. The hall was divided into two floors, many timbers were replaced, and flues and chimneys, two of which survive, were installed. Throughout the hotel the timberwork is richly carved and moulded; the wose, or wild man of the woods, in the lounge, is perhaps early Tudor, while the main door-case carries the date 1649 and the initials WD for Walter Drew, whose family owned the Bull for three generations. (Drew was the landlord in July 1648 when a wealthy yeoman, Richard Evered, was murdered in the inn by one Roger Greene, who subsequently hanged.)

Long Melford is a curious village, strung out for over a mile along a very straight, broad road. The theory is that the road was surveyed by the Romans, who went so far as to build the ford over the Stour in the village, but never completed the work. But the turnpike owners made good use of this preliminary survey in building the London–Bury St Edmunds–Norwich coach road, from which the whole village benefited. The Bull itself became an important stop along the way, while many of the small houses that line the road have had frontages added during the coaching era. Long Melford also boasts not one but two Elizabethan manor houses, Melford Hall and Kentwell Hall.

THE MIDLANDS

DERBYSHIRE

Ashbourne, The Green Man & Black's Head Royal, Victoria Square

The Green Man, as the hotel is generally known nowadays, is first mentioned in 1710 when a new church organ at St Oswald's in the town was dedicated. Choirs from Lichfield and Lincoln cathedrals, augmented by brass and strings as well as the new organ, performed at the ceremony and were afterwards feasted by the parish at the Green Man, where, after their dinner, they struck up with an impromptu concert. But the Green Man is older than that, and by then had already become an important inn. Throughout the eighteenth century it served as the Magistrates' Court for the Low Peak Hundred, and was also the local centre for cock-fighting—apparently the two functions were not considered incompatible, although the cock-fighting was always attended by heavy betting which was completely illegal, and of which the magistrates must have been aware (if indeed they did not take part themselves). In 1777 Dr Johnson and Boswell stopped for lunch while awaiting a post-chaise, and Boswell reported that it was 'a very good inn' with a 'mighty civil' landlady who presented him with an engraving of the inn-sign.

The rather cumbersome name results from a take-over in the early years of the nineteenth century. The Blackmoor's Head was a smaller inn some way up the street, now a shoe-shop. It is last recorded as a separate concern in Cary's *New Itinerary* of 1802. Shortly afterwards it was bought out and closed down by Mr Brooks of the Green Man, who retained the name and the goodwill of his former rival, erected the gallows sign which still spans the street and entertained the Duchess of Kent and her daughter Princess Victoria, thus adding the 'Royal' to the inn's title.

Ashbourne's ancient and famous Shrove Tuesday Football begins in the car-park behind the Green Man, which was once a meadow. The game takes two days, and as many as two hundred local men take part. It is very similar to Swaying The Hood at Haxey, near Doncaster, in that almost anything goes as the great scrimmage develops round the ball, and if only one bone is broken it is accounted a peaceful year's game. The townsmen who take part are divided into two teams, the Upards from north of Hensmore Brook, and Downards from

---

(*opposite*) The Green Man And Black's Head Royal Hotel, Ashbourne, Derbyshire, boasts both the longest name of any English pub and one of the few surviving gallows signs, which came into vogue in the seventeenth century

190

south of it. The goals are stone pillars three miles apart. On the first day the ball is 'thrown up' by a local dignitary, on the second by a visiting celebrity. Such games are supposed to date back to prehistoric ritual mock-battles, and were certainly common in the Middle Ages as trials of strength between neighbouring villages—thus in Swaying The Hood the men of Haxey challenge the men of Westwoodside. In Ashbourne's case the game had died out and was revived in the 1830s.

The rafters supporting the carriage arch of the Green Man are studded with hooks, for at one time it acted as a meat-store, not only for the inn-kitchen, but also for the seven butchers who traded in Victoria Square. This was once a common practice, for it was found that carriage arches tended to act like wind-tunnels, and meat hung there (wrapped in muslin to keep off the flies) would be well chilled and would keep fresh for days, while also becoming more tender the longer it was hung.

The Peacock, Rowsley, Derbyshire. This ceramic peacock stands proud guard in the entrance hall

Rowsley, The Peacock

The Peacock, with its crenellated porch tower, its stone mullioned windows and its massive chimneys, is a seventeenth-century gem. It was built as a country home for John Stevenson of Elton, and the inscription over the doors reads:

IONSTE
16   52
VENSON

After its builder's death, it was sold to the Duke of Rutland, whose former seat at Haddon Hall is no more than two miles away. For about a hundred years it served as Haddon's dower-house, but after the dukes moved their residence to a rebuilt Belvoir Castle in the late eighteenth century, the Peacock became first a farm and then, in the 1820s, an inn. With its gardens sloping down to the River Derwent and fishing rights on the River Wye, it has always been an angler's paradise, and it was one of the inns that benefitted rather than suffered from the railways (for Rowsley once had its own station). In fact, when cars and charabancs began bringing tourists to the area in the early part of the twentieth century, the two elderly sisters who ran the Peacock used to refuse to serve anyone who was not equipped with rod and creel.

The inn's name comes from the coat of

arms of the dukes of Rutland; there is a peacock carved in stone strutting, tail spread, on the porch's crenellations, and a second peacock, ceramic this time, stands on a plinth in an alcove in the hall.

The ceramic peacock was modelled in the 1850s by Paul Comolera of Limoges for Minton's. Only five were made, all of hand-painted majolica. This one was on its way to Australia for an exhibition in 1878 when the ship carrying it, the *Loch Ard*, went down off Moonlight Head, Victoria. The vessel remained on the bottom for some years, and when it was eventually salvaged the Minton peacock was found in perfect condition, still sealed in its crate. It was brought to England in 1937 and found its way to the inn which bears its name.

The hotel, which was bought from the Rutland estate by Ind Coope, is a designated national monument in the Peak District National Park.

HEREFORDSHIRE

Ledbury, The Feathers, High Street
The Talbot, New Street

Thickly wooded Herefordshire is famous for its half-timbered buildings, and the small market town of Ledbury is generously sprinkled with them. The Market House, the Tudor House and the House on Props are all splendid examples of sixteenth-century timber framing, as are two of the town's oldest inns, the Feathers and the Talbot. In the Middle Ages, visitors to the town and travellers passing through were accommodated in St Katherine's Hospital, founded in 1232. But during the Reformation this guest-house was converted into almshouses for the local

poor—as it is today—and three inns were built to fill the gap. The oldest of these, now the Tudor House, dates back to 1530 and was the King's Arms until 1778, when it lost out in the fierce competition for the coaching trade. In its heyday it had a banqueting hall and extensive stabling, but its entrance arch was too narrow for coaches and could not be widened, so it went to the wall.

The Feathers, built in 1565, was the main beneficiary of its demise. Originally a two-storey building, an extra floor with five gables was added in the seventeenth century when the inn took its present name, either from Prince Henry, James I's elder son who died young, or Prince Charles, who succeeded him as Prince of Wales and became Charles I in 1625.

As Ledbury's principal coaching inn, the Feathers continued to expand and when in 1784 mounted post-boys were superseded by mail coaches, the inn became the halt for the Aberystwyth to Cheltenham Royal Mail, and many other coaches both private and public also made it their regular port of call. Fortunately the management resisted the temptation to pull down the heavily timbered frontage and rebuild in the classical style; they only went so far as to insert fashionable sash-windows and plaster over the old-fashioned timbers. But a Georgian wing was added at the rear to accommodate the extra business, and with it went a great assembly room, built over the yard on pillars. At the same time the house next door, built in about 1570, was incorporated into the inn.

The Feathers' coach trade lasted well into the nineteenth century. Until the dawn of the motor age those who wanted to get about either walked, rode or drove in a pony-and-trap, and the two latter

193

classes were well catered for by the Feathers' stables.

The plastering over the frontage was removed by Trust Houses, who took over the inn early this century, but in the late 1960s it was sold and is now part of a small chain. The Prince of Wales' feathers are carved into the timber-work, and a projecting lantern of embossed glass on an iron bracket is a souvenir of coaching days.

The Talbot Hotel was built in 1596; the date is to be found over the entrance door with its Ionic piers and on a carved overmantel in the panelled dining-room. The big bay window over the door, however, was added later.

Two bullet-holes in the dining-room's panelling were made in April 1645, when the town was the scene of a brief but fierce battle between Royalists under Prince Rupert and Parliamentarians under Colonel Massey, who was Governor of Gloucester. Massey's column, which was marching through the town, was surprised by Rupert's cavalry charge but managed to barricade the road with carts and wagons. A second charge carried the barricade, and a third put the Parliament troops to flight. The battle degenerated into a series of skirmishes and running fights as the Roundheads scattered; some were holed up in the Talbot, and were flushed out in hand-to-hand fighting. More bullet-

---

(*opposite*) The Feathers, Ledbury, Herefordshire. A coaching inn which survived both the craze for rebuilding of the coaching era and the coming of the railways, which sent many similar establishments to the wall

holes are to be seen in the church door, and the sword on display in the chantry belonged to a Roundhead officer who was shot through the head.

Pembridge, The New Inn

Built in the fourteenth century as a farm, local tradition has it that it was here that Henry VI signed his crown over to Edward IV after the Battle of Mortimer's Cross, fought six miles away in 1461. In fact Henry was not at Mortimer's Cross, and the decisive battle was fought at Towcester some weeks later. But the tradition may have some basis in fact: the commander of the beaten Lancastrians, Owen Tudor, was beheaded after the fight. Was it here that the nineteen-year-old Edward caught up with him?

That the farm was already an alehouse by the time of the battle, however, is almost certain. It would have brewed its own ale, and when the Wool Market which stands in the forecourt was busy, the farmer would have made extra money by selling refreshments to the merchants and possibly putting them up for the night. Certainly by the sixteenth century, when the two projecting wings with their carved finials were built, it was not only an inn but also served as the local court-house, a function which it maintained for two centuries. The court-room was a first-floor chamber which is now a bedroom, and the holding-cell for prisoners awaiting trial was located in the cellar.

After its wool market declined in the seventeenth century, Pembridge's importance waned and the court was wound up, but, like the Feathers at Ledbury, the New Inn stood on the Cheltenham to Aberystwyth road, and although it never became a major coaching inn, it was used as a regular lunch stop, known locally as the Inn With No Name. A souvenir of those days is the whip-rack beside the fire in the public bar. In the same bar is a huge round-backed settle which is said to have originally formed a section of the local cockpit until cock-fighting was banned in 1849.

There is a quoits table, and the pub has a team in the local quoits league. There are also two ghosts, a man and a woman. The man has been seen and even spoken to in the gents!

NOTTINGHAMSHIRE

Nottingham, The Trip to Jerusalem, Castle Road
The Flying Horse, Poultry

The Trip To Jerusalem's claim to be the oldest inn in England is utterly bogus and deserves to be comprehensively de-bunked. It gives the year of 1189 as an unsupported date of origin which, even if it were true, would not make the Trip as old as the Ostrich at Colnbrook in Buckinghamshire, whose date of 1106 is well attested. But it would appear from the name of the square in which it stands—Brewhouse Yard—that the building on the site at that date was the castle's brewery, which may also have been a convenient cover for a sally-port used by the garrison in times of siege. Brewhouse Yard was at one time an atrocious slum of a couple of acres of close-packed hovels, supervised by an overseer. Before the Police Acts of the 1820s, the Parish Constables had no jurisdiction there, and so it became a refuge for criminals on the run. But slum clearance has left only a dozen or so

buildings, one of them the Trip, grouped round a quiet garden.

Having disposed of its mythical age, the Trip To Jerusalem is still a fascinating and indeed unique pub in that it is almost all cavern. The eighteenth-century building which makes up the front of the Trip is neither impressive nor extensive—it comprises only two rooms, a large cellar cut out of the rock and a small cavern bar. The latter, which contains a sixteenth-century chest called the Armada Chest and the padlocks and keys from the old stocks, once had a flight of stairs running up to the castle and may have been the sally-port or postern. There is also a stairway running down from the castle to the River Leen, called Mortimer's Hole after Roger Mortimer who murdered Edward II in 1327 and was arrested at Nottingham Castle in 1330. (He was subsequently hanged, drawn and quartered at Tyburn.)

At one time the Trip was not unique in its construction, for Brewhouse Yard had a second pub, the Gate Hangs Well, which was also carved out of the rock. In fact Nottingham has a long tradition of cave-dwelling, because the sandstone is particularly soft and easy to work. It has another advantage over harder stone in that it is extremely porous, and the inhabitants of the caverns would not therefore suffer from damp and condensation. They say at the Trip that any beer spilt in the cellar is absorbed into the stone floor before it can be mopped up. In the seventeenth and eighteenth centuries, many of the inhabitants of Brewhouse Yard lived in caves, which interconnected like a maze, and in which it was impossible to find any fugitives the law might be looking for. These were not merely criminals: they might also be religious dissidents, as were the 'Family

The Trip to Jerusalem, Nottingham. The Trip's much-trumpeted claim to be England's oldest inn is bogus; nevertheless, tucked beneath the battlements of Nottingham Castle, it still has much to commend it

of Love' who met here secretly in the 1660s.

Less well known than the Trip, but probably just as old, is the Flying Horse, named after a medieval fairground game in which a rider mounted a swinging 'horse' to catch a ring on a cord with a dummy sword. Now a Schooner Inn, it has been very badly knocked about in recent years, but it is largely Tudor. It is first mentioned, however, in 1392 when it was the home of the Plumptre family; it became an inn in 1483. In the eighteenth century it was a prominent coaching inn, and was the headquarters of the town's Tories. Later on it was much favoured by actors. The five-gabled, heavily timbered frontage is still highly attractive; the interior can best be described as disappointing.

Southwell, The Saracen's Head

Southwell's splendid Norman Minster was founded in 1110, but it is possible that the Saracen's Head predates it, for fragments of the timber frame have been tentatively dated as eleventh century. But it was definitely the King's Arms by 1194, when it was visited by Richard I. He was the first of a whole string of royal visitors; his brother John in 1213; his nephew Henry III in 1223 and 1258; Edward I in 1281; Edward III in 1331; and Richard II in 1395, 1396 and 1398. In 1396 the inn was leased by Thomas Arundell, Archbishop of York, to one John Fisher, who carried out a rebuilding programme, and more alterations were made in the sixteenth century. Edward IV stayed in 1481, and Cardinal Wolsey after his disgrace in 1530.

James I passed through Southwell on the way to his coronation in 1603, and was much impressed by the Minster. 'By my blude', he is reported to have said, 'this kirk shall justle with York or Durham or any other kirk in Christendom.' His son, Charles I, had cause to know Southwell and its inn better; he stayed at the King's Arms in 1642 when he was raising his standard at Nottingham to begin the Civil War; he did not dare stay in Nottingham itself for fear of the mob. For the next four years the inn was popular with local Royalists, and Charles ate his last meal as a free man here in May 1646. Next day he surrendered to the Scots Commissioners, hoping to continue the war with their armies. But they trusted him no more than he should have trusted them: they sold him to Parliament for £400,000, and three years later he was beheaded.

To be connected with so many kings was not politic in the years of Cromwell's Interregnum; Charles II's Worcester campaign of 1651 must have been the last straw, for in the same year the name was changed to the Saracen's Head. This was nothing to do with the crusades; it came from the turbanned-head stamp on barrels of tobacco imported from the Balkans.

The Saracen's Head later became a profitable posting-house between Nottingham and the Great North Road at Newark; it was also for a time the local Inland Revenue office. The timbered front was stuccoed over, sash windows were inserted and in 1805 the town assembly rooms next door were incorporated into the inn. At about this time Lord Byron was living with his mother on the Burgage by the Minster; he hated her and he hated Southwell.

Saracen's Head, Southwell, Nottinghamshire. A typical coaching yard

The Mytton and Mermaid, Atcham, Shropshire. This Georgian coaching inn was built at the spot where Watling Street, now the A5, crossed the Severn

The inn has recently been restored, and the stucco taken off. Underneath it the timbers were found to be their natural golden colour, for the plaster had protected them from the fashionable pitch-pot so enthusiastically wielded in Victorian days.

SHROPSHIRE

Atcham, The Mytton & Mermaid

Two miles east of Shrewsbury on the old Watling Street, near the Roman city of Viroconium, is the village of Atcham with its red-brick Georgian coaching inn, the Mytton & Mermaid. Surrounded by trees with the village church behind it and a garden sloping down to the Severn, it is, as Pevsner described it, stately; so stately that it looks more like a wealthy country mansion than a pub.

But it was actually purpose-built as a coaching inn, and still does well on the A5 traffic. It was originally called the Talbot in honour of the earls of Shrewsbury; later it changed its name to the Berwick Arms, after the Hills of Attingham who bore the title Lord Berwick and whose stately home, Attingham Park, is just visible from the village.

Steam killed the Berwick Arms; after less than fifty years as an inn it was sold as a private house, and so it remained until the 1930s, when it was purchased by Sir Clough Williams-Ellis, the archi-

The Three Tuns, Bishop's Castle, Shropshire, perhaps the most famous of the 'home brew' pubs

tect of Portmeirion, who reopened it to the drinking public. The present name derives from the mermaid in his coat of arms and from Mad Jack Mytton, MP for Shrewsbury in the eighteenth century, whose body rested at the inn on its way home from the London debtors' gaol where he died.

Bishop's Castle, The Three Tuns, Salop Street

The Three Tuns is perhaps the best known of the small but ever-growing band of pubs which brew their own beer. From 1880 to 1976 the pub was kept by three generations of the Roberts family, and the brewery was built by the first John Roberts soon after taking over. It is of the tower type: all the necessary materials are hoisted up to the top, and each stage in the brewing process takes place on a successively lower floor. At the top is the grain-hopper, on the next down are the mash-tub and liquor-tank, while on the first floor are a steam boiler and the copper bath in which the wort cools and clears. Fermentation, barrelling and steam-cleaning of the oak casks all take place at ground level.

Although the brewery itself is Victorian, most of the pub and its outbuildings are from the sixteenth or seventeenth century. Inside there is a Jacobean staircase, and the small timber-framed shed now used as a store shows the corresponding joint marks which indicate that it was designed and pre-fabricated in the builder's yard and then brought to the site for assembly.

The last John Roberts retired in 1976 and the Three Tuns was taken over by Peter Milner, who introduced two new beers, Carlisle Bitter and Steamer draught porter. Their names recall the Bishop's Castle Railway (*Carlisle* was one of its engines) which operated from 1886 to 1936, running to Craven Arms a few miles away. It was originally intended to become the main line for the Irish ferry at Holyhead, but was never a success and spent most of its life in the hands of the Official Receiver. But it left its mark on the life of the town—one bar at the Three Tuns is lavishly decorated with mementoes, and Bishop's Castle has become famous for its annual steam fair, a rally of old traction engines and farm equipment which draws enthusiasts from all over the country.

Cleobury Mortimer, The Talbot

Set on the southernmost edge of the Clee Hills, with (on a fine day) awe-inspiring views of the Herefordshire plain far below, the village takes its name from the Mortimers, the mightiest of the medieval Marcher barons. Roger Mortimer was the murderer of Edward II in 1327, Edmund Mortimer was the claimant to the throne in the Percys' revolt put down by Henry IV at Shrewsbury in 1403, and another Roger Mortimer was the grandfather of Edward IV and Richard III.

The splendid half-timbered Talbot, however, takes its name from the family which became earls of Shrewsbury in 1422 when Sir John Talbot took command of the English forces in France towards the end of the Hundred Years' War. It was built in 1561 on the vaulted cellars of a very much older building, and local legend has it that in these cellars is the entrance, now bricked up, of a tunnel which once led to Mawley Hall, over a mile away. This tunnel, like so many others, is said to have been used by Roman Catholics escaping their persecutors in the sixteenth and seventeenth centuries.

With its entrance arch, large courtyard and generous stabling (recently extended), the Talbot was a thriving posting-house in the coaching era, but afterwards declined and became simply the village pub. The courtyard was for generations the site of an important market, and a small market is still held there. The atmosphere of antiquity inside the inn is fostered by the heavy oak beams and the original fireplaces, while the beer, Wood's, comes from the Plough at Wistanstow a few miles away, where the landlord has recently started brewing and distributes beer to many south Shropshire pubs.

Ludlow, The Feathers, Corve Street
The Bull, Corve Street

Ludlow Castle was one of the great Marcher fortresses, built around 1090 to keep the wild Welsh in check. The town was 'planted' around it, but its market and its wool trade, with the prosperity they brought, soon softened the harshness of frontier life. During the Wars of the Roses, Ludlow was firmly Yorkist, and was sacked by the Lancastrians in 1459. Edward IV, when he came to the throne in 1461, rewarded the townsmen by incorporating Ludlow as a borough.

The Feathers, Ludlow, Shropshire. This seventeenth-century royal coat of arms adorns the ceiling of what is now the resident's lounge

He took over the castle for his own use, and when he died in 1483 his young son Edward set off from there to London to claim his inheritance. On the way the boy was met by his uncle Richard, who arrested his escort and delivered the Prince to the Tower to join his little brother. Some months later Richard was crowned, and no one heard of the two princes again.

In 1475 the castle became the seat of the Council of the Marches, set up to rule the border country. In its new guise as an administrative centre, Ludlow survived the decline of the wool trade, and

both the Bull and the Feathers date back to a sixteenth-century heyday. The Bull is in fact the older of the two, but it cannot rival the fantastically elaborate carved timbers of the Feathers' façade which have made it one of England's best-known hotels.

There was an inn on the site of The Feathers in 1521, of which only the heavily studded front door remains. The present building is dated 1603. It was at first the town house of the Foxe family, but the lease was taken six years later by Rees Jones, who eventually bought the premises and renewed the licence. He

202

gave the house its present name in 1616 to commemorate a visit by the Prince of Wales, later to become Charles I; the decoration of the first-floor residents' lounge, including an intricate oak over-mantel, a cast-iron fireback and moulded plaster-work ceiling, all bearing the royal coat of arms, date back to his tenure.

The Council of the Marches was wound up by William III in 1689, and the town fell on hard times. The Feathers was forced out of business, and it was not until 1752, when Ludlow's fortunes were beginning to revive, that the inn was reopened by Samuel Corne as a posting-house with stabling for sixty horses. It has never looked back: even the collapse of coaching was not a disaster, for the Feathers became a local base for both 'commercials' and tourists.

The frontage was completely restored in 1970, and the hotel holds awards from both the Civic Trust and the British Tourist Authority.

Just across the street is the Bull, an unassuming white-painted pub selling Marston's. Until very recently it was a hotel, but it had to stop taking guests because it could not meet modern fire regulations. This was not the Bull's first brush with fire: if the frontage seems modest it is because a blaze in 1800 swept away all the timbers, and they had to be replaced with brick.

But the timbering, thought to be the oldest in the town and dated by the local historical society to about 1390, is very much in evidence in the inn yard, where a once-open gallery reaches back to a seventeenth-century stone cottage. Above these rises the magnificent Perpendicular tower of St Laurence's, one of England's largest parish churches. Together the ascending group of buildings makes a very picturesque skyline.

Shrewsbury, The Lion, Wyle Cop
The Golden Cross, Golden Cross Passage

The best known of many fine pubs in this historic border town is the Lion in Wyle Cop, a group of fifteenth- and eighteenth-century buildings, which has been licensed since 1618 and became one of the most famous coaching inns in the country.

The story of the Lion and its entrepreneurial landlord, Robert Laurence, is told in Chapter 5; but considerably older than the Lion is the Golden Cross, tucked away down a narrow alley and known for much of its life as the Sextry because it was originally the sacristy of Old St Chad's Church. The building has been much altered during its long career; the oldest parts are a stone arch and a timber doorway which date back to the reign of Henry III in the thirteenth century. The ground floor is largely fifteenth-century, probably about 1480, and the half-timbered upper floor is late sixteenth- or early seventeenth-century. It was originally used by the church-wardens and by the church's staff of priests, who used a bridge connecting it to Old St Chad's when going to say their midnight office.

Although it was primarily religious, it had another function: it was the brew-house for the church ales, which were sold to raise money for the maintenance of the church and clergy and for the relief of the parish poor. By 1495 this side of its function appears to have largely usurped the purely ecclesiastic use; in the next century it lost its connection with the church altogether.

During the Civil War it was a favourite rendezvous for the local Royalists; they included the Governor, Sir Francis Ottley, and his successor, Sir Michael

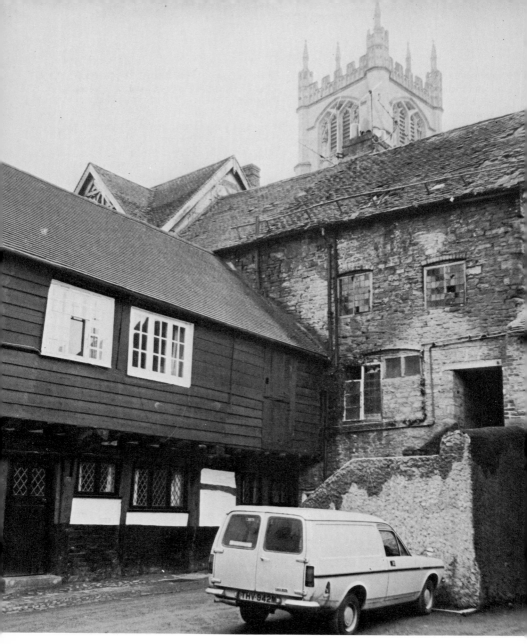

The Bull, Ludlow, Shropshire. Once an open gallery, the rear wing of the Bull adjoins a seventeenth-century stone cottage. Behind them rises the Perpendicular tower of St Laurence's Church

Ernley, Ottley's brother Richard and other cavaliers like Sir Thomas Lyster and Sir William Vaughan. But after 1643 the Sextry disappears from the town's records for nearly a hundred and fifty years, reappearing in 1780 as the Golden Cross. There is no way of knowing whether it remained open all that time, or whether it closed down and was revived, as seems likely.

In 1788 Old St Chad's suddenly collapsed during the night. A new St Chad's was built on the town walls, and in 1794 the bridge connecting the Golden Cross to the ruins of the old church was pulled down.

WARWICKSHIRE

Stratford-on-Avon, The White Swan, Market Square
The Shakespeare Hotel, Chapel Street
The Garrick, High Street
The Falcon, Chapel Street

A merchant's house of about 1450, the White Swan is chiefly famous for its wall-paintings. These are to be found in what was once the great hall and were executed in about 1560. They depict the story of Tobias and the Angel, from the Apocryphal Book of Tobit, and consist of three panels in which Tobit and his wife, their son Tobias and the Archangel Raphael are all shown in Tudor dress. The colours are still remarkably fresh, perhaps because the paintings were panelled over in Jacobean times and lay hidden until they were rediscovered in 1927 by workmen carrying out restoration work for Trust Houses, who had just taken over the hotel.

The date of these paintings appears to coincide with the opening of the house as an inn—either the King's House or the King's Hall—and were possibly commissioned by its first licensee. By the time the turnpiking of the local roads was completed in 1770, it had become the King's Head and attracted much of the coaching trade. The railway came to town ninety years later, but by that time Stratford's hotels were already prospering on the name of their most famous citizen, and were not too badly affected. It was at about this time, too, that the inn changed its name, perhaps to cash in on the 'Swan of Avon'.

The Shakespeare's link with the bard is more obvious, and is genuine. The southern end of the building is a sixteenth-century house originally known as Five Gables, but the northern end was built in 1486 as a home for the rich wool-merchant Sir Hugh Clopton, a benefactor of the town who became Lord Mayor of London and died in 1496. His descendants were the builders of New Place, which was leased to the Bard himself in the 1590s. He would presumably have visited their house every quarter day to pay his rent along with all the other tenants.

Stratford was the scene of much fighting in the Civil War, and an explosion which destroyed the town hall in 1643 also damaged the Clopton's house. Afterwards the building was rebuilt with a plastered brick front, and at some time in the early eighteenth century it seems to have been united with the Five Gables as an inn. Certainly it was licensed when the actor David Garrick visited Stratford in 1796 to declare open the new town hall; for it was he who suggested naming all the bedrooms after Shakespeare's plays and characters.

Between 1882 and 1920 much restoration and rebuilding work was car-

The Garrick, Stratford-upon-Avon, a near-neglected gem amidst the grandeur of Stratford's famous hotels

The Falcon, Stratford-upon-Avon, one of the town's many impressive hotels

ried out. The brick front of 1643 and a classical portico of 1820 were removed, and four dormers were added at the northern end to harmonise with the roof-line of the Five Gables.

These are only two of Stratford's many ancient pubs and hotels. The Garrick is an exquisite little tavern sandwiched between the Tudor House and Harvard House in the High Street. It was built in 1595 after a fire had swept away its predecessor, was opened as a tavern called the Reindeer in the early eighteenth century and changed to its present name in 1796. The Falcon in Chapel Street was a private house built

in the sixteenth century and became an inn in about 1640. Its landlord from about 1660 to about 1680 was Joseph Phillips, a man of substance who issued trade tokens and supplied wine to the corporation. The Shakespeare Club was founded here in 1823.

One of the best and most famous of the pubs has now gone for ever. This was the Red Horse, an eighteenth-century building in Bridge Street standing on the site of an earlier inn known first as the Peacock and later the Golden Lion. In coaching days it was Stratford's 'head inn', and it was here that Garrick stayed during his 1796 visit. But the Red Horse has always been best known for its connection with Washington Irving. It was one of his favourite places: he is known to have made prolonged visits at least three times, in 1815, 1819 and 1821, and it was here that he wrote much of his *Sketch-Book*, using the pseudonym 'Geoffrey Crayon'. It was while sitting in his parlour at the Red Horse late one night that he wrote:

> To a homeless man, who has no spot on this wide world which he can truly call his own, there is a momentary feeling of something like independence and territorial consequence when, after a weary day's travel, he kicks off his boots, thrusts his feet into his slippers, and stretches himself before an inn fire . . . He is, for the time being, the very monarch of all he surveys. The armchair is his throne, the poker his sceptre, and the little parlour, some twelve feet square, his undisputed empire.

Alas, the Red Horse is a homeless man's empire no more. It was closed in 1980, and is currently being converted into a branch of Marks and Spencer's.

WEST MIDLANDS

Kinver, The Whittington Inn

By the time Kinver's manor house became an inn in 1783, it already had over four centuries of history behind it. Built in 1310 of local oak by Sir William Whittington, Dick Whittington's grandfather, it passed from the family to Thomas de la Lowe in 1352 when Dick's father was outlawed for marrying without royal consent.

The manor remained in the de la Lowe family until the fifteenth century, when the male line died out, and the heiress married a Grey. The manor was added to the Grey estates: Lady Jane, queen for ten days in 1553, spent part of her childhood here, and her unhappy ghost still roams the upstairs corridor. At about this time some Jesuits related to the Greys took refuge here, and although their secret chapel in the attic, complete with font and piscina, is now unsafe, there is still a priest's hole to be seen in the floor of the corridor connecting the old barn (now the wine bar) with the main building.

Charles II, on his flight into exile after Worcester in 1651, snatched a few hours' sleep here. He left Worcester at about 6.00pm on the day of the battle (3 September) and stopped three times on the fifty-mile journey to Boscobel in Shropshire—at the King's Arms at Ombersley, where he and his companions, Lord Wilmot, Lord Derby and Charles Giffard, were offered food and drink, here at the manor and finally at a house in Wordsley. They reached Boscobel at about 3.00am next day. His niece, Queen Anne, also stayed a night at the manor in 1711.

In 1783 a man named Dunn took over the old Whittington Inn in the village, and transferred the licence to the manor house. (The former inn is now Whittington Cottage.) The bull-baiting shows which he held proved a magnet for the less reputable characters of the district, and in 1805 William Howe, a local ruffian, was arrested while having a drink in the parlour after he had robbed and murdered Squire Robins of Dunsley Hall, who was returning from market with money he had made selling cattle. Howe was hanged and gibbeted, but in the struggle to arrest him, his lantern was left where he had put it, hanging from a rafter. There it remained until 1926, when the landlord had it destroyed.

The Whittington Inn is still a free

The Fleece, Bretforton, Worcestershire, mecca for beer connoisseurs and tourists alike (*see page 210*)

house, but only because no brewery would pay the £1,500 asked for it when it was sold in the 1920s. The present owners have spent £200,000 on it, but conscientiously. The old and new blend satisfactorily, and although the inn is visited by its share of tourists and businessmen, it still has a place in the purely local community, playing host to the local hunt, the film society and the car club.

WORCESTERSHIRE

Bretforton, The Fleece

A fourteenth-century building, the Fleece had been in the family of Miss Lola Taplin for four hundred years when it was acquired by the National Trust on her death in 1977. Originally it was a farm, but in 1840 it became a beerhouse and it has changed remarkably little since then.

The internal arrangements of the Fleece (which is managed by CAMRA) are something of a history lesson. Until recently there was nothing a modern drinker would recognise as a bar. Instead there was a hatch in the hall which served all three parlours (they could hardly be called bar-rooms). Behind the hatch there was a room which doubled as a beer-cellar, and it is this room which gives us the word 'tap room'. In the days when the Fleece had its own brewhouse, the conditioned beer was stored in a shed outside, and the day's supply was brought into the tap room every morning. There it could be kept cool, and the pot-boy or the maid would come up to the hatch with a ewer to be filled direct from the barrel, would hand over the customer's money to the landlord or landlady and receive the change. Things

have changed somewhat: there are no pot-boys or maids any more, hand-pumps have been installed and the hatch has been recently enlarged until it almost constitutes a normal bar-counter. But for all that, the original concept is still very much in evidence.

Of the three parlours, one is of particular interest. The uneven floor has white lines painted over the cracks between the stone flags to keep witches from getting in through them. The hearth boasts an iron fire-back dated 1670 and has a high round-backed settle drawn up close to keep out the draught. The family china is on display on a dresser, as is the family pewter which was collected in the late seventeenth century to replace the silver requisitioned by one side or the other during the Civil War. A grandfather clock beats time solemnly, and there are hooks in the rafters from which once hung strings of sausages, hams, slabs of bacon, joints of mutton and beef and bunches of onions. Indeed, here is the cottage kitchen-turned-alehouse kitchen as it has been for five hundred years or more, and almost untouched by time. Even the selection of cask-conditioned beers is as close to the original article as any modern brewer achieves. If you can distance yourself from the real-ale pilgrims and culture-crazed Americans, you can come closer to the spirit of the past at the Fleece than you can almost anywhere else.

Broadway, The Lygon Arms

Situated in the broad main street that gives this most-visited of Cotswold villages its name, the Lygon Arms is first mentioned in the parish records of 1532. But the inn's name at that time—the Whyte Harte—suggests the reign of Richard II (1377–99), when the Cotswold wool industry was at its peak, as a likely date of origin, and this is backed up by a fourteenth-century fireplace in one of the bedrooms. There are also two fifteenth-century door-cases.

The four-gabled Jacobean frontage in mellow stone was built in 1620 by John and Ursula Trevis, who engraved their names and the date upon it. A four-poster bed has the same date carved on the oak bed-head. John Trevis kept the Whyte Harte from 1604 to 1641, and his descendants kept it for a century after that. Charles I is said to have conferred with his supporters in a panelled room approached by a secret stair, although he had no need for secrecy, for the area was staunchly Royalist until the very end of the Civil War. But the inn also played host to Oliver Cromwell, on his way to the defeat of Charles II at Worcester in 1651.

In the eighteenth century the house became a flourishing coaching inn, with stabling for thirty horses. Extensions were carried out in the 1760s, when Giles Attwood was licensee; and it was one of the very few inns to be praised by the diarist Viscount Torrington, who toured the country in the 1780s and '90s. 'There cannot be a cleanlier, civiller inn than this', he wrote—high praise from a man who usually condemned all inns and everything connected with them in the roundest possible tones.

It was in about 1830, when General Sir Edward Lygon purchased it, that the White Hart became the Lygon Arms. Lygon, a relative of the earls Beauchamp, had commanded a division

The Lygon Arms, Broadway, Worcestershire. From its humble origins as a drovers' alehouse, the Lygon Arms has grown into one of the country's most renowned hotels

under Wellington at Waterloo. The inn was managed by his former butler, and the white hart of Richard II was replaced on the signboard by the two lions of the Beauchamps. The decline of the coaching trade hit the Lygon Arms hard, but in the closing years of the nineteenth century it was taken over by a noted sportsman, Charles Drury, who persuaded the North Cotswold Hunt to make the inn the regular venue for their opening meet.

In 1904 the Lygon Arms came into the hands of Sidney Bolton Russell, and since then it has never looked back, going from country pub to luxury hotel. Russell brought in his collection of antique furniture, and attracted much of the new motor-borne trade. Under his son, Don, and grandson, Sir Gordon, the hotel expanded into neighbouring buildings, gained four stars, entertained Prince Philip and won a Queen's Award for Industry. Of a new extension at the rear, Pevsner said: 'A perfect twentieth-century extension, just to show that such a thing can be done and should be done.'

Inkberrow, The Old Bull

According to local legend, Charles II hid here after the Battle of Evesham, ten miles to the south, and he fled so hurriedly that he left his maps behind. However, the Battle of Evesham was fought in 1265 between Edward, Prince of Wales, and Simon de Montfort, but as with Pembridge, there may be a basis of fact behind the legend. Charles did pass very close twice on his flight from Worcester—once on his way north to Boscobel and the famous oak tree, and a week

The Old Bull, Inkberrow, Worcestershire, the model for the Bull at Ambridge in the BBC radio series *The Archers*

later on his way to Stratford. If he himself did not stop at the Old Bull, there were 16,000 officers and men in his army, who were scattered to the winds after the battle. Perhaps the dimly remembered fugitive was one of them?

The three-storeyed, timber-framed Old Bull dates back to the sixteenth century, and was probably built as a barn. It later served as a farriery, and became an alehouse by the often-trod path discussed in Chapter 1. As to when this happened, local legend once again offers an answer. William Shakespeare, they say, used to refresh himself at the Old Bull while visiting his aged mother, who lived nearby. This may not be true, but the forge might have become an alehouse by then, for even if local legends should not be overestimated, they usually contain at least a germ of fact.

But it is both true and legendary that the Old Bull served as the prototype of the Bull at Ambridge in the BBC Radio series *The Archers*. Photos of members of the cast adorn the walls, and Phil Archer was 'married' at Hanbury Church not far away, whose recorded bells can sometimes be heard on the programme.

THE NORTH

CHESHIRE

Brereton, The Bear's Head

The Bear's Head is another of the splendid half-timbered buildings for which Cheshire, like Herefordshire, is famous. In fact Cheshire is better endowed with timber-framed houses than most other counties because its stocks of oak lasted longer. Timber-framing was still common here in the late seventeenth century, when most other areas had gone over to the use of brick; as we will see, the Bear & Billet and the Old Hall are dated 1664 and 1656 respectively, and timber-framing in Cheshire reached heights of sophistication unknown elsewhere.

The Bear's Head is older than the Bear & Billet and the Old Hall; the date inscribed here is 1615. Its outstanding feature is the tall porch with its arched doorway and large gable, on which the date is inscribed along with the initials Wm.B. for William Brereton, and the coat of arms of his family, whose manor-house this originally was. Eventually the Breretons built themselves a more splendid home, Brereton Hall, the model for Washington Irving's Bracebridge Hall; their former home became an inn, taking its name from the device on their coat of arms.

The A50 beside which the inn stands was then the main London–Liverpool coach road, and the Bear's Head soon became a prominent coaching and posting-house. The pleasant but undistinguished Georgian brick wing was added at this time, and across the road was a magnificent brick stable-block, with a great central pediment supported by two pilasters over the carriage arch, and projecting wings at each end. Although a yard behind the inn was the more usual arrangement, the location of stabling across the road was by no means uncommon; other examples were at the Saltersgate Inn near Pickering and the Wagon & Horses at Beckhampton. But in most cases, as in this, they have been pulled down, and where they once stood is now a large car-park.

What looks like a converted stable-block beside the pub is in fact a range of bedrooms built of reclaimed brick and apparently designed to look like old stables. Inside, the ceilings are low and heavily beamed; but unfortunately it cannot be said that the decor lives up to the promise of the exterior.

Chester, The Bear & Billet, Lower Bridge Street

Built in 1664 as a town house for the earls of Shrewsbury, the Bear & Billet is one of the most splendid of timber-framed buildings in a city renowned for them. The frontage consists of a gable of four storeys end-on to the street; the timber-mullioned windows of the first and second floors extend across the

The Bear and Billet, Chester, seen through the eighteenth-century Bridgegate

whole façade, and all the woodwork is most delicately carved in intricate patterns.

The earls of Shrewsbury needed a town house in Chester because of their hereditary function as Serjeants of the Bridgegate, which almost adjoins the inn. The Serjeant's primary function was, of course, the organisation of the defence of the gate and its stretch of wall; but by 1664 this role was very much a ceremonial one. More important at the time was the collection of tolls from those using the gate; eventually this, too, was superseded by the Turnpike Trusts, and in 1721 the earl leased out his house as an inn, on the condition that a suite of rooms be reserved for his use should he ever need it. By 1740 he had never used this suite, and therefore gave up the condition.

The inn was not called the Talbot, as one would expect; it was at first the White Bear. It became something of a coaching inn, and some of the stable buildings survive at the rear. Unusual features are the double hoist-doors in the top floor, just under the eaves: they are supposed to have been used to winch up fodder for the horses, which was stored in the attics before being dumped down the other side into the yard. It was at about this time that the interior timbers were plastered over.

When the earl finally sold the property in 1867 to Quellyn Roberts & Co, a firm of wine-merchants who also own the Boot in Eastgate, it was called the Bridgegate Inn; subsequently it adopted its present name, which is more confusing still, for the bear and ragged staff, or billet, are the arms of the earls of Warwick, who never had anything to do with the place.

In recent years the interior has been restored, and the plaster has been re-moved from the beams. Some were found to be rotten, and have been replaced; the originals that survive have escaped the Victorian pitch-pot and retain their natural mellow golden colour.

Sandbach, The Old Hall

From the road the Old Hall looks too fine to be a mere pub; its four black-and-white gables, all of oak from the Mondron Forest near Nantwich, gaze out serenely across the market-place with its Saxon crosses like the stately home of some ancient blue-blooded family. In fact that, as its name suggests, is what it once was.

The mansion that occupied the site in medieval times was the hall of the Sond-baches; in those days it was a fortified manor-house, and occupied a much more prominent position than it does today, for the road and market-place were lower then than they are now. By 1597, when the charter for the Thursday markets was granted, it had come into the possession of the Radclyffe family. All that remains of those times are a large barn in the yard at the rear, and a spiral staircase with a right-hand twist in order to free the sword-arm of a defender retreating upwards while hampering that of his attacker advancing from below.

The inscription on the front of the house gives the date of its rebuilding as 1656, and much of the panelling, the exposed beams and the three fireplaces with their carved overmantels date from this time. It was then the home of the earls of Crewe, and when they left it for not being secluded enough, it became an inn. It had a brisk coach trade; the carriage arch giving access to the yard is on the right-hand side of the building. Like many country inns of the time, it

Tan Hill Inn, Tan Hill, County Durham. The highest and surely the remotest pub in the country, the Tan Hill is all that survives of a once-flourishing mining community

brewed its own beer; it was still doing so when Charles G. Harper visited it in 1906 and only stopped when World War I made the necessary materials scarce. It had also a pair of dog-gates across the top of the stairs to prevent the household pets reaching the bedrooms; these have had to be removed because of hotel fire regulations.

COUNTY DURHAM

Tan Hill, The Tan Hill Inn

Not only the highest inn in England (at 1,732ft above sea-level, it beats the Cat & Fiddle at Buxton by 27ft), the Tan Hill must also be the most remote. Keld, the nearest village, is five miles away;

Kirkby Stephen, the nearest town of any size, is twelve. The pub enjoys no mains services whatever: gas is stored in a tank outside, electricity is provided by a generator and the water is pumped up from a well. Even the telephone is a radio-telephone. Every winter it is cut off by the snows; it closes from October to Easter. It stands in the middle of a primal landscape of bleak turf moor; all that is visible around it is rolling acres of coarse grass.

Yet it has always been immensely popular, and has never wanted for custom. When it was built in 1737, the moor teemed with coal-miners operating one-man or father-and-son shafts; the now-blank heath was studded with their cottages and pitted with their workings. Some of these were in use within living memory, and although they have all now vanished, walkers still have to beware of falling into open shafts.

It was not only the miners who came to the Tan Hill Inn. Hawkers, pedlars and drovers were glad of a night's company and a roaring fire to sleep beside, and there are a surprising number of farmers in the apparently empty region. They hold their May Sheep Fair outside the inn every year, when the landlord takes on twenty extra staff to help out.

But the major part of the Tan Hill's custom comes from the droves of walkers on the Pennine Way, which comes conveniently right up to the pub's front door. The Tan Hill has been a Mecca for them ever since the pub at Keld was closed—by the local Methodist preacher, according to the landlord of the Tan Hill. The walkers come not only for food and drink; many of them are fed up with tenting and are only too pleased to be able to spend a night under a proper roof. But the inn's three bedrooms are quickly filled, and so, like the wandering hawkers before them, the ramblers lie down on the bar-room floor in their sleeping bags beside the fire to sleep.

Tan is the old Celtic for fire; the feast of Beltane, when cattle are driven between two fires to ward off sickness, recalls the pagan god Belenos. Whether the inn's name means the hill was formerly a beacon, or that the tribes who once inhabited the region knew of and exploited the seams of coal, is not certain. But fire has not always been the pub's friend. In 1974 it was badly damaged when the gas-holder exploded. The sturdy stone walls were unharmed, but the interior was gutted and has been entirely rebuilt. An extension was added, built of the tumbled stones of the old miners' cottages.

CUMBRIA

Keswick, The George

The small town of Keswick with its grey stone houses is called the Capital of the Lakes, and has been England's most popular inland resort ever since the Romantic poets flocked to Cumbria at the beginning of the nineteenth century. But its prosperity before then depended partly on the manufacture of pencils, which began in 1566, and partly on the German silver-miners and silversmiths from Augsburg, who had first arrived to work in the hills in 1561.

When the Germans arrived, the George & Dragon, as the inn was then named, was already the town's largest inn, and possibly its largest building after the church. No one seems to know how long it had been there, but it was the natural choice for the counting-house and revenue office for the silver brought down by pack-mule from the Goldscope and Borrowdale deposits which the Germans had come to work. Their smelting house in the town was destroyed during the Civil War, by which time the ore had largely been extracted. For the eighty years during which the mining went on, Keswick must have resembled a Wild West boom-town. The George & Dragon was not only used for official purposes: it was also the centre of a lively black market in ore filched by the miners to avoid taxes.

The inn dropped the Dragon from its title in 1714 on the death of Queen Anne and the accession of German George. In 1715 the Old Pretender raised his standard in Scotland, and one of the rebels who set off to join him was the Earl of Derwentwater, who lived on Lord's Island in the lake beside which Keswick stands. The last the town saw of its Earl was when he called at the George for a last tankard of ale before joining the rebellion. By the end of the year he was dead, executed on Tower Hill.

In the later eighteenth century the George became a prominent coaching inn, and the frontage was rebuilt in the Georgian style. It was at this time that Coleridge arrived; he lived in the town from 1800 to 1809. Southey came to live near the town in 1803, and stayed for forty years. Keats, De Quincey and Charles Lamb were all frequent visitors; Shelley lived in a cottage on Chestnut Hill. They say nothing of the George, but it would be surprising if they had not known it well. What was the kitchen in their day is today the bar, but the snug front parlour can have changed very little in nearly two centuries.

Penrith, The Gloucester Arms, Cornmarket

From the outside the Gloucester Arms looks like a smart Elizabethan town house, clearly the home of a wealthy and influential gentleman. And indeed that is what it was; the initials IW on the porch, next to the date 1580, stand for John de Whelpdale, scion of an old and armigerous Penrith family and co-founder of the town's grammar school. But the house had existed long before his time.

Its former name, by which it is still known to many locals, was Dockray Hall; for in the Middle Ages it was the home of the Penrith branch of the Dockray or Docwra family. Their house was the southern half of the present building, but just how old it is is hard to say. The rise of the family began in the thirteenth century, and they had left the town by the middle of the sixteenth. About their house it is difficult to be more specific, since the cruck frame and many other original features are of a type common throughout the Middle Ages. But it certainly existed in 1471 when Richard of Gloucester, later Richard III, lived in it for a time while Penrith Castle was being altered for his use. The Docwras were a numerous and important family in Cumberland at that time and later; Sir Thomas Docwra was Grand Prior of the English Langue of the Knights of St John from 1501 to 1527.

The old building was restored by Whelpdale at the same time as he built the northern half. Only four of the mullioned Tudor windows survive; two have been cut through to make doors, and the rest were replaced in the eighteenth century. But there are many Tudor and later fireplaces; much plasterwork of the period, including the ceiling in the Gloucester Room which Richard is supposed to have used, and the panelling of various dates includes a fine Elizabethan oak screen. One plastered ceiling bears the impaled arms of the Whelpdales and the Carletons, indicating a marriage between the families, but the craftsmen have fashioned the Carleton arms the wrong way round, making what should be a bend dexter into a bend sinister—the mark of bastardy.

The house was sold by Andrew Whelpdale in 1684 to Thomas Webster, by Webster to William Rowell in 1719 and by his descendants to Jeremiah Savage in 1787. Between then and 1829 it became an inn, called the Golden Lion: the name was changed in about 1860 to take advantage of the connection with Richard III. It has been suggested that this connection is a complete fabrication, made up for commercial reasons; the best evidence for this is the fact that Richard's arms over the front door are wrong. They show, correctly, the royal arms supported by Richard's two boars, but there is no label or 'file' identifying him as the heir, and the motto is the royal 'Dieu et mon droit', instead of 'Loyaute me lie', which Richard used until his accession. This coat of arms is, in fact, a Victorian fake, and a clumsy one at that; the very door over which it appears was originally a window, and was probably cut through at the time when the house became an inn. The original main entrance is in the porch over which the Whelpdale arms appear. On the other hand, Richard could not have lived in the castle while it was being rebuilt for him, and the home of the important Docwra family was near enough for him to oversee the work that was being done on it. He had to live somewhere: Dockray Hall is as good a candidate as any for the honour.

GREATER MANCHESTER

Bolton, The Old Man & Scythe, Churchgate

Certainly Bolton's, and possibly Lancashire's, oldest inn, the Old Man & Scythe claims a date of 1251, the year in which the weekly market held in Churchgate until 1826 was given its charter. The present building dates only to 1636, but the cellars are medieval, and there could quite easily have been a market inn or alehouse on the site in the Middle Ages.

The present Market Cross was erected only in 1912; its predecessor had been removed in 1786 on the insistence of coachmen using the Swan, who said it obstructed the traffic. This was the scene of many activities: the pillory where felons were flogged stood here until 1837, and in 1748 John Wesley attempted to preach to a very hostile crowd from the Market Cross steps. Some started throwing stones, and others climbed up behind him to push him down; God or bad aiming intervened, however, and the stones meant for the preacher hit those trying to push him. Evidently the crowd saw the funny side of this, for after a while they desisted and let him finish.

On 15 October 1651 James Stanley, Earl of Derby, was executed at the Market Cross, having been tried at Chester for his part as a Royalist leader in the Battle of Bolton in 1644. The sentence was determined before the trial was held, and on the night before his death Derby was imprisoned at the Old Man & Scythe. A very rustic chair which furnished the room in which he was held is preserved in the bar, as is an old pewter tankard engraved 'Sacred to the Memory of the Earl of Derby'. A larger tankard holds half a gallon, is dated 1778 and belonged to Isaac Pennington, a churchwarden of St Peter's.

The pub's curious name is allowed three possible explanations. One is that it was copied from the figure of the grim reaper which once formed the church weathervane (there is a similar weathervane at Lord's Cricket Ground). Another, more romantic, story concerns William Trafford of Swithamley, a wealthy Royalist whose valuables were to be sequestered by local Parliamentarians during the Interregnum. When a troop of horse arrived at his house to collect the goods, however, they found it deserted except for a senile old man who was threshing in the barn, chanting idiotically to himself: 'Now thus; now thus' as he worked. But the old man, so the story runs, was Trafford himself, who had concealed his plate and money

The Gloucester Arms, Penrith, Cumbria, owes its name not to a geographical quirk but to a connection with Richard of Gloucester, later Richard III

under the threshing-floor. The inn-sign is supposed to commemorate him; but the third version is more likely, if more prosaic. It is that the figure of the grim reaper and the motto 'Now thus, now thus' formed the coat of arms of the family on whose land the pub stood—although unusual from a heraldic point of view, it is by no means improbable.

HUMBERSIDE

Beverley, The Beverley Arms, North Gate Within

Originally the Blue Bell, the first mention of the inn occurs in 1666, when it was used by Sir William Dugdale, the Garter King of Arms, on his Herald's Visitation to the area, where all those who wished to register their coats of arms with the College of Heralds could come and meet him. To be used for such a purpose, it could be no mere alehouse, and must have already been a commodious and reputable house. A lease of 1689 describes it as having been formerly two tenements, but no trace of them has survived two complete rebuildings, in 1700 and 1790.

It was at the Blue Bell in 1738 that Dick Turpin was arrested. He was not recognised, but the horse he was riding was: it was a black gelding with a little star on the forehead, and Turpin had just stolen it. At that time the magistrates were using the Blue Bell as their court-room. Although they did not realise who it was they had caught, they did not like the look of him, and committed him to York for trial, under his assumed name of Palmer. From York he wrote home to Essex, asking his brother to stand bail for him, but he neglected to pay the postage, and his brother refused

to accept the charge. The letter was returned to the post office, where it was spotted by his former schoolteacher, who identified his handwriting immediately. He was hanged at York, for horse-stealing, on 10 April 1739.

The present Georgian brick building, with its graceful porch and carriage arch, dates back to 1790, at which time the old name gave way to the present one. The long room or assembly room where dances and functions were held is to be found in its usual place, at the front on the first floor; it gives on to the balcony over the porch, from where victorious election candidates used to address the populace. Almost all that remains of the earlier incarnation is the stone-flagged kitchen with its five fireplaces, made famous by the Victorian artist F. W. Elwell RA, who painted it twice. The old kitchen is now a lounge, and one of Elwell's paintings is on permanent loan and hangs in the reception area. The other is in the Tate. The old stables have gone, and have been replaced by new buildings; the coach-yard is now a patio.

Hull, The Old White Hart, Silver Street
The White Hart, Alfred Gelder Street

Dating from the late sixteenth century, the Old White Hart was the Governor's House in 1642, and it was here that one of the first dramas of the Civil War took place. The Governor of the city, which included a formidable arsenal, was Sir John Hotham; he had been appointed by Charles I in 1628 and was also MP for Beverley. One of the King's first acts after raising his standard at Nottingham was to march on Hull in order to seize the arsenal for his army; naturally he

The Beverley Arms, Beverley, Humberside, and the gates of St Mary's Church

expected that Hotham would be only too happy to let him in. It was not to be. Whatever the Governor's own feelings, a conference with the borough's MPs, who included the staunch Parliamentarian Sir Harry Vane the Younger, convinced him that the people of Hull would not support the King; so when Charles arrived on St George's Day, he found the gates shut against him, and since he had no powder, there was no way of opening them. It was the first of many cruel blows, but Hotham was to regret it later; he was executed by a vengeful Parliament in 1645 for attempting to change sides. The first-floor 'Plotting Room' in which the conference took place is panelled and has many superb carvings, some of them Masonic; there is also in one of the two cupboards flanking the fire-place a hundred-year-old Guinness bottle which appears to be haunted; strange things are said to happen if it is moved.

Much of the old building was swept away in a fire in the late eighteenth century; the scars of it are still to be seen on the banisters of the remaining stair-

The White Hart, Hull. A late Victorian gin-palace, the inspiration of the design appears to be more seventeenth century than Tudor. The two stone door-cases are particularly elaborate

case. After the fire, the building remained a private house until 1881, when it was first licensed. Much rebuilding was carried out; a new frontage was added, and two Civil War cavalry sabres were found in a wall where they had presumably been hidden; they are now on display along with a large collection of other militaria. During restoration work in 1937 a blocked-off room was uncovered in the attics; in it were found the skull of a woman of about thirty and the jawbone of a child of about six or seven. They are now preserved in a case in the bar.

The White Hart is an unexceptional Victorian pub with an amusing façade of fake half-timbering with stone embellishments, presumably intended to look seventeenth century. The inside of this pub has been opened out into two large bars, where originally it would have been several small parlours; the only survival from its early days is an amazing horseshoe bar-counter in the front bar, all in ceramics and complete with glass-fronted mahogany cupboards and fittings in the alcove behind. It was designed by a local man named Robinson who died in the 1890s, and was probably installed in the 1870s or '80s; it is quite remarkable that such a relic should have survived the many redecorations and strippings-out which the pub has undoubtedly undergone. It proves that while the Victorian imagination may not have had much room for taste, it certainly knew how to have fun.

LANCASHIRE

Ribchester, The White Bull

The White Bull is a late Tudor or early seventeenth-century building, but the foundations upon which it stands are very much older than that. In fact the masonry in the cellars is reputed to be Roman, although it would take a proper dig to confirm it. But there could be something in it: during the summer of 1700, severe drought caused the level of the Ribble to drop dramatically, and many Roman remains were temporarily exposed. As many of these fragments as possible were recovered, and most found their way to museums. But four complete Roman columns support the porch, and the date of its construction, 1707, is carved on the wall beside it.

For many years the local magistrates used the White Bull as their courthouse. One room was used as a holding cell, and the rusted remains of a set of manacles were found embedded in an inside wall during redecorations. Half a mile away is Gallows Lane, but of course the magistrates tried only petty offenders, and all the more serious criminals were committed for trial at Lancaster Castle, which is still in use as a court. But until 1805 the bodies of executed villains were returned to the scene of their crime to be gibbeted in chains as a warning to others; Gallows Lane was probably the site of the local gibbet.

The crudely carved white bull that surmounts the porch is of wood, and looks to be early sixteenth-century or even older. However, it is probably an eighteenth-century copy of an original model. The old stables, still largely intact and now used for storage, have room for only half-a-dozen or so animals, for the White Bull was never a coaching or posting-house of much note. A mounting-block of three very worn steps stands beside the front door. The forecourt is used by the Garstang Morris Men; other teams of dancers also visit the White Bull from time to time.

The Fauconberg Arms, Coxwold, Yorkshire, stands on a site occupied by an alehouse for a thousand years or more

NORTH YORKSHIRE

Coxwold, The Fauconberg Arms

Coxwold is best known for its connection with Laurence Sterne, the author of *Tristram Shandy* and *Sentimental Journey*, who was vicar from 1760 to 1768 and lived in the fifteenth-century Parsonage House, christened Shandy Hall by his admirers and today a place of pilgrimage. As well as being an acute and pithy writer, he was a man of great charity and devotion. His flock loved him, and in return he loved his Yorkshire home. 'I am as happy as a prince at Coxwold,' he wrote in 1767; '. . . it is a land of plenty.'

The village already had seven or more centuries of history behind it when Sterne arrived: in the Domesday Book it is Cucvalt, the Crying Wood; and the layout of the houses with their long garths running down behind them is as it was in 1605 when it was first mapped, and as it was in feudal times. The Fauconberg Arms is a seventeenth-century building, but it stands on a building-plot whose boundaries have not changed in a thousand years. It seems to have been an alehouse since it was built, and it may well have replaced a much older alehouse on the site.

It was at first the Bellasis Arms, after the family who had had Newburgh Priory since it was dissolved in 1538 and who owned most of the village. Thomas Bellasis, who in 1662 founded the village almshouses or Poor Men's Hospital, was created first Earl Fauconberg in 1682, despite the fact that he was Oliver Cromwell's son-in-law; legend has it that the

226

missing bones of the Protector are kept in a secret sarcophagus at Newburgh. The Bellasis Arms changed its name in 1823, at which time it had been kept by the Barwick family for at least half a century and possibly for very much longer. The last Earl Fauconberg died in 1832, and Newburgh passed by marriage to the Wombwells, who are there still.

An L-shaped stone building with nineteenth-century porch and windows, the pub does not look its age from outside. The interior, however, with its stone-flagged floor, massive joists, and great open hearths, tells a different story. Until recently the inn-sign was an enormous plaque, 8 or 10ft square, bearing the Fauconberg coat of arms and their motto 'Bonne et Belle Assez'. The present sign is of the same type, and carries the same device, but is of more modest proportions.

Helmsley, The Black Swan, Market Square

Originally established in the sixteenth century, the stone-built Black Swan has come a long way since it was the principal resort of Ryedale farmers bringing wool down from the hills. It was then a mere pack-horse inn, but was of necessity endowed with generous stables and barns, which came into good use in the eighteenth century, when Helmsley's position at the junction of roads to York, Scarborough and Teesside made it an important coaching town. The Black Swan shared the trade with the Crown, then called Cooper's Posting House; the inn's stone frontage and sash windows were added during this period.

By the time of the demise of the coaching trade, Helmsley had developed into a centre for tourists enjoying the

The Black Swan, Helmsley, North Yorkshire. The somewhat incongruous half-timbered building on the left was originally a Tudor vicarage and was added to the hotel in the 1950s

Yorkshire Dales, a circumstance which ensured not only the Black Swan's survival, but its further expansion. From 'coaching inn' it changed into 'country hotel': the Sunnington Foxhounds met there regularly, and its dining-room was the venue of the Duncombe Estate annual rent dinner, when tenants of Lord Feversham's Duncombe Hall, built by Vanbrugh, met to pay their rent and claw back as much of it as possible in food and drink. To dignify the hotel, Jacobean panelling was brought in from the church in 1860, and a Tudor doorway was rescued from the ruins of Helmsley Castle and installed at the top of the cellar steps.

Despite its increasing importance in the local scheme of things, however, the Black Swan was still very much a village pub, much favoured by (amongst others) the boys of the neighbouring public school, Ampleforth. After the war, it began its climb to its present status of luxury hotel. The next-door building, a fine Georgian house containing an elegant curving staircase, was incorporated in 1947, and the Tudor vicarage next to that was added on in 1954. Thus the Black Swan now occupies the whole of the north side of the market-place, and one cannot escape the feeling that it is far too elevated these days to entertain anyone common enough to allude to it by its former affectionate nickname of 'the Mucky Duck'.

Saltersgate Inn, Lockton High Moor, Yorkshire. The radomes of Fylingdales lie just over the horizon

Lockton High Moor, The Saltersgate Inn

At about 900ft above sea-level, the Saltersgate Inn is almost as remote as the Tan Hill Inn, but since it is on a main road it has nothing of the Tan Hill's sense of isolation. Cars whizz by on their way to the seaside, there are walkers and cyclists by the gross, and on fine days the pub gets a great deal of custom from the hang-gliders on (or off) Lockton Low Moor and the swarms who turn out to watch them.

Originally a farm, the Saltersgate has been an inn probably since the early eighteenth century, and a peat fire is kept burning perpetually in the black-leaded hearth. This is a fairly frequent custom, which lost its meaning when closing hours were introduced; originally travellers and others would be coming in more or less round the clock, and a good fire would be the first thing they wanted. As so often happens, the custom has fostered a legend: in this case it concerns the Old Man of Horcum, a recluse who lived in the miniature Grand Canyon that cuts deeply through the moor, called Horcum Hole. He would come up to the inn to warm his cold bones, threatening to lay a curse on the house if ever the hearth should grow cold. One day he suddenly threw himself into the fire and vanished shrieking up the chimney, upon which it was realised that he was, of course, the Devil; the fire has been kept burning ever since in order to ward off his reappearance.

Until World War II the inn was the Wagon & Horses; post-boys used to change horses at the now-ruined stables across the road, and there are cots in the attic where they used to snatch an hour or two's sleep. The name was changed in memory of the days when the landlord's had a sideline in salt fish. The inn is only ten or so miles from the North Sea: pack-trains would bring the raw ingredients inland, and the drying racks used in the process are still to be seen in the cellars. Romance has it that this trade was conducted in secret to escape the crippling taxes imposed on salt during the Napoleonic Wars; this is rather hard to believe. Salt fish was a staple of the industrial working classes because it was so cheap; in order to make a reasonable profit, therefore, the production had to be a bulk operation. It is a little difficult to swallow the idea that pack-trains could move across 10 miles of trackless moor at night, or that a bulk salting operation could be carried on without the revenue men finding out about it pretty quickly and putting a stop to it. In fact the goods in which smugglers generally dealt—French brandy and lace, Italian silk, and so on—are all expensive luxury goods, easy to conceal and transport, and yielding a maximum return for a minimum effort.

Tadcaster, The Angel & White Horse, High Street

The home of Sam Smith's, John Smith's and a branch of Bass Charrington, Tadcaster is today best known as a brewing town almost rivalling Burton-on-Trent. But in the eighteenth century it was equally well known as a coaching town astride the Great North Road ten miles or so from York. Some fifty public coaches passed through every day, as well as a great number of private post-chaises, carriages and chariots, and among the many coaching inns were two side by side: the White Horse and the Red Hart.

The Red Hart had been in existence since Tudor times; some half-timbering is still visible at the side. Its landlord in the early eighteenth century was Edward Marshall, who became the town's postmaster, servicing and providing horses for the post-boys who passed through. In 1784 mail coaches replaced post-boys. Shortly afterwards a stone front with two bays was added to the inn, and the Red Hart became the Angel, with a stone figure of an angel as its sign. It survived until 1855, when it went out of business.

The White Horse, also with two bays but a taller and rather more elegant brick building possessing a dignified porch, was kept by the Backhouse family from 1777 until 1840, when it went broke and closed down. It was reopened fifteen years later by Lord Londesbrough to accommodate his guests at Tadcaster Races, since his own home, Grimston Hall, was too small. It was named the Londesbrough Hotel, and by a curious twist of fate its first landlord was Matthew Kidd, who had kept the Angel at the time of its closure.

As the Londesbrough, it survived until 1976, when Sam Smith's stepped in to reverse history. For now it was the turn of the Londesbrough to go out of business and its old rival, the Angel, to reopen.

After its closure, the Angel had been converted into two shops, occupied by a dressmaker and a cobbler. When Sam Smith's decided to reopen it, they stripped off the rendering, and replaced the odd patches of brick they found under it with original stone and put up a new figure of an angel to replace the one taken down in 1855. But perhaps the most important part of their work was carried out inside, where they made and installed a whole new set of panelling, made from oaks planted by the Admiralty for shipbuilding at the time of

Trafalgar. All the work was carried out by the brewery's own joiners, and the customer can be excused for not realising that it is, in fact, all only a few years old. The Londesbrough also had the rendering stripped off it; it now houses the brewery architects' department. But so that it should not be forgotten, the brewery decided to incorporate its original name into the title of the revived Angel. They also commissioned a sign by the artist Terence Cuneo showing Barrel, one of their team of Shire horses.

The story of John Smith's and Sam Smith's, the two main breweries, is almost as confusing. The Old Brewery, which is just behind the Angel & White Horse, was Beaumont's in 1772 (and it was nearly a century old then) when it was purchased by the Hartley family. John Smith bought it in the 1850s, and on his death his son William built the new brewery, which kept the name John Smith's. In 1886, however, Samuel Smith, John's grandson and William's nephew, re-equipped the Old Brewery and ran it in direct competition with his uncle. Since then the two have grown further apart: John's is now part of the Courage empire and produces no real ale; Sam's is one of the country's leading independent breweries and produces nothing else.

As well as its team of dray horses, Sam's maintains a foreman, three journeymen and an apprentice in its cooperage, using tools like jointers and crozes whose design is hundreds of years old.

(*opposite*) The Angel and White Horse, Tadcaster, Yorkshire. An apprentice at work in the cooperage of Sam Smith's brewery behind the car park

The coopers repair barrels and sometimes make small casks for presentations; but the cost of making new large barrels of wood is prohibitive. It is highly labour-intensive, and since English oak is unsuitable for barrel-making, German oak has to be imported at great expense. There are coopers in Sheffield and Cheshire, however, who replace old barrels at the end of their forty-year life.

Sam's is also one of the few breweries still using the traditional Yorkshire squares for fermentation. These are, as their name suggests, square rather than round; each one holds from 25 to 75 barrels (a barrel being 36 gallons) and they are made of thick slate slabs. Squares are also used by Theakston's at Masham.

York, The Black Swan, Peasholme Green

Originally built in the fourteenth century, the Black Swan was the home of the Bowes family, ancestors of the Queen Mother and wealthy merchants in the city. William Bowes represented York in four Parliaments under Henvy V and Henry VI, was Sheriff of York in 1407 and Lord Mayor in 1417 and 1428. His son William was Lord Mayor in 1443, and his grandson, Sir Martin, who was born in the house but later moved to London, was a goldsmith who became Lord Mayor of London in 1545 and was Court Jeweller and Treasurer of the Mint to Elizabeth I. It was Sir Martin who presented to his native city the sword of state which is still borne before the Lord Mayor on occasions of ceremony. It seems unlikely that such an important family would have anything to do with Papists, but tradition has it that Margaret Clitheroe, one of the Catholic Forty Martyrs recently canonised, was arrested in the house. She was pressed to death under a door for refusing to plead.

In 1683 the house came to Edward Thompson, Lord Mayor in that year and MP for the city. His grandson was James Wolfe, the general who captured Quebec in 1759. Tradition has it that the general lived in the house as a child; but he was born in 1727, and the first vague mention of a licence is in 1715, so the point must remain unresolved.

When it did become an inn—whether in 1715 or later—the Black Swan was still equipped with all the refinements of a prosperous house. The front parlour has moulded plaster ceiling and elegant seventeenth-century panelling and doorcases, and the staircase of about 1700 is equally elegant; but the pride of the house is an upstairs room which was probably the original family dining-room. This is panelled like the parlour and there are similar plaster mouldings on the ceiling, but in this case the panelling was covered from top to bottom and all round the room with chiaroscuro paintings of the sixteenth century. In time these paintings all faded and are now mere marks on the wood, largely indecipherable; but in 1930 one panel, over the fireplace, was restored. The scene shows the Blessed Virgin and St Elizabeth with Jesus and St John the Baptist in a rustic landscape; it is possible, if the subject-matter was repeated in the other paintings, that they were deliberately scrubbed out during the iconoclastic Interregnum, when idolatrous images all over the country were destroyed. This room also possesses a fireplace surrounded with Delft tiles of the eighteenth or nineteenth centuries.

Despite these amenities, the Black Swan never became a major coaching

232

inn. (The George, which was the town's chief terminus, has now been demolished.) Indeed, it became something of a dive. An engraving of about 1800 shows a rather ramshackle porch at the front, the house is covered with peeling stucco and the chimneys look distinctly unsafe. In 1884 a bricklayer conducted an auction at the inn: Lot 1, the only lot in the sale, was his wife; he got 1/6d (7½p) for her. By 1900 the porch had gone, and horses were being led through the inn's main hall to the blacksmith who had a forge in the back yard.

The whole place was restored in 1930. The stucco was pulled off, and many missing timbers were replaced. The decline was arrested and reversed, and the Black Swan became the smart town pub it is today. Unfortunately the beautifully carved barge-boards which decorated the gables vanished during this restoration: they were probably too rotten to be rescued.

NORTHUMBERLAND

Blanchland, The Lord Crewe Arms

Blanchland is a remarkable village. Hidden in the depths of rural Northumberland, but with the towers and chimneys of Consett steelworks visible five miles away, it seems more Mediterranean than English; for it is constructed entirely round a courtyard or quad which was originally the outer courtyard of Blanchland Abbey. In fact the cottages, the church and the Lord Crewe Arms were constructed on the layout of the abbey—a layout which has therefore remained unaltered since 1165.

The Premonstratensian Canons were founded by St Norbert of Xanten in 1120; their first English house was founded in 1143. The Abbey of Blanchland was established after the Order was given a small estate, then known as Wulwardshope, by Walter de Bolbec in 1165. It was never a large community; there were no more than twelve Canons, who were hard-pressed to carry out the great amount of pastoral work expected by their Order. The income from their estates was small, they were constantly in debt and in 1536, when there were only seven Canons and two novices, the house fell within the scope of the first Act of Suppression in that its income was less than £200 a year. However, it was allowed to continue until 1539, when the nine members of the community were pensioned off.

The abbey and its lands were then purchased by the Radcliffes, an old Northumbrian family. Uniquely, the buildings were not plundered, but were converted to dwellings. Only the church itself was allowed to decay; one side-chapel was preserved for the use of the family. It was the Radcliffes who created the manor-house which was later to become the inn. This was composed of the abbot's lodgings, which were built out from the south-west corner of the church, the abbot's guest-house adjoining it, and beneath them the former abbey kitchens and some store-rooms. The transformation into a small manor was complete by the time the Forsters of Bamburgh bought the estate from the Radcliffes in 1623; nearly all the internal divisions are either Elizabethan or Jacobean, although the Dorothy Forster room was probably made into a parlour in the reign of Charles I.

The Forsters were strongly pro-Stuart. They were Royalists in the Civil War, and Jacobites after the Glorious Revolution. Dorothy Forster married

Lord Nathaniel Crewe, Bishop of Durham, who performed the marriage service of James II and Mary of Modena; Dorothy's nephew, Thomas Forster, was later to become a Jacobite general and eventually died in exile at the court of the Old Pretender, having escaped from Newgate three days before he was due to be tried for high treason.

Dorothy and Thomas succeeded to the two estates of Blanchland and Bamburgh in 1701, and in 1704 Lord Crewe bought them out. By this time the manor was no longer in regular use as a residence, and after Crewe's death in 1721 it became an inn. Crewe used his enormous wealth to set up the Lord Crewe Trust, which still helps pay for schooling and almshouses, and meets the stipends of many clergy in the diocese. The present condition of the village is due to the work of the Trustees: during the 1750s they rebuilt all the cottages surrounding the village square and reconstructed the choir of the old abbey church to serve the parish. The buildings opposite the hotel were at that time used as a refinery, for lead and silver were mined in the hills around. It was at about this time, too, that the hotel dining-room was built as a ballroom in the Gothic style.

The Lord Crewe Arms still contains a good deal of medieval work, including the twelfth- or thirteenth-century abbey kitchen fireplace, but tales of a priest's hole for fleeing Jacobites need not be taken too seriously.

Battlesteads Inn, Wark, Northumberland, a village and a pub which have seen much military activity over the centuries

Wark, The Battlesteads Inn

Like Tewkesbury's Gupshill Manor, the Battlesteads was a farm which took in paying guests until about World War II, and has only been a pub for some thirty years. The public bar is housed in a new extension, and many villagers remember the cocktail bar when it was still the farmer's private parlour.

On the lintel over the front door the date 1747, together with some initials now too worn to be made out, can be seen, but the building contains masonry at least a hundred years older than that, and it has been suggested that for some years in the seventeenth century it served, as it does again today, as the village alehouse. Its present name stems from the belief that at that time it was used by the moss-troopers or reivers, small private armies who spent their time plundering across the Scottish border or fighting off similar raids by their Caledonian counterparts. In the eighteenth century it was a billet for British troops engaged in putting down the Jacobite rebellions of 1715 and 1745.

Opposite the inn is the earthwork which gives the village its name. It is known as Mote Hill, and local legend has it that it was built by the women of the district, who carried the stones on which it is founded from the bed of the North Tyne. It is claimed that the earthwork dates back to Saxon times, when the Tynedale Moot was held on it; certainly Wark was once the capital of Tynedale, and a Manorial Court was held here to deal with such crimes as sheep-stealing and cattle-rustling. However, Mote Hill is probably the motte on which an early Norman castle of mud and timber once stood; it is unlikely to be Saxon, but it would be quite usual for the Manorial Court to be held in the castle.

APPENDIX: INN SIGNS

The study of inn-names and inn-signs can be most revealing, both in dating inns and in giving some hints about their pasts. Names had their period of vogue, and some of them can be definitely associated with some individual, family, or trade. Often an inn takes its name from the feudal landholder: for instance, a Bear & Ragged Staff will have formed part of the estates of the earls of Warwick, this symbol being part of their arms. This can be useful in dating, too: an inn called the Talbot will have come by its name after 1422, when John Talbot was created Earl of Shrewsbury for his part in the Hundred Years' War. Other inns can be dated by this means to a particular reign: the White Hart was Richard II's badge, the Antelope was the badge of the Lancastrians Henry V and Henry VI. An Angel or a Mitre will have had Church connections, while a Boar's Head, an Elephant & Castle and a Golden Ball will have been connected with one or other of the many medieval trade guilds.

All of these symbols come from some part of the coat of arms or achievement of the person or body concerned; normally from the arms themselves, or the crest, or the supporters. (The other parts of the achievement are the wreath, the helmet, the mantling and the motto.) Until the late Middle Ages most people, including many nobles, were illiterate, so it was no good writing, say, 'The King Henry V' on the wall of your alehouse. Nor was it any good painting a portrait of him: most people had no idea what he looked like. But the Antelope, one of the supporters, was instantly recognisable—more so than his coat of arms itself, which would have so many quarterings that only an expert could tell it from the arms of any other king.

Not all pictograms came from coats of arms, though. If the inn was dedicated to the Blessed Virgin Mary, one might commission a sign commemorating the salutation. Regulars would then call the inn the Salutation, or they might pick a recognisable figure from the scene and call the inn the Angel.

The earliest alehouse sign was, as is commonly known, a branch of greenery tied to a pole, and known as the bush or alestake. This custom dates back to the Romans, who used a vine branch for the same purpose. There are today many pubs called the Bush, or the Hop Pole, which is the same thing, but in early days they would have had no names and would have been known by the name of the owner. The first inn-names as we know them came in the twelfth century, when monks began to build hospices on a large scale for pilgrims. The Ostrich at Colnbrook is the earliest of these; its name may also be the oldest in the country. It is in fact a rebus or canting sign—a heraldic pun. As we have seen, it was no good writing the word 'hospice' on the wall; nor was there any obvious pictogram as there would have been with a coat of arms. So an ostrich was painted up instead. In fact this joke backfired, for the locals knew nothing of ostriches and thought the bird was a rather poor representation of a crane, so the Ostrich was known as the Crane for many years. Much more common amongst these early religious names was the Golden Cross; the inn of that name in Oxford was founded in the 1190s.

The advantage of erecting a hanging sign rather than merely painting on the wall was that it could be seen by potential customers at a distance, and in a village where there were several alehouses, the landlords would compete for the largest, gaudiest and most attractive sign—medieval neon, in effect. In 1375 an act had to be passed limiting the alestake's projection over the roadway to 7ft, and in time the inn-sign had become so universal that the uprooting of a sign by the authorities signified the suppression of the inn.

Inn-signs reached a peak of artistry and opulence in the seventeenth century, when gallows signs were often built stretching from one side of the road to the other. These are still to be seen at the George at Stamford, the Green Man & Black's Head Royal at Ashbourne, and the Fox & Hounds at Barley in Hertfordshire; but the most famous of all in its day was at the White Hart at Scole on the London–Norwich coach road. When erected in 1655 it cost over £1,000 and comprised twenty-five figures carved in oak representing the mythical story of Diana and Actaeon. (Actaeon was a hunter who was turned into a stag by Diana and torn in pieces by his own hounds after he had stumbled across the chaste goddess and her nymphs bathing in a pool.) This has now vanished, as have many others: the George at Crawley, the Greyhound at Sutton, the Greyhound at Croydon, the Four Swans at Waltham Cross and the Old Star at York all had gallows signs.

At the same time, hanging signs were proliferating in the towns. They were attached not only to taverns but also to ordinary shops, which often traded under symbols. A druggist could be identified by the civet cat on his signboard, a hatter would have a beaver and a bookseller a Bible. Modern pawnbrokers still hang out the three roundels of Lombardy. In Charles I's time these signs had to have a clearance of at least 9ft to allow horsemen safe passage; after the great fire of London in 1666 a vain attempt was made to ban them altogether. During the great rebuilding that followed the fire many crsftsmen involved in the work carved signs in their spare time to make a little extra cash; a now featureless wooden panel preserved in the Cock & Bottle, Fleet Street, is said to have been carved by Grinling Gibbons himself, but was more probably the work of one of his employees. The presence of great numbers of these skilled men, and the fierce competition between rival traders, led to a great increase in both the quantity and extravagance of these signs, which were necessary because there was no system of street-numbering.

But they could be confusing. When premises changed hands, they often retained their old name—hence the Rainbow coffee-house in Fleet Street, founded in 1657, occupied a former dyer's shop. Or it might keep its old sign and be given a new one too—one

Three Kings: Jacks Booth, Sulhampstead, Berkshire. One of the rare examples of a pub licensed with two names. The most likely origins of the names are that the pub was first known as the Jack Boot, by dint of its use by drovers making their way to London; then, despite the evidence of the modern pub sign, the Three Kings was added in 1603 to celebrate the accession of James I

can only imagine what might have been sold at the Civet Cat & Three Herrings. Addison, writing in the *Spectator* in 1710, commented: 'I have seen the Goat set up before a perfumer's, and a King's Head before a swordcutler's.' In time it reached the point where the sign alone would not tell a potential customer whether the premises was a goldsmith's or a brothel; and although the hundreds of gaily painted signboards swinging overhead must have made a very colourful street-scene, there was a constant danger of one of them falling and causing a nasty injury. Finally in 1762 all hanging signs except those belonging to taverns and pawnshops were banned from the City of London, in 1764 from Westminster as well and in 1768 the street-numbering system we know today was instituted.

An innkeeper wanting a particularly fancy sign would generally turn to a coach-painter for it; many well-known artists started life in this trade. They include John Cromer the Elder of Norwich, Thomas Wright of Liverpool and J. F. Herring and his younger brother Charles in Doncaster. Even such luminaries as Sir William Beechey RA, Robert Dalton (who was keeper of pictures to George III) and Ralph Kirby, who was George IV's art master, had painted inn-signs before fortune beckoned them upwards. Hogarth himself did a sign for the Man Loaded With Mischief in Oxford Street. For a struggling painter, a commission to do an inn-sign could make the difference between mere hunger and actual starvation. The classical landscape painter Richard Wilson, who died in penury in 1782, and George Morland, who died in similar misery in 1824, both kept body and soul together in this way. Morland in particular would dash off an inn-sign for the price of a supper.

What was for Morland and Wilson an absolute necessity, and for Cromer, Wright and the Herrings a part of their apprenticeship, became an indulgence of whimsy for the fashionable painters of Queen Victoria's reign. David Cox's sign, painted in 1847 as a gift to the landlady of the Royal Oak at Bettws-y-Coed, became the bone of contention in a legal wrangle when the lady retired. She

The Crown and Cushion, Minley, Hampshire. This attractive sign, in mock Bayeux Tapestry style, refers to the local legend that King Harold was crowned nearby in 1066. In fact he was the first King of England to be crowned at the new Westminster Abbey

claimed it as her own property; the brewery maintained it was a fixture of the inn and therefore belonged to them. (The judge ruled for the brewery.) Millais executed a sign for the George & Dragon at Hayes Common, Middlesex. G. D. Leslie and J. E. Hodgson took a side each of the sign at the George & Dragon at Wargrave-on-Thames in 1874, and Leslie later painted signs for the Row Barge, Wallingford and the King Harry at St Albans. In 1902 Walter Crane painted a sign for the Fox & Pelican at Graysholt, Hampshire.

The study of names can be both interesting and useful; it can also be thoroughly misleading. When one sees the Unicorn, for instance, it can mean three things: it can signify a link with medieval and Tudor apothecaries, who used narwhal horn as a remedy against poisoning; James I, whose arms were supported by unicorns; or a type of carriage drawn by three horses. The Red Lion can signify Edward I, the hammer of the Scots whose arms figure the red lion, James I, John of Gaunt, founder of the Lancanstrian dynasty, or Cardinal Wolsey. The Three Kings can signify the Magi, the union of the kingdoms of England, Scotland, and Ireland (James I yet again), or the Mercers' Company, who used the three crowns of the city of Cologne in their arms because it was stamped on the barrels of flax imported from Germany. Apart from these confusions, inns have always been subject to changes of name. The Saracen's Head at Southwell was the King's Arms until kings went temporarily out of fashion in the 1650s, while the White Hart at Lewes was a private house until 1717 and took its name from a tavern which closed when it opened.

Many pubs possess odd, fanciful names which seem to bear no relation to anything and defy easy explanations. What does the 'Goat & Compasses' mean? 'God encompasseth us' has been suggested, but it could merely have been the home of a mason or joiner. Bag O' Nails—'Bacchanals', or merely the former home of a nail-maker? Pig & Whistle—'Pige Washail' ('Pige' here meaning a wooden tankard or piggin)? 'Pyx & Housel', both used in the Mass? Or simply Bear & Ragged Staff, the staff normally being shown with sawn-off stumps of branches closely resembling the stops on a flute? Do the Bull & Mouth and the Bull & Bush recall Boulogne harbour ('Bush' here being a corruption of 'bouche'), and if so, why? Does the Cat & Fiddle commemorate Caton le Fidele, a governor of Calais renowned for his loyalty, or the anonymous maker of catgut lute strings? These and other teasers— the Case Is Altered, the Original Ball, the Happy Union, Cabbage Hall, the Old Man & Scythe—are an accepted feature of the pub scene and provide an unending source of argument. I cannot accept that they are mere whimsy, even where the original meaning is lost; but Thomas Burke, in *The English Inn*, complains:

> The learned Smelfungus is never happy with the poet's fancy . . . and having demolished our folk-tales and nursery rhymes . . . he has got busy on our inn-signs. He will tell you that such a sign as the Pig & Whistle is a corruption of the Anglo-Saxon 'Pige Washail' . . . Corruption my knee-cap! The fellow is so incapable of understanding fancy that to him everything fanciful must be an over-dressed fact. He can't see that to call a house the Pig & Whistle is just what an Englishman, left to himself, would do. . . . The first innkeeper who named his house the Pig & Whistle doubtless did so . . . because he saw that it would bring questioning customers like Smelfungus & Co . . . Smelfungus always was unaware of that human failing, facetiousness.

This is clearly absurd, especially when there is so much recent evidence of how foreign names are corrupted in English. Wipers and Bully Wood were both places well known to British troops on the Somme; Burke would doubtless hold that the names were invented by the Tommies as an example of English facetiousness, when the Tommies would tell him they were merely corruptions of the French Ypres and Bois de Bouillet. There is no reason to suppose that an identical process did not occur in the Middle Ages, when so many nobles spoke Norman French. Besides, Burke misses half the fun in such odd names—which is tracking down what they really mean.

Here, at any rate, is a short (very short, given the variety available) list of some common and not-so-common inn-names and their possible derivations:

Adam & Eve Understandably, the arms of the Fruiterers' Company; but also standing for the City of London whose sign of the zodiac is, for some reason, Gemini—thought by the illiterate, when painted on an inn-sign, to represent Adam and Eve.
Admiral Vernon Captor of Portobello in 1739, he is one of

many military heroes who decorate inn-signs. **Wellington** and **Nelson** are most common; another is the **Marquis of Granby**, victor of Minden in 1759. Modern warriors so honoured include **Lords Roberts, Kitchener, Montgomery**, and **Earl Mountbatten**.

Anchor Clearly nautical, but there is a religious significance as well, Christ being the anchor of the soul. Other religious signs, apart from the Angel, the Salutation and the Mitre already noted, include the **Golden Cross**, the **Cross Keys** (for St Peter), and the **Pelican**.

Axe & Compasses Anything with compasses in it refers to masons and joiners; that includes the Goat & Compasses, more imaginative explanations notwithstanding, and the **Square & Compasses** is also sometimes seen.

Bay & Say Not as puzzling as it seems. Both were varieties of woollen cloth in the sixteenth century, the first being fine, the second coarse.

Bear & Billet A variation on Bear & Ragged Staff from the arms of the Nevilles, earls of Warwick and Westmorland. Their crest was the **Bull's Head**. The male line died out in 1495, when the heiress married a Dudley, whose own arms included the **Green Lion**, seen occasionally on inn-signs.

Beetle & Wedge The beetle was the heavy hammer used to drive in the wedge; this sign is therefore associated with builders, shipwrights and foresters.

Black Bull A Yorkist sign; a supporter of the arms of George, Duke of Clarence (brother of Edward IV and Richard III) who met his end in the butt of Malmsey. The **Sun** or **Sun in Splendour** is the most common Yorkist name; this was a device affected by Edward IV. The **White Lion** and **White Rose**, less common, also come from his arms. The **White Boar** was Richard III's crest; because of it he was known as the hog. He and three of his ministers, Catesby, Ratcliffe and Lovell, are commemorated in a piece of doggerel current at the time:

The cat, the rat, and Lovell our dog
Rule all England under a hog.

After Richard's defeat and death, many White Boars were repainted blue, the **Blue Boar** being the crest of his enemy, the Earl of Oxford. The **Falcon** is another Yorkist sign.

Black Lion One of the oldest inn-names, it comes from the arms of Edward III's queen, Phillipa of Hainault, who was Flemish. Many of her countrymen settled in England in the reigns of Edward and his grandson Richard II; hence the **Golden Lion** from the arms of Flanders. Rarer is the **Fleur de Lys**, adopted from the arms of France by Edward himself; but the common **Plume of Feathers** was part of the arms of his son, the Black Prince, and may signify any Prince of Wales from then on.

Blue Ball Said to depict the gipsy fortune-teller's crystal ball.

Blue Bowl Blue Bristol ware punch-bowls were common in the eighteenth century; hence also the **Punch Bowl**. Punch was the favourite tipple of the Whig Charles James Fox, so the landlord of a Punch Bowl or Blue Bowl was likely to be a supporter of his—as was the landlord of the **Intrepid Fox**, named after the politician, not the animal.

Boar's Head From the arms of St Blaise, patron saint of weavers and woolcombers.

Boot Either a former cobbler's shop, like the **Last**, or from the arms of the Hussey family.

Brunswick Commemorates the accession of George I in 1714, as do the **White Horse** and the **Running Horse**, from the arms of Hanover.

Butchers' Arms Butchers, miners, bricklayers, smiths and other artisans do not generally possess grants of arms; the habit of ennobling them on inn-signs grew up in the late eighteenth century. This particular name refers as much to drovers as to butchers; alehouse-keepers who had a side-line in butchery are often recalled by the **Shoulder of Mutton** and, in one case, the **Shoulder of Mutton & Cauliflower**. Smiths are also commemorated on the sign of the **Horseshoe(s)**.

Case is Altered A rational explanation is hard to find for this one; four stories are told to account for it. A lawyer advised a farmer that if his cows got into another man's turnips, the farmer would be legally liable, but when his own cows strayed he remarked: 'The case is altered'. More likely is that it is a reference to a Popish priest named Casey and his portable altar during the years of persecution, and more likely still is a Peninsular War veteran turned innkeeper who named his house after the 'Casa de Salter' where he used to dance in Spain. On the Ypres-Wipers progression this seems, to us at least, fairly plausible. Finally it is conjectured that it was a corruption of 'La Casa Alta'—'the high house' or 'the house on the hill'.

Catherine Wheel St Catherine was put to death on the wheel by the Emperor Maximinus; one of the lesser fighting orders of the Crusades was the Knights of St Catherine of Sinai. Nottingham's **Trip to Jerusalem** is another pub with crusading memories; but surprisingly, this is not so with **Saracen's Head, Black's Head, Turk's Head** and **Black Boy**. The first three hark back to the early days of smoking, when Balkan tobacco arrived from the Ottoman Empire in casks stamped with a turbanned head. The Black Boy dates from about the same time but is a reference to Charles II, a very swarthy man whose appearance owed more to his Medici than his Plantagenet ancestors.

Cock Along with the **Cross Keys**, from the arms of St Peter. Not to be confused with **Cock & Bottle**, in which 'cock' means spigot; hence a pub selling both draught and bottled beers; also **Jug & Bottle**.

Crutched Friar Not a drunk monk, but one of the Cruciatei or Canons Regular of the Holy Cross.

Dandy-Roll A device used for water-marking; hence a printers' pub. Another such is the **Devil**, the printers' devil being the errand-boy who also performed such menial tasks as inking the plates.

Eagle & Child From the arms of the Stanleys, best known for their swift change of sides at Bosworth.

Goat in Boots Supposed to be 'Godes Bode', or the Gospel.

Golden Ball The arms of the Mercers' Company, from the golden bezant of Constantinople, centre of the silk trade until routes to China were opened up.

Goose & Gridiron Swan & Harp. Similarly **Mucky Duck** or **Dirty Duck** for the Black Swan.

Green Man Originally Jack o' the Green, the Celtic god; generally refers either to archers or verderers.

Hind From the arms of Sir Christopher Hatton, one of Elizabeth I's chief ministers.

Ladas In Epsom, one of many racehorses celebrated on sign-boards. Another is the **Amato** in the same town; also the **Brigadier**, near Manchester, after Brigadier Gerard, and the **Cadland** near Chilwell, Nottinghamshire.

Lamb (& Flag) The Knights Templar, who owned several hospices in the Middle Ages; but also in the arms of the Merchant Tailors and of Charles II's queen, Catherine of Braganza.

Lion & Castle From the arms of the royal family of Castile, identifies a wine importer, as does the **Three Tuns. Elephant & Castle** is from the arms of the Cutlers' Company.

Maid's Head From the arms of the dukes of Buckingham.

Ram Along with the **Fleece** and the **Woolpack**, recalls the wool trade of the Middle Ages. Oddly enough, so can the **Ship**. At Chirk Castle there is a painting of Llanrhaiadr Falls with a number of large yachts floating in the pool at the bottom. This pool is only about 3ft deep, but the story is that a local farm-labourer, watching the painter at work, remarked that the picture wanted a few ships in it, so the artist obligingly put some in. But like many inn-signs, the yokel was actually saying 'sheep'.

Rose & Crown One of the commonest inn-signs of all, it is a symbol of the triumph of Henry VII. Another common Tudor symbol is the **Red Dragon**. The **Raven** was the personal badge of Mary Tudor (1553–8) but is also part of the arms of the Corbets, a Shropshire landowning family.

Star Generally a religious symbol; also the **Star of Bethle-**

hem. But it can also be heraldic, particularly when it is found as the **Star & Garter**.

Swan Henry IV's personal badge, and thus a Lancastrian symbol like the **Red Rose**. The **Chained Swan**, however, comes from the arms of the de Bohuns, earls of Hereford.

Two Chairmen Once common in London; sedan-chair carriers. This belongs with a whole range of small urban pubs from the seventeenth century on, generally known as the **Tap, Vaults** or **Shades**, which signified a haunt of servants. Major inns such as the White Hart at Lewes, the Spread Eagle at Midhurst and the George at Stamford actually had separate taverns set aside for servants of guests.

White Bear Bearing in mind our naval past, we have surprisingly few pubs named after ships; even the **Ship** and the **Anchor** are not necessarily nautical. The **Golden Hind** is one that is; so is this.

INDEX